THE END OF TERRITORIALITY?

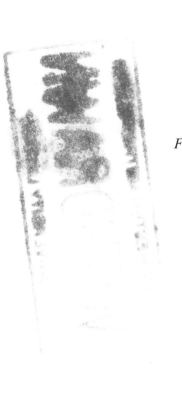

For my grandmother, Maria

The End of Territoriality?
The Impact of ECJ Rulings on British, German and French Social Policy

ANDREAS J. OBERMAIER

ASHGATE

Published by
Ashgate Publishing Limited
Wey Court East
Union Road
Farnham
Surrey, GU9 7PT
England

Ashgate Publishing Company
Suite 420
101 Cherry Street
Burlington
VT 05401-4405
USA

www.ashgate.com

British Library Cataloguing in Publication Data
Obermaier, Andreas J.
  The end of territoriality? : the impact of ECJ rulings on
  British, German and French social policy.
  1. Court of Justice of the European Communities--
  Influence. 2. Law--European Union countries--
  International unification. 3. Great Britain--Social
  policy. 4. Germany--Social policy. 5. France--Social
  policy. 6. Public welfare--Law and legislation--Great
  Britain. 7. Public welfare--Law and legislation--Germany.
  8. Public welfare--Law and legislation--France.
  I. Title
  344.2'403165-dc22

Library of Congress Cataloging-in-Publication Data
Obermaier, Andreas J.
  The end of territoriality? : the impact of ECJ rulings on British, German and French social policy / by Andreas J. Obermaier.
    p. cm.
  Includes bibliographical references and index.
  ISBN 978-0-7546-7827-4 (hardback) -- ISBN 978-0-7546-9628-5
(ebook) 1. European Union countries--Social policy. 2. Public welfare--European Union countries. 3. Public welfare--Law and legislation--European Union countries. 4. Freedom of movement--European Union countries. I. Title.
  HN377.O28 2009
  320.6094--dc22

2009031355

ISBN 9780754678274 (hbk)
ISBN 9780754696285 (ebk)

Printed and bound in Great Britain by
MPG Books Group, UK

Contents

List of Figures

List of Tables

Acknowledgments

This book was written over a period of six years, in three different academic contexts. First of all, I would like to thank the Graduate School of Social Sciences at the University of Bremen. Its staff and especially Prof. Steffen Mau and Werner Dressel never failed to offer me an open ear and sympathetic attitude. Second, my thanks go to the Department of Political Science at the Institute for Advanced Studies in Vienna. The head of the Department, Prof. Gerda Falkner, facilitated a scientific internship for me in the summer of 2006 and was so kind to provide me with an interesting job opportunity afterwards. And finally, I thank the Austrian Academy of Sciences, the Institute for European Integration Research; my last academic stop. The following colleagues and friends in Bremen and Vienna stimulated the ideas presented in this book: Nicole Alecu de Flers, Kerstin Blome, Dawid Friedrich, Daniela Kroos, Kathrin Leuze, Nadja Meisterhans, Christian Möllmann, Stephan Renner, Thomas Richter, Claudia Ruddat, Scott Siegel, Reinhard Slepcevic, Chris Swader, Florian Trauner, Oliver Treib, Christian Völkel, Clemens Wiedermann, Caroline Wörgötter, Sonja Wrobel, and Lorenzo Zambernardi. I would also like to thank the Hans-Böckler-Stiftung for providing me with a very generous stipend and unbureaucratic help in all kinds of situations. The experts I interviewed during this project provided me with new insights: Thank you for that. My special thanks go to Prof. Stephan Leibfried and Prof. Klaus Sieveking. Hillary Marzec, thank you for proofreading this manuscript!

Andreas Obermaier

List of Abbreviations

AIM	Association Internationale de la Mutualité
AOK	Allgemeine Ortskrankenkasse
BKK	Betriebskrankenkasse
BMGS	Bundesministerium für Gesundheit und Soziale Sicherung
BSG	Bundessozialgericht
BVA	Bundesversicherungsamt
CDU/CSU	Christlich Demokratische Union Deutschlands/ Christlich-Soziale Union in Bayern
CLEISS	Centre des Liaisons Européennes et Internationales de Sécurité Sociale
CNAM	Caisse Nationale d'Assurance Maladie
CNAMTS	Caisse Nationale d'Assurance Maladie des Travailleurs Salariés
CPAM	Caisse Primaire d'Assurance Maladie
CSP	Code de la Santé Publique
CSS	Code de la Sécurité Sociale
DACI	Division des Affaires Communautaires et Internationales
DG	Directorate General
DGS	Direction Générale de la Santé
DHOS	Direction de l'Hospitalisation et de l'Organisation des Soins
DoH	Department of Health
DSS	Direction de la Sécurité Sociale
DSS/DACI	Direction de la Sécurité Sociale/Division des Affaires Communautaires et Internationales
ECJ	European Court of Justice
EEA	European Economic Area
EEC	European Economic Community
EHIC	European Health Insurance Card
EP	European Parliament
EPHA	European Public Health Alliance
ESIP	European Social Insurance Platform
EU	European Union
FDP	Freie Demokratische Partei
GKV	Gesetzliche Krankenversicherung
GMG	Gesundheitssystemmodernisierungsgesetz
GP	General practitioner
KBV	Kassenärztliche Bundesvereinigung

KZBV	Kassenzahnärztliche Bundesvereinigung
LG	Landesgericht
LSG	Landessozialgericht
MP	Membre du Parlement
NHS	National Health Service
OGH	Oberster Gerichtshof (Austria)
PS	Parti socialiste
RPR	Rassemblement pour la République
SBK	Siemens Betriebskrankenkasse
SG	Sozialgericht
SGB	Sozialgesetzbuch
SPD	Sozialdemokratische Partei Deutschlands
SpiK	Spitzenverbände der gesetzlichen Krankenkassen
TK	Techniker Krankenkasse
UK	United Kingdom
VdAK/AEK	Verband der Angestellten Krankenkassen/ Arbeiter-Ersatzkassen-Verband
VfGH	Verfassungsgerichtshof (Austria)
VwGH	Verwaltungsgerichtshof (Austria)

Chapter 1

Introduction: De-territorialization versus Justice Contained

Welfare state change is among the most important and most controversially debated social and political issues of our times. Many authors argue that welfare states in the European Union (EU) have succumbed to numerous pressures and have changed their systems of social security accordingly. In the on-going de- and re-structuring pressure stemming from the EU-level, the rulings of the European Court of Justice (ECJ) have been identified as a major source for change. In the existing literature on the ECJ there is a clear-cut divide between those who affirm the destructive potential of ECJ interference and those who deny it.

Two Opposing Camps

On the one hand, in the quasi-absence of "positive" social policy integration at the EU-level, "innovative" ECJ rulings are considered to be "path-breaking" in a positive or negative sense in that they significantly change the internal institutional configuration of domestic social security systems and gradually weaken or tear apart the exclusive national spatial demarcation lines and closure practices of domestic systems (see, for example, Ferrera 2005, Leibfried 2005, Martinsen 2005a).[1] However, scholars who voiced these concerns also conceded that the actual influence of ECJ rulings on social security systems remained "opaque and continuously contested" (Leibfried 2005: 265).

On the other hand, ECJ rulings are believed to be systematically "contained" by the Member States, understood as the application of legal innovation to the individual ECJ rulings at hand, without acknowledging the broader implications, specifically when it comes to social benefits (see, for example, Conant 2003, Kingreen 2003).[2]

---

1 Stephan Leibfried distinguished between "positive" social policy initiatives "taken at the 'centre' by the Commission and the Council" to develop uniform social standards at the EU level, "negative" reforms "through the imposition of market compatibility requirements," and "indirect pressures" of European integration (2005: 244–245).

2 Lisa Conant (2003) introduced the concept of "justice contained," that was developed particularly in the study of the law in the United States, into the studies of the ECJ (on this transfer, see Wincott 2003). It means that compliance with an ECJ ruling is consciously and systematically contained by Member States. They typically apply legal

Did EU Member States – through implementing ECJ rulings – weaken or abolish the principle of providing social benefits exclusively within their territory? Did they have to alter the internal functioning of their domestic welfare states? If this is the case, what does this impact look like, and have these changes really taken place because of the ECJ jurisprudence? If the assumptions of those scholars who affirm the destructive potential of ECJ rulings hold (partially) true on empirical grounds, the consequences for the structure and the financing of domestic social security systems will be enormous. And this will only be the beginning: in the quasi-absence of "positive" social policy initiatives at the EU-level, it is foreseeable that the ECJ and national courts will be increasingly concerned with social policy issues in the future. Ultimately, a court-driven process could change the very structure of social security systems as we know them today. These issues are therefore central to the future of European welfare states and will be elucidated in the present publication.

This book will challenge both of the aforementioned views on ECJ rulings. The detailed analysis of the *Kohll/Decker* jurisprudence – a key series of ECJ rulings – and its implementation will allow me to fulfill this task. This line of decisions on patient mobility started with *Kohll* and *Decker*, both decided by the ECJ on April 28, 1998. The two rulings challenged Article 22 (which deals with health care entitlements abroad) of one of the oldest EEC regulations, that is Regulation 1408/71 on the application of social security schemes to employed persons and their families moving within the European Community.[3] Also, the ECJ applied the passive free movement of services, that is the freedom to receive a service, and the free movement of goods to patients moving within the Community and thus provoked a new challenge for the EU Member States. *Kohll* and *Decker* were so important that according to an anecdote from the German Ministry of Health, the very day of the pronouncement of the rulings, a high-ranking official drove by car to Luxembourg in the middle of the night to obtain the written version of the rulings, which only available in English at the time. In the following weeks, months, and years, these ECJ decisions were intensely discussed and contested in the political, administrative and academic arenas, as well as in the media. Many articles and books were written on *Kohll* and *Decker* and their potential impact (see, for example, Eichenhofer 1999, Hervey and McHale 2004, Jorens 2004, Kaczorowska 2006, Leibfried 2005, Nihoul and Simon 2005, Palm et al. 2000, Sieveking 2007). In some accounts, the possible destruction of the domestic social security systems was evoked (see Ferrera 2003), while others reacted in a much more reserved way (see Becker 1998). However, *Kohll* and *Decker* were only the beginning: follow-up rulings fine-tuned these cases, extending and limiting

---

innovations only to the individual ECJ decisions at hand and negate further legislative and administrative implications.

3   Regulation (EEC) No 1408/71 of the Council of June 14, 1971 applies social security schemes to employed persons and their families moving within the Community, Official Journal L 149, July 5, 1971, p. 0002–0050.

their scope simultaneously. The so-called *Kohll/Decker* jurisprudence that has emerged comprises eleven rulings which were delivered between 1998 and 2007; of high importance were the consequences of this jurisprudence for the principle of territoriality enshrined in the national social security systems. In addition, the financial, political and structural costs of the implementation of the *Kohll/Decker* jurisprudence were considered to be extremely high. Therefore, this series of cases was contested by most of the EU Member States; its impact on the individual social security systems was denied and implementation refused. Despite this initial fierce resistance by governments/administrations and the majority of health care actors, the ECJ jurisprudence was fully incorporated into domestic legislation in France and Germany and partially incorporated in the UK. Why could the opposition against the *Kohll/Decker* jurisprudence be overcome? What role – if any – did national court cases play in the implementation processes?[4]

In the book I show, first, that Member States indeed had to relax their territorial principles to a minor degree. However, the internal functioning of their social security systems has remained unharmed: Member States continue to exert considerable control over their domestic systems. Secondly, I demonstrate that this rather minor impact is mainly due to the ECJ's fine-tuning of the jurisprudence.[5]

I argue thus that the UK, Germany, and France put themselves in conformity with the *Kohll/Decker* jurisprudence through rather minor adjustments. Member State governments and insurance funds representatives, as well as political and legal science scholars feared from the beginning that this series of ECJ rulings could not be limited to cross-border cases but that, on the contrary, these rulings would endanger the principle of territoriality. In addition, they feared that *Kohll* and *Decker* would affect the domestic functioning of the delivery of health care and thus destabilize entire social security systems. In the course of the implementation, though, the limitation to cross-border cases turned out to be feasible. Legislative and administrative changes were necessary to comply with the jurisprudence, but they were not far-reaching. In addition, the most important health reform projects since the 1990s in the UK, France, and Germany were either not concerned with these rulings at all or they needed only minor adjustments in order to implement them. The national reform trajectories followed their own paths and were not driven by ECJ rulings, be they even as important as the *Kohll/Decker* jurisprudence. In the short and middle run the postulated tremendous impact of these rulings can thus be considered rather minor. In the long run, though, their general destabilizing potential remains a threat.

---

4   I speak of processes because implementation involves three steps: interaction among multiple types of political or private actors; interpretation and settlement of disputes; and internalization of EU law into domestic legal systems (see Siegel 2007).

5   Fine-tuning will be understood here as the extension and/or limitation of the scope of judicial doctrines elaborated in a leading case in the follow-up rulings.

Innovative Contributions

This book is located in the intersection of political and legal sciences and contributes to both worlds equally. It makes four innovative contributions to the fields of Europeanization, implementation of/compliance with EU law, and social policy research.[6] First, I analyze in detail how EU Member States implemented ECJ rulings at the national level and what impact this had on their social security systems. Most scholars focus on the legal doctrines elaborated by the ECJ and their potential impact, and not on the actual implementation of these doctrines. The latter is of extreme importance, though, because without such analyses, scholarly research can only speculate and the actual impact will remain opaque. I am able to overcome these shortcomings by tracing the political processes in detail and by linking specific rulings to specific policy responses.

My second contribution is that I do not discuss isolated influential rulings in one single country as is often done by (legal) scholars (see, for example, Becker 1998, van der Mei 1999), but I examine a longer series of rulings – the *Kohll/ Decker* jurisprudence – from 1998 to 2007, and I do so for three selected EU Member States: France, Germany, and the United Kingdom. Examining such a line of cases allows me to integrate the dynamics of the development of the ECJ jurisprudence – a key variable in understanding implementation processes and outcomes – into the analysis.

Thirdly, in contrast to existing studies with a bias toward single causes, in order to explain implementation I focus on the combination of factors such as domestic political preferences, enforcement through national court rulings, enforcement and management strategies of the European Commission, and the fine-tuning of the jurisprudence by the ECJ.

And lastly, I contribute to the debate of whether the established historical periodization of the role of the ECJ (early "judicial activism" versus "self-restraint" in a later phase) is tenable, or whether it has to be modified.[7]

EU implementation/compliance studies usually focused on directives (see, for example, Börzel 2000, Héritier et al. 2001, Falkner et al. 2005, Linos 2007).[8] This book treats compliance with ECJ rulings. This "third form of compliance" started

---

6   "Europeanization" has been defined as the formal and qualitative changes induced by European decisions in domestic policies, politics and polity (see Héritier 2001: 3). The majority of the abundant literature on Europeanization deals with the effect of EU institutions on the political systems of the Member States and their efforts to adapt to European requirements. ECJ jurisprudence is only a subfield in this literature but will be in the focus here.

7   Judicial activism refers to ECJ rulings that usurp the rule and policy-making powers of the Member States. Judicial self-restraint describes situations in which ECJ judges defer their rulings to some extent to the objections of the Member States.

8   EU directives – in contrast to regulations which are directly applicable – are binding on the Member States as to the result to be achieved, but leave it to them to decide the means.

to receive increasing attention in the late 1980s and early 1990s (see Tallberg 2003: 48–52).[9] In 2005, the European Commission characterized compliance with ECJ rulings as being of utmost importance:

> In a Community governed by the rule of law, it is of utmost importance that judgments of the ECJ are fully complied with by the Member States. Otherwise, legal certainty, individual rights, the conditions under which market participants operate in various parts of the Community, equal treatment of the 25 Member States as well as the balance of rights and obligations of Member States under the Treaties could be seriously called into question. Non-compliance with a judgment of the ECJ thus strikes at the heart of the legal order of the Community. (2005a: 1)

Case Selection

I am interested in the question of whether ECJ rulings perforate or abolish the principle of territoriality of domestic social security systems and de-structure their internal functioning. In order to investigate these contested questions I had to select a series of cases that was critical to the concept of increased de-territorialization and de-structuring triggered by ECJ rulings (for the relevance of choosing crucial cases see, for example, Eckstein 1975: 118, Gerring 2001: 219–221, 2007).

I collected all the relevant rulings first to get an insight into the universe of ECJ rulings. In the course of gathering the rulings, an interesting line of cases came to the fore: the *Kohll/Decker* jurisprudence. These rulings do not fall into the usual ECJ social policy categories, such as free movement of workers, free movement of third country nationals, and worker's protection and equal treatment, but they concern the passive free movement of services and the free movement of goods of patients moving within the European Community. This line of rulings started with *Kohll* and *Decker* in 1998, and was followed chronologically by *Vanbraekel* and *Geraets-Smits/Peerbooms* in 2001, *Müller-Fauré/van Riet* and *Inizan* in 2003, *Leichtle* in 2004, *Keller* in 2005, *Watts* and *Acereda Herrera* in 2006, and *Stamatelaki* in 2007.

If ECJ rulings do trigger de-territorialization and internal de-structuring, we should detect both effects in the implementation outcomes of the *Kohll/Decker* jurisprudence. This jurisprudence concerned health care systems in general and patient mobility in particular. *Kohll* and *Decker* determined that domestic health care systems had to be operated in a way that was compatible with the free movement of services and goods. Health care is indeed only one aspect of social policy (see Hatzopoulos 2005: 112–113). However, Leibfried has estimated that

---

9   The first form is compliance in the implementation of directives, the second compliance in the practical application of EU rules.

the importance of the health area with regard to the struggle between domestic and European rules is particularly high:

> The health area is a first, *and crucial* [emphasis in original, AJO], Europe-wide testing ground for the turf battle between national welfare states and the EU plus the market, as represented by private insurance, producers, etc. (2005: 268)

Leibfried points to three reasons for this particular role of health:

> Compared with pensions, health insurance has more 'market traces' in most national systems, is more fragmented by provider groups already operating in markets (medical instruments, pharmaceuticals), or quasi-markets (doctors in sick fund private practice), and has been traditionally exposed to substantial private provision in most countries. In recent decades, national reforms have pointed increasingly to 'market cures'. (2005: 268)

From the overall EU impact on the health area, I will isolate and analyze the influence of the *Kohll/Decker* jurisprudence which supposedly undermined important elements of the sovereign welfare states: the exclusive control of Member States over the beneficiaries of benefits, over the territorial borders of the consumption of benefits and over the design of the respective policies, that is whether a social benefit is delivered in cash or in kind (see Leibfried and Pierson 1995). *Kohll* and *Decker* and subsequent rulings were supposed to show that the ECJ had a direct impact on the way social policy is organized in the Member States, in this case the reimbursement of health care costs. Maurizio Ferrera stated that *Kohll* and *Decker* "are unquestionably of great importance for the neutralization of territoriality conditions in EU health care systems." According to his assessment, from the rulings originated "a destructuring potential that ... may lead to significant changes in the institutional configuration of this sector of the welfare state" (2003: 22). Hans Vollaard equally considered the *Kohll/Decker* jurisprudence as being "à l'encontre du principe de territorialité" [being in opposition to the principle of territoriality, AJO] (2005: 230). With regard to compliance with the *Kohll/Decker* jurisprudence, Derek Beach found that

> the faithful implementation of the rulings has potentially extremely high costs for EU governments ... as the doctrine can in theory undermine national attempts to contain health care costs by enabling citizens to avoid waiting lists and poor service in their home countries by seeking medical treatment abroad, with the bill being footed by the citizens' own national health care system. (2005: 114)

The main interest of this study is to examine whether or not all these developments took place and what impact the ECJ rulings had on domestic social security systems.

Country Selection

In order to show the differential responses of EU Member States to the ECJ jurisprudence, I examined France, Germany, and the United Kingdom. These EU Member States represent three distinctive European social (health care) systems. When we compare them we can distinguish between two ideal types: a Beveridge model (national health service) and a Bismarck model (social insurance system). The Beveridge model covers all citizens and is marked by a direct state-run administration, financing through taxes and service provision through public law organizations, whereas the social insurance Bismarck model relies on a solidaristic self-governed financing structure based on income. These two models, though, do not exist in their pure form. In order to oversimplify, in the "old" EU-15, nine have a national health service, three a social security system based on the provision of cash benefits, and three a social security system based on the provision of in-kind benefits. The health care systems of the Scandinavian countries (Denmark, Finland, and Sweden) with strong communal and regional autonomy and those from Anglo-Saxon countries (UK and Ireland) marked by centralist control are financed predominantly through taxes. Four southern European countries (Greece, Italy, Portugal, and Spain) have at the same time tax-based as well as contribution-based financed components. Predominantly financed through contributions are the systems in the remaining six countries. While cash benefits dominate in Belgium, France, and Luxembourg, in Austria, Germany and the Netherlands in-kind benefits prevail.[10]

In addition to the theoretically grounded reason for the country case selection, it should be noted that in the internationally booming comparative literature on welfare states political scientists rarely do the comparison between Germany and France. France is especially not among the intensely researched countries (see Lepperhoff 2004: 23–24).

Method

I examine a critical line of ECJ social policy decisions: *Kohll* and *Decker* and subsequent rulings from 1998 to 2007. With these innovative rulings, the ECJ supposedly challenged the exclusiveness of domestic social security systems and enhanced the exportability of welfare state benefits with the help of the fundamental freedoms. How these ECJ decisions were implemented in France, Germany, and the UK, and which effects were triggered by the jurisprudence, will be the central questions of this book.

There is a multitude of different pressures exerted on EU Member States when it comes to the (re)shaping of their welfare state features. I am specifically

---

10   For an overview of the different health care systems in the EU see for example Knieps (1998a, 1998b), Kingreen (2003), and Palm et al. (2000).

interested in the impact of ECJ rulings. Through careful and detailed process-tracing (see, for example, George and Bennett 2005) I attribute a specific policy response at the Member State level to a specific ruling. I pay special attention to the time sequencing of social policy changes and I can thus separate the impact of ECJ rulings from other possible factors, such as changing domestic policy preferences.

I gathered and analyzed both national and EU-level documents. At the national level: rulings by national courts, legal texts dealing with legislative or administrative changes as a response to ECJ and national court cases, legal text drafts, ministerial circulars, parliamentary debates, newspaper articles, press releases, documents from the domestic insurance funds, and documents from other concerned actors. Complementary to this, I assembled and analyzed documents from the EU-level in order to be able to show the interaction between domestic and supranational processes: the ensuing ECJ rulings, the concerned EC regulations, European Commission documents that deal with the implementation of the ECJ jurisprudence, documents from the European Observatory on Social Security for Migrant Workers, and other relevant documents.

Having analyzed these various documents I then refined my findings with the help of 25 problem-centered expert interviews in Germany, France, the UK, Austria, Brussels and Luxembourg. On the one hand, I conducted interviews with actors on the supranational level: members of the legal staff of the DG Internal Market who were engaged in monitoring and promoting the implementation of EU Member States, staff members of the DG Employment, Social Affairs and Equal Opportunities who were monitoring the correct implementation of Regulation 1408/71, staff members of the DG Health and Consumer Protection who were keeping a watch on health being incorporated into all Community policies, and members of European interest groups, such as the *Association Internationale de la Mutualité* and the European Social Insurance Platform. On the other hand, more importantly, on the Member State level, in Germany, France, and the UK, I interviewed ministerial officials who were concerned with the implementation of ECJ rulings, officials of compulsory health insurance funds who were dealing with European law, and independent academic experts who followed the respective internal and European processes. The interviewees are listed in the annex. The expert interviews helped me to fill missing links in my analysis and generated information that was partly not deducible from the examined documents. The assembled expert interviews have been coded and analyzed in "atlas.ti", a qualitative document analysis software package. The results were incorporated into the analysis.

Structure of the Book

In Chapter 2, I theorize implementation processes of ECJ rulings. I develop the three main questions of my book and the theoretical approaches used to answer them. First, I want to know how EU Member States implement ECJ rulings. I argue that contrary to conventional assessments, even crucial ECJ cases like *Kohll* and *Decker* are implemented in a comparatively timely and correct fashion. There seems to be a growing implicit *erga omnes* effect. Second, I ask about the driving forces behind the implementation of the ECJ jurisprudence. The goodness-of-fit approach will help me to evaluate the *Kohll/Decker* jurisprudence. The most promising explanations for the implementation are domestic party political preferences, national court litigation, the fine-tuning of the jurisprudence by the ECJ in follow-up decisions, and the management and enforcement activities of the European Commission. Several of these factors have to interact with each other in order to guarantee smooth compliance with the ECJ jurisprudence. Lastly, I put forward an answer to the central questions of the book, whether the implementation of the *Kohll/Decker* jurisprudence perforated or abolished the territorial principle enshrined in domestic social security systems, whether the rulings caused internal de-structuring processes, and whether the implementation of the rulings caused financial destabilization.

In the third chapter, I discuss the different concepts of the ECJ as a policy-maker in general and in social (health care) policy in particular. This allows me to evaluate the implementation of the *Kohll/Decker* jurisprudence.

In Chapter 4, I describe the secondary law that inspired *Kohll* and *Decker*, that is the Coordination Regulation 1408/71 for migrant workers, and then detail the series of cases central to this book, as well as the legal discussion surrounding that line of cases. Starting with the rulings *Kohll* and *Decker*, continuing with *Vanbraekel* and *Geraets-Smits/Peerbooms*, and so forth, I show how the originally rather general material ECJ doctrines, which were directed toward countries providing health care predominantly through cash benefits, were progressively extended to other types of health care systems, to other countries, and to additional areas.[11] I show how simultaneously the doctrines were narrowed and restricted step by step by the ECJ.

In Chapters 5 to 8, I present the empirical results of the implementation of the *Kohll/Decker* jurisprudence. In Chapter 5, I assess the implementation in twelve "old" EU Member States in order to provide an overall picture. In Chapters 6 through 8, I detail the story of the implementation of the *Kohll/Decker* jurisprudence in three EU Member States: Germany, France, and the UK. The three detailed case studies follow a common structure: first, I very briefly describe the central principles of the respective health care system and the individual cross-border provisions which existed prior to the *Kohll/Decker* jurisprudence; then, I determine the status quo against which the following changes have to be seen, that

---

11   I adopt the distinction between structural and material doctrines by Joseph Weiler. For him a structural doctrine lays down a "normative framework that purports to govern fundamental issues, such as the structure of relationships between Community and member states", whereas a material doctrine does "the same in relation to, for example, the economic and social content of that relationship" (1994b: 512).

is the degree of misfit with the jurisprudence; finally, I chronologically scrutinize the different pathways of the implementation in the three countries.

In Chapters 9 and 10 I look at the interaction between the supranational and domestic levels. The fine-tuning of the jurisprudence by the ECJ (Chapter 9), that is the restriction and extension of the material doctrines, and the initiatives of the European Commission (Chapter 10) both influenced domestic implementation processes and outcomes.

I make sense of the empirical results in Chapter 11. I explain the reasons for the initial non-implementation of the *Kohll/Decker* jurisprudence, then compare the diverse pathways of the implementation processes, examine the driving forces behind the implementation, and lastly look at its de-territorializing, internal de-structuring and financially destabilizing effects. In the concluding chapter, I draw five lessons from the findings of the book.

Chapter 2
Theorizing Implementation Processes of ECJ Rulings

I argue in this book that the ECJ and its rulings do have an impact on domestic (social) policy. In order to assess this impact, I first trace domestic social policy changes, changes of disputed laws and changes of disputed administrative practices. Assessing the significance of the modifications requires examining the implementation processes and outcomes in the three selected Member States in detail. It is important to look at the process of implementing an ECJ ruling as such an analysis brings to the fore the importance and intention of the changes made.

The main explanatory factors for (the degree of) implementation are the existing institutional arrangements in the Member States, domestic political preferences, national court rulings, the management and enforcement initiatives of the European Commission, and the fine-tuning of the jurisprudence achieved in due course through the ECJ itself. This book provides answers to the following three interrelated complexes of questions:

- Under which conditions and by which pathways do EU Member States implement ECJ rulings? What strategies do they employ to deal with rulings that relate to social benefits, and are the strategies different?
- What accounts for the variation in the national modes of implementation?
- Do de-territorialization, internal de-structuring and financial destabilization effects result from the implementation of the jurisprudence?

How do EU Member States Implement ECJ Rulings?

First of all, I am interested in the way EU Member States implement/comply with ECJ rulings in the area of social policy.[1] The concept of compliance with Court rulings according to Bernadette Ann Kilroy is a complex one:

---

1 The meaning and scope of implementation and compliance vary: both concepts are fuzzy and difficult to grasp. Kal Raustiala and Anne-Marie Slaughter distinguished between compliance and implementation: "Implementation is the process of putting international commitments into practice: the passage of legislation, creation of institutions (both domestic and international) and enforcement of rules. Implementation is typically a critical step toward compliance, but compliance can occur without implementation; that is, without any effort or action by a government or regulated entity. ... [I]mplementation is

> Compliance with EC law is not simply giving effect to the Court's ruling in the concrete case at issue. If this were so, the actual impact of any Court decision would be quite limited. More significantly, full compliance means that the member state amends, repeals or annuls national provisions that the ECJ has deemed incompatible with EC law, or it incorporates EC directives and other measures directly into the national legal order. (1999: 80)

For practical reasons I adopt this broad meaning for my study and use compliance and implementation synonymously. Many implementation/compliance studies do not restrict their analysis to "simple" legislative and administrative implementation but distinguish between three stages of the implementation process. Tanja Börzel and Thomas Risse distinguished between output, outcome and impact. First, the output dimension refers to legal and administrative measures that put a European policy or rule into administrative effect. Second, the outcome dimension captures the effect of these policy measures on the behavior of the target actors. Third, the impact dimension tries to detect the further effect of policy measures on their socio-economic environment (2002: 143–144). Similarly, Falkner et al. distinguished between three stages of compliance: legal transposition (with administration, government, parliament, and interest groups involved), enforcement (involving administration and courts), and practical application (norm addressees such as administrations and companies) (2005: 11–12).

Applied to this study, output (legal transposition) is effected through the change of disputed parts of the social security legislation and disputed administrative practices on the national level. The outcome dimension (enforcement and practical application) is represented in the behavior of the indirect addressees of the ECJ decisions, the insurance funds. The impact dimension would be the behavior of the "target actors," in my case individual patients.

The output dimension will be of central importance in this study, whereas the other two dimensions of compliance, outcome and impact, play only a minor role. However, I assume that the legislative and administrative modifications on the national level are generally respected by the insurance funds. The French insurance funds are under the direct "tutelle" (public guardianship) of the ministry of social security. In Germany, the legislator and the Federal Insurance Authority supervise the insurance funds. And the NHS in the UK is directly state-run. The third element of compliance, the behavior of the "target actors," the individual patients – with my political science approach – can only be traced with limits.

When we look at the output dimension, the Member States as rule addressees have to:

---

conceptually neither a necessary nor a sufficient condition for compliance, but in practice is frequently critical" (2002: 539). In this definition "implementation and compliance are two sides of the same coin" (Treib 2008: 4). The first focuses more on the process of how a norm is translated into practice, the latter on the outcome of implementation. Other authors used both concepts synonymously (see, for example, Kilroy 1999).

- Implement a ruling completely and correctly into national law and amend, repeal and annul, if necessary, contradicting national legislation;
- Provide the administrative apparatus and the resources necessary for implementing the ruling and for monitoring the compliance of the rule targets; and
- Promote compliance of the "rule targets" via effective monitoring, provide for positive and/or negative sanctions and look after their enforcement (see Börzel and Risse 2002: 144).

Do EU Member States implement ECJ rulings? There is no consensus in the literature on this question. Some authors like Ernst-Joachim Mestmäcker and Stacy Nyikos took it for granted that "there is the habit of obedience to Community law" (Mestmäcker 1994: 623) and that we can assume an "implementation prejudice," i.e. that national courts "overwhelmingly" implement ECJ rulings (Nyikos 2003: 413).

Other scholars like Lisa Conant assumed that ECJ rulings – especially regarding social benefits – are being contained consciously and systematically. Her conclusion was that "social benefits is one of the areas in which prior ECJ judgements have faced the most overt noncompliance" (2003: 206). According to Conant, national governments are free to contain compliance in this field, as well as overrule or pre-empt ECJ decisions (2003: 206–207).

This study will show that Member States implement ECJ rulings systemically, meaning that they change their legislation. Certainly this is a messy process: Member States deny the transferability to their systems, they start with small steps, and they tend to neglect essential parts of required changes. Overall, however, EU countries seem to be increasingly aware of the binding effect of ECJ rulings and veer toward faithful implementation.

We still know too little about how EU Member States implement ECJ rulings. What we seem to know is that they do not implement ECJ rulings uniformly – a process analogous to directives (for example Duina 1997) – although uniform interpretation according to Francis G. Jacobs "is essential if the Community, and particularly the single market, are to work at all" (1994: 32). Héritier et al. (2001) observed a differential rather than a uniform impact of European requirements on the Member States because

> … the political reality of European policymaking is 'messy' insofar as it is uneven across policy areas and member states, institutionally cumbersome, and subject to the dynamics of domestic politics, each with its own particular logic. As a consequence, the outcomes of European policymaking tend to be much more diverse than one would expect and preclude any simplistic explanation of Europe-induced changes. (2)

This study will show that ECJ rulings do not necessarily lead to a differential domestic impact. The processes of implementation, that is the pathways through which EU Member States come to grips with EU rules, are indeed rather diverse,

although the implementation outcomes resemble each other: a weakening of the
principle of territoriality, which is enshrined in domestic social security legislation,
stood at the end of the implementation in all Member States studied; in Germany,
France, and the UK.

In order to capture the variation in implementation and to be able to classify the
modes of implementation through EU Member States, I compiled possible outcomes
in the court phase and the legislative/administrative phase (see Table 2.1).

Table 2.1 Implementation processes of ECJ rulings:
Court phase and legislative/administrative phase

Mode of implementation		Explanation	The disputed domestic laws and administrative practices …
COURT PHASE			
Non-application by National Courts		A (referring) court applies national law clearly deviant from the ECJ interpretation. The reason for this deviation might be, e.g., a poorly formulated question, rules of evidence and miscomprehension.	… remain unchanged
Evasion	**Re-referral**	A court sends the same or an only marginally different question to the ECJ.	… remain unchanged
	Reinterpretation	A (referring) court bases its decision on a different interpretation of the law, or determines that the facts of the case have changed when they have not or that the ECJ decision is valid but does not apply to the facts of the case.	… remain unchanged
Application by National Courts		A (referring) court applies an ECJ ruling without deviation.	… remain unchanged
LEGISLATIVE AND ADMINISTRATIVE PHASE			
Justice contained		Compliance is consciously and systematically contained by the EU Member States, which negate further legislative and administrative implications for the universe of parallel situations.	… remain unchanged
Partial implementation		A disputed national law or an administrative practice is changed, but limits and exceptions are inserted.	… are changed partially
Full implementation		A disputed national law or an administrative practice is changed and no limits and exceptions are inserted.	… are changed fully

In the court phase, a national court sends a preliminary reference question to the ECJ who gives its interpretation (see Figure 2.1). Subsequently, the national court may:

- Refuse to apply this ECJ ruling correctly to the case at hand;
- Evade the ruling by either re-referring or reinterpreting the question; or
- Apply the ECJ ruling without deviation, without causing legislative and administrative changes.

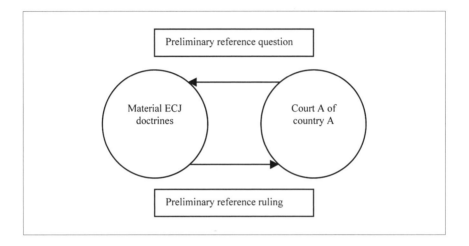

Figure 2.1 First phase of court application

It is possible that implementation is terminated at this stage, if national legislation and administrative practices are in full conformity with the ECJ ruling. In my study I will not deal with the court phase, but rather concentrate on the second phase in which the national legislator/national administration has to consider the broader implications of the ECJ ruling. The legislator/administration here may:

- Negate further legislative and administrative implications for the universe of parallel situations;
- Partially incorporate the doctrines of an ECJ ruling into legislative and administrative actions and policy instruments, but also insert limits and exceptions and discriminatingly implement elements of a ruling; or
- Fully change the disputed national law or administrative practice without deviation.

For the purpose of this study, I will distinguish between "direct" and "indirect" implementation/compliance (see Figure 2.2). First, a Member State, more precisely a national authority, may be a direct party to a preliminary reference ruling. In this case, it has to comply directly with the ruling. Second, a Member State, without being a party in a preliminary reference ruling, may take active part in the written and oral proceeding in order to influence the outcome of the ruling in particular, and the development of European Community law in general. The Member State may then indirectly comply with the ruling in that it accomplishes appropriate legislative and administrative reforms. The three EU countries selected for a detailed analysis were first only indirectly concerned, and became in the course of the unfolding of the jurisprudence direct parties.

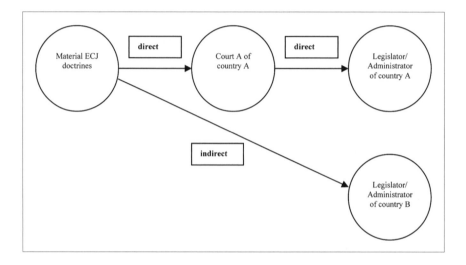

Figure 2.2 Direct and indirect implementation/compliance

Nyikos (2003) in her study on implementation behavior looked only at countries that were directly concerned with a specific case. However, this limitation excludes those EU Member States that are also affected by the same ruling. Among law scholars, there is a controversial debate about whether ECJ rulings, and more precisely in my case preliminary rulings, are binding *inter partes* (between the parties), or if they are binding *erga omnes* (for all EU Member States). Kilroy distinguished between the binding force, i.e. a legal obligation for all concerned parties, of an ECJ ruling and its legal effects, i.e. there is no legal obligation but an effect on the interests and legal position of other parties. According to her, "the binding force extends to the parties to the dispute only," whereas "the legal effects of a decision may reach beyond those parties" (1999: 334). As far as preliminary rulings are concerned, Kilroy concluded that although they do not create the obligation "to repeal, amend, or adopt a provision or provisions of national law," they have a general effect based on Article 234 EC Treaty on national courts

(1999: 354).[2] Michael Schweitzer and Waldemar Hummer in their standard work on European law claimed that ECJ rulings not only bind the referring court when it affirms the relevance of the preliminary ruling for the referred case, but also create a quasi-binding effect through setting precedents for other courts: every court confronted with the same question has to conform to the preliminary ruling or refer the issue anew (1996: 164–165). Kieran St Clair Bradley similarly referred to a 'multiplier effect' of ECJ rulings for all Member States faced with the same issue (2002: 125).

As the *Kohll/Decker* jurisprudence was implemented, the Member States reproduced this very normative debate. Some simply refused to accept that the rulings held for their system and that horizontal effects reached out to areas similar in nature. However, the evidence produced in this study strongly supports the position that there is a binding effect for all Member States and for similar situations. I show that the successful implementation of the *Kohll/Decker* jurisprudence in a Member State is uncoupled from its being party to an ECJ ruling, a result that empirically supports an *erga omnes* effect.

What are the Driving Forces behind the Implementation of ECJ Jurisprudence?

A second series of questions in this study concerns the factors that drive the implementation of the *Kohll/Decker* jurisprudence. Alexander L. George and Andrew Bennett have pointed out that studies that rely on process-tracing need to consider alternative explanations (2005: 217). Therefore, I take into consideration several possible explanations for why EU Member States comply with ECJ rulings (see Table 2.2).

The most prominent and promising for my study are: the goodness-of-fit argument which explains implementation with the congruence between EU requirements and domestic provisions; the behavior of national courts is another promising approach; the various activities of the European Commission might also explain compliance; domestic political preferences were stressed by Gerda Falkner et al. (2005) as a key variable; and finally the fine-tuning of the jurisprudence by the ECJ itself in follow-up cases offers a promising explanation. I introduce each of these competing factors very briefly, discuss their strengths, and propose a working hypothesis for each of them. In Chapters 6 through 8 I discuss the process of implementation in Germany, France, and the UK against the background of these explanations. In the analytical Chapter 11, I take up these factors and comparatively assess their power in explaining implementation in the three EU Member States involved in this study.

---

2   With "EC Treaty" I am referring to the treaty establishing the European Community, the consolidated text from 2006 (Official Journal C321E of December 29, 2006).

Table 2.2 Cross-national variation of implementation

Competing explanations for the cross-national variation of implementation	Process/mechanism
Goodness-of-fit model Match or mismatch model	Congruence or incongruence of European arrangements and existing legal and administrative domestic structures
Domestic Politics	Domestic concerns prevail over European requirements and each individual case of implementing an ECJ ruling tends to require a fresh cost-benefit analysis
Influence of the European Commission	Overall interaction between the European Commission and the Member States (formal and informal)
National judicial system	National courts adjudicate cases in accordance with ECJ jurisprudence and force the legislator or the administration to act
Fine-tuning of the material doctrines by the ECJ in further decisions	In the process of extending and restricting its jurisprudence the ECJ exercises self-restraint and facilitates compliance by Member States

Several Variants of Goodness-of-Fit

In the 1990s, the impact of "sticky" institutions on implementation received considerable attention from neo-institutional scholars who worked on the implementation of EU policies in Member States, especially environmental policy. These scholars had the parsimonious hypothesis that compliance depends on the degree of fit or misfit between new EU rules and pre-existing domestic policies and structures, the latter leading to various adjustment pressures for domestic governments and translating into varying degrees of compliance.

This goodness-of-fit explanation can be subdivided into two arguments whose differences are not always clear-cut, one focusing on the policy dimension, that is on the actual content of the policies, and the other on the institutional dimension, that is on the regulatory styles and the institutional structures. According to Tanja Börzel, the principal cause of implementation failure is a match or mismatch between European rules and domestic policy standards, policy instruments, and problem solving approaches (2000). Authors like Christoph Knill and Andrea Lenschow stressed the significance of domestic institutional arrangements and traditions (2000). Thomas Risse, Maria Green Cowles, and James Caporaso have tried to provide a more integrated understanding of the misfit concept (2001).

Simplifying the argument, Börzel stands for goodness-of-fit that stresses policy fit. For her, policy misfit is the necessary cause of implementation failure:

> [T]he individual Member States face different levels of pressure for adaptation depending on the extent to which an EU policy 'fits' the national approach and

standards. The more an EU policy challenges or contradicts the corresponding policy at the national level, the higher the adaptational pressure a Member State faces in the implementation process. (2000: 225)

Knill and Lenschow stand for goodness-of-fit that sees more likely effective implementation, that is the degree to which formal transposition and the practical application correspond to European requirements,

> ... if the adaptation required by European policies can be achieved by changes *within* rather than a change *of* the core of national administrative traditions. In other words, general characteristics shaping administrative practices and structures within a country, which follow from the specific constellation of the macro-institutional context, including the state tradition, the legal system, as well as the political-administrative system. (2000: 257–258)

Building on these two approaches to the goodness-of-fit problem, Risse, Green Cowles, and Caporaso argued that European rules, regulations and collective understandings interact with domestic institutional settings, rules and practices. They assumed that "the degree of adaptational pressure generated by Europeanisation depends on the 'fit' or 'misfit' between European institutions and the domestic structures" (2001: 7). In general they claimed that "no single EU member state ... is more likely than others to change its institutional structure in response to Europeanisation pressures" (2001: 226). As an exception they identified Germany because its institutional structure and political culture is characterized by many factors that facilitate change. In order to explain why domestic reforms in response to adaptational pressures were impeded or facilitated, they identified five mediating factors: the number of veto points, the mediating formal institutions, political and organizational cultures, differential empowerment of actors, and potential for learning. Their conclusions were that Europeanization processes faced very different domestic institutional structures and accordingly adaptational pressures varied (2001: 221).

Some authors saw satisfactory explanatory value in the goodness-of-fit approach. Imelda Maher, for instance, referred to an edited volume (see Daintith 1995) that included five case studies on the legal implementation of Single European Market directives and concluded that "confluence between British and Community law and policy is of central importance to implementation" (1996: 578). According to Ian Bailey, goodness-of-fit remained the key factor in differentiating between the British and German implementation strategies regarding EU environmental directives (2002: 805–808). However, even its supporters have heavily criticized the goodness-of-fit explanation – especially since the late 1990s – for its limited explanatory value and its overall rather disappointing results.[3] Most authors who criticized the approach nonetheless worked with it. They abandoned the purely

---

3 For an overview of this criticism, see for instance Mastenbroek (2005).

institutional hypothesis and introduced complementary as well as auxiliary actor-based variables to overcome the shortcomings.

Adrienne Héritier and Christoph Knill, for instance, noticed "the limited explanatory relevance of the congruence/incongruence perspective in order to account for the domestic impact of Europe" (2001: 289). Neither the degree of change nor the direction of change could be accounted for. The goodness-of-fit approach for them was simply a first analytical step. In order to overcome its deficits, they pleaded for "a more dynamic approach that conceives of European policies basically as input into the domestic political process, which might be exploited by national actors in order to enhance their opportunities for achieving their objectives" (2001: 288). Héritier and Knill saw domestic change as being "contingent upon the dynamic interaction with two further variables: the level of sectoral reform capacity and prevailing beliefs and ideological orientations" (2001: 289). According to Markus Haverland, the goodness-of-fit approach helps to identify adaptation pressure as an important source of domestic opposition to an EU directive, but it "cannot explain the pace and degree of adaptation to European requirements" (2000: 100). Instead, he stressed the importance of institutional veto points for explaining the timing and quality of compliance with EU directives (2000: 100). Börzel also developed a more dynamic pull-and-push model in which she identified domestic pressure for adaptation from "below" (the pull factor) and external pressure for adaptation from "above" (the push factor). The general argument of this model was as follows:

> First, implementation problems only arise if European policies impose considerable costs for the public administrations of the Member States. The less a European policy fits the legal and administrative structure of a Member State, the higher the adaptational costs in implementation and the lower the willingness of the public administration to ensure effective implementation. Second, the willingness and/or ability of the public administration to bear the costs of implementing poorly fitting EU policies is influenced by additional pressure for adaptation from 'below' by societal actors mobilising against ineffective implementation at the domestic level (pull), and from 'above' by the European Commission introducing infringement proceedings (push). (2000: 224–225)

Concerning the empirical results of the goodness-of-fit approach, Falkner and others found that the implementation of six important EU directives in labor law did not support the misfit explanation (2005: 289–291). A great number of other authors expressed similar reservations vis-à-vis this approach.

Despite its shortcomings, the goodness-of-fit argument still figures among the most prominent approaches for explaining the implementation of EU directives. I will apply it to the stream of ECJ rulings researched here and examine the following hypothesis:

Working hypothesis 1   The de-territorializing and de-structuring pressure, brought to bear by the ECJ rulings, varies by country, because the "filters" of different social health care systems lead to varying results at the national level. This variation in implementation results mainly from differences in the institutional environment. Countries with social security systems based on in-kind benefits and national health systems should have been under tremendous pressure, hampering the smooth implementation of the requirements laid down in the *Kohll/Decker* decisions, while those relying on health care systems based on cash benefits should have found it rather easy to put themselves in line with the requirements displayed by the ECJ.

In the empirical Chapters 6 through 8 I first determine the degree of misfit with the *Kohll/Decker* jurisprudence for each of the three countries studied. I operationalize the concept of misfit like Falkner and her colleagues did in their study on EU social policy directives (2005: 27–32). They grasped the overall misfit in three dimensions: first, a misfit can be substantive, that is the contents of European requirements are not reflected in national laws or administrative practices which would need to be changed accordingly. This can be a gradual difference or one of principle. Second, a misfit can result from a mismatch with existing procedures, having repercussions for politics and/or the polity. Third, there can be a cost misfit, depending on the estimated economic consequences of EU requirements. Falkner et al. claimed that it is virtually impossible to determine the exact costs of adapting to an EU directive (2005: 30). The same should be true for ECJ decisions. Since additional problems come up in the analysis of ECJ rulings, determining costs becomes even more difficult. A line of rulings is a moving target for EU Member States and its financial implications are nebulous because of judicial uncertainty. Still, I try to determine the possible economic consequences for the three countries studied to assess an overall misfit. When aggregating the three dimensions of misfit, Falkner et al. argued that "no dimension of misfit can eradicate or soften adaptational pressure in another dimension" (2005: 32). Therefore, a high degree of misfit in one of the three dimensions needs to be rated as a high overall misfit. In establishing the misfit for Germany, France, and the UK as regards the *Kohll/Decker* jurisprudence, I proceed accordingly. Against the background of the overall misfit, I then assess whether any adaptation was necessary and which one was to be expected. Finally, in the analytical Chapter 11 I probe the explanatory value of the goodness-of-fit approach for the *Kohll/Decker* jurisprudence.

In order to establish the overall misfit with respect to this ECJ jurisprudence, it is necessary to determine how relevant the goodness-of-fit approach is. At the same time, as Falkner and others have pointed out, "establishing in a detailed manner both the status quo ante in the member states and the demands embedded in any European Directive [in the case of my study ECJ rulings, AJO] is crucial" (2005: 27). The first analytical step of the analysis is to establish the overall misfit. This will also facilitate the checking of the relevance of any alternative explanations for implementation, because it enables me to compare the status quo ante with the effected legislative and administrative changes.

ECJ jurisprudence has several peculiarities with respect to misfit. First of all, the jurisprudence unfolds over time; the degree of misfit is therefore a moving target. Consequently, I assess the overall misfit in 1998 in respect to the whole *Kohll/Decker* jurisprudence. Second, because of the judicial uncertainty generated by the ECJ rulings, the interpretation of the "misfit space" varies according to the position of the actor. Therefore, I determine the misfit in Germany, France and the UK with regard to the *Kohll/Decker* jurisprudence after a careful analysis of the different perceptions of the main actors involved in implementation.

Domestic Politics

The majority of empirical implementation/compliance studies have shown that the goodness-of-fit argument is ill-suited to explain domestic implementation of European requirements satisfactorily. Many authors tried to introduce more dynamic auxiliary or complementary variables without completely abandoning the goodness-of-fit approach. Many of these newly introduced variables indirectly attested to the importance of domestic politics. Therefore, Ellen Mastenbroek and Michael Kaeding suggested to drop the goodness-of-fit concept completely and to bring domestic politics back in, that is to focus on the beliefs or preferences of the domestic actors involved in an implementation process (2005: 4–8). Also, the evidence of Falkner and others suggested that national preferences and ideologies play an important part; in implementing EU directives, some countries form a specific cluster – a "world of domestic politics" – in which domestic preferences and ideologies usually prevail in case of a conflict of interest. This cluster has to be differentiated from the two other worlds of compliance: the world of law observance and the world of neglect. According to Falkner and others, implementation processes of EU demands link up with political processes at the domestic level and could add conflicts, be neutral or have an accelerating or facilitating influence (2005: Chapter 15). In a preceding study, Oliver Treib had found that party political interests within governments, trade unions and employers' federations play a central role in the digestion of EU directives (2004: 246–259). The analysis of this role unearthed indirect effects for the implementation of EU law, which were related to the *Eigenlogik* of the national political systems. Therefore, Treib noted:

> Gewählte Regierungen sind in der Regel keine Umsetzungsmaschinen, sondern haben häufig neben der Befolgung europäischer Richtlinien auch noch andere Reformziele, die sie gegebenenfalls gemeinsam mit (oder zusätzlich zu) europäischen Vorschriften zu verwirklichen trachten. (2004: 260)[4]

---

4 "Elected governments usually are not implementation machines. In addition to compliance with European directives they have often other goals of reform that they try to achieve should the occasion arise together with (or in addition to) European directives" (translation of the author).

These findings for EU directives could also be applied to the implementation of ECJ rulings. In countries belonging to the world of domestic politics, according to Falkner and others, domestic concerns should prevail over European requirements and each case of implementing an ECJ ruling should happen grounded in a fresh cost-benefit analysis. Falkner and others did not think the factor of domestic politics generalizable. Nonetheless, I examine the following hypothesis:

Working hypothesis 2   Domestic party political preferences shape the timing and the extent of compliance with the *Kohll/Decker* jurisprudence.

Activities of the European Commission: The Centralized Compliance System

In order to understand the dynamics of implementation processes, one must take into account the enforcement and management activities undertaken by the European Commission to ensure Member States' compliance.

The Commission is part of the centralized EU compliance system (see Tallberg 2002: 614). According to Article 211 EC Treaty, it is the "guardian of the Treaty" and in this "police" function, it is responsible for the timely and correct implementation of the ECJ rulings. A central aim of the Commission is to increase overall compliance of EU countries. It monitors the implementation performance of Member States, identifies laggards and publishes reports on their implementation record. The Commission has been characterized as managing or, more importantly, enforcing compliance, or alternatively, as combining "instruments of coercive enforcement with mechanisms of managerial problem solving" (Tallberg 2002: 632). According to Jonas Tallberg "[t]he combination of compliance mechanisms takes the form of a highly developed 'management-enforcement ladder' – a twinning of cooperative and coercive measures that step by step improve states' capacity and incentives for compliance" (2003: 143). He identified several strategies of the Commission to prevent violations of European law. One of the strategies particularly relevant to this study is that it issues interpretative guidelines to decrease uncertainty about the content of a rule (Tallberg 2002: 615). According to Francis Snyder, since the 1980s the Commission developed the "quasi-legal form of the communication," it being either informative, declaratory, or interpretative. With this instrument, the Commission explains ECJ rulings, identifies their settled and their disputed aspects, and spells out their implications for Member States and other parties concerned (Snyder 1993: 33).

The Commission fulfills the monitoring function to detect arising violations of European law in a "two-track approach":

> On the one hand, it actively and systematically collects and assesses information on state compliance through in-house monitoring. On the other hand, the Commission operates an informal procedure through which it records and examines complaints lodged by citizens, firms, non-governmental organizations, and national administrations. (Tallberg 2002: 616)

The central instrument of the Commission to realize its compliance function is the infringement procedure (Articles 226 and 228 EC Treaty).[5] This time- and resource-consuming instrument is employed when a violation has already taken place. Before an infringement procedure is initiated, the Commission first informally consults the Member State concerned and "weeds out cases that may have arisen due to legal uncertainty and misunderstandings" (Tallberg 2002: 617). Therefore, only strong intentional violations of European law result in an infringement proceeding (see Tallberg 2003: 50). If the informal talks are not successful, the Commission may opt to move through the three formal stages of the infringement procedure: the Letter of Formal Notice, followed by a Reasoned Opinion, and finally the referral to the ECJ.[6] The Formal Notice delimits the subject matter of the dispute and does not require a formal statement by the Member State. If the normally ensuing negotiations fail, the Commission issues another statement articulating the reasons why it believes that the Member State has breached European law (see Snyder 1993: 28). This "administrative" or "conciliatory" phase is "characterized by flexibility in the procedure and a margin of discretion for the Commission" (Audretsch 1986: 415). If the Member State does not comply after the Reasoned Opinion, the Commission may refer the case to the ECJ, which then, judges independently on the issue (see Falkner et al. 2005: 205–206). In practice, the Commission system to ensure compliance combines negotiation with the threat of adjudication. Francis Snyder found that since the mid-1980s, the Commission has terminated many infringement procedures at the first stage, and characterized the relationship between negotiating and adjudicating as follows:

> We usually think of negotiation and adjudication as alternative forms of dispute settlement. It may be suggested, however, that in the daily practice and working ideology of the Commission, the two are not alternatives but instead are complementary. The main form of dispute settlement used by the Commission is

---

5   For information on its monitoring function, see the Communication from the European Commission (2003a).

6   The Commission found that "[a]ccording to the statistics for 2001, approximately half (49 percent) of the suspected infringements recorded gave rise to a letter of formal notice; slightly more than half (54 percent) of the letters of formal notice were followed by reasoned opinions and approximately a fifth (21 percent) came to court. In the end, only about a tenth (10.3 percent) of the suspected infringements originally recorded culminated in infringement proceedings" (2003a: 4). Regarding the access to these different stages of the infringement procedure, Ciavarini Azzi noted: "Since 1996, it has been standard practice to publicize decisions on reasoned opinions and referrals to the Court by issuing press releases. The same applies to letters of formal notice concerning failure to notify national measures implementing directives, and failure to comply with Court judgments; these are, by their nature, public infringements. Conversely, in the case of other letters of formal notice, the principle of confidentiality is respected, because at this preliminary stage it is more conducive to regularizing the infringement" (2000: 64).

negotiation, and litigation is simply a part, sometimes inevitable but nevertheless generally a minor part, of this process. (1993: 30)

Christer Jönsson and Jonas Tallberg divided the "seemingly formal and inflexible framework of the infringement procedure" into a strictly judicial surface and a highly political souterrain:

> On the surface, the Article 169 procedure [today Article 226, AJO] is a strictly judicial process in which the Commission initiates and pursues infringement proceedings against member-states which have committed clear and objectively identifiable violations of Community law. Beneath the surface of neutral and objective law, however, Article 169 proceedings are highly political and subject to substantial discretion on the part of the Commission. (1998: 390–391)

The Commission has considerable room to maneuver within the formal infringement structure regarding

> the decision of whether to initiate infringement proceedings or not, the decision of what the time limits should be within which member-states will have to comply in order for the Commission not to bring the case yet one step further in the procedure, and the decision of when and how to close formal infringement proceedings. (1998: 391)

This allows for compliance bargaining and compromises between the Commission and the Member States (1998: 391).

In the extensive body of literature on compliance or non-compliance with EU requirements, the literature on enforcement or management activities of the Commission is relatively small. About the Commission and the ECJ, Tallberg remarked, "[p]olitical scientists studying European integration have been largely oblivious of the enforcement functions of the supranational institutions" (1999: 38–39). The predominant focus of the enforcement literature is the infringement procedure, that is the quantity and evolution of the main enforcement instrument of the Commission (see, for example, Audretsch 1986, Dashwood and White 1989, Snyder 1993, Mendrinou 1996, Jönsson and Tallberg 1998). Sporadically, studies have looked at enforcement by the Commission as a side product of an analysis of the implementation of EU rules at the national level. Andrew Jordan, for instance, found in a study on the implementation of European Community coastal-bathing water policy in Britain from the mid-70s to the mid-90s that the Commission's various devices, for example the complaints procedure and the annual compliance reports, led to what he called "cultivated spillover," "outflanking" the government and building informal alliances with sub-national actors (1997: 61).

For this book it is important to determine the role of the Commission in implementing European law, specifically ECJ rulings. The question of whether or not the enforcement strategies of the Commission lead to the proper implementation of EU directives or ECJ rulings, and indeed which strategies may have lead to this, is an important desideratum of research. The enforcement mechanism is the most important instrument of the European Commission for bringing about compliance. We have to keep in mind, however, that the Commission may rely on other initiatives as well, which are more managerial in nature.

The relatively few studies on the role of the Commission in implementation found the following: The qualitative studies that dealt with the implementation of legal EU requirements in Member States have not attributed a great role to the Commission. Authors like Börzel and others (2003) who assumed that Member States do not obey European law sufficiently, postulated that the enforcement and management activities of the Commission to overcome the implementation gap were unsatisfactory. In line with this skeptical approach, Gerda Falkner and others have concluded that "in overall terms, infringement proceedings as they are practiced today are a rather inadequate instrument for assuring compliance, even though the situation would be worse if there were none at all" (2005: 227).

Claus-Dieter Ehlermann criticized as early as 1987 that the infringement mechanism is too ponderous, appropriate for normative legal instruments and general administrative practices, but inappropriate for controlling single administrative decisions (208). In addition, the evident resource constraints of the Commission would lead to superficial monitoring of Member States' compliance. Moreover, the increase in proceedings of the Commission brought before the ECJ would risk increased non-compliance with the rulings (Ehlermann 1987: 212).

According to Maria Mendrinou, the Commission changed its monitoring approach in the late 1980s with the internal market on the horizon. Supposedly, it shifted to a more rigorous and consistent monitoring policy: the number of infringement proceedings has risen dramatically since then (1996: 16–17). Similarly, Jonas Tallberg found that the Commission tried to enhance the infringement procedure in the 1980s through "internal reforms streamlining the handling of cases, the shift to a firmer enforcement policy, the encouragement of complaints to the Commission, the development of a shaming strategy, and the intensification of compliance bargaining" (1999: 258). However, both authors refrained from concluding that the Commission enacted a more successful infringement policy.

I demonstrate in Chapter 10 that the Commission employed both management and enforcement activities to make EU Member States implement the *Kohll/Decker* jurisprudence. I clarify in this chapter, first, which strategies were used for which country. Second, I examine what role, if any, the activities of the Commission play in actually making Member States implement the *Kohll/Decker* jurisprudence. Given the particularities of ECJ jurisprudence and its implementation, the results of the research on compliance with EU directives do not automatically hold here. Building on the theory-driven literature presented above, I examine the following hypothesis:

Working hypothesis 3   If the European Commission utilizes enforcement activities, the implementation of the *Kohll/Decker* jurisprudence will be accelerated.

The National Judiciary: The Decentralized Compliance System

The role of the national judiciary in enforcing European Community law, particularly following ECJ rulings, has been largely neglected by empirical legal and political science research. Existing research has categorized the role of the national judiciary as either shielding national legislation from the ECJ primarily by withholding preliminary references (Article 234 EC) or as serving as its "sword" to foster integration and to force policy change on reluctant governments. These contradicting views, however, have not been empirically assessed to a satisfying degree. This reluctance stems in part from the methodological difficulties to find a direct link between national court cases and the (legal) implementation of ECJ cases at the Member State level. The example of the ECJ patient mobility jurisprudence used in this book provides an opportunity to assess the role of the national judiciary.

Tanja Börzel and Thomas Risse noticed that the sheer willingness of national courts to engage in a legal discourse on a given subject does not necessarily lead to compliance (2002: 164). However, in alliance with the ECJ, the national judicial branch is a crucial element for explaining the implementation of ECJ jurisprudence. Links between the ECJ and national courts seem to be a key mechanism in fostering compliance. Joseph Weiler, Karen Alter and others developed distinctive branches of this basic explanation. They explored the motives of national courts for engaging in such linkages, and found not only cross-national variation but also variation among different types and levels of courts within individual countries.

According to Weiler, the national judicial branch is the most interesting and consequential interlocutor of the ECJ (1994b: 518). The national judiciary has been a two-fold partner of the Court. First, it gradually accepted the so-called constitutionalization of the legal and political order of the European Community: the structural key doctrines of direct effect, supremacy, pre-emption, implied powers, state liability, and so on (see, for example, Weiler 1991, Lenaerts 1992, Slaughter et al. 1998, Weiler 1999).[7] Weiler observed in 1994 that,

> ... in all member states, in practically all matters likely to be the subject of litigation, domestic courts will accept that Community law must be regarded as the law of the land, which judges must uphold, and that, within the field of application of Community law, in cases of conflict between a Community norm and a member state norm, the former not the latter, must be applied. (1994b: 518)

Weiler also looked beyond the doctrinal content of the ECJ jurisprudence and found a second way that the national judiciary was a partner of the Court of Justice: it got increasingly involved in "administering" the law of the European Community (1994a: 135). The interpretative claims made by the ECJ exerted

---

7   A structural doctrine lays down a "normative framework that purports to govern fundamental issues, such as the structure of relationships between Community and member states" (Weiler 1994b: 512).

a considerable "compliance pull" on the Member States. More precisely, the piecemeal acceptance of the ECJ doctrines of direct effect and supremacy was willingly transformed by the national courts into procedural and social reality (see Weiler 1994b: 512–518). National courts thus have become "the principle vehicle for imposition of judicially driven Community discipline" (Weiler 1994a: 135–136). The national courts await the preliminary rulings, and are obliged to use them in a domestic final decision.

According to Weiler, the compliance and enforcement mechanisms in the relationship between the ECJ and the national judicial branch work as follows:

> When a national court *seeks* the Reference it is, with few exceptions, acknowledging that, at least at face value, Community norms are necessary and govern the dispute. This very issue may be of huge political significance and the subject of controversy among governments or between the Member States as a whole and, say, the Commission. But, the very fact that 'their own' national courts make a Preliminary Reference to the European Court of Justice, forces governments to 'juridify' their argument and shift to the judicial arena in which the Court of Justice is pre-eminent (so long as it can carry with it the national judiciary). When a national court *accepts* the ruling, the compliance pull of Community law becomes formidable. When European Community law is spoken through the mouths of the national judiciary it will also have the teeth that can be found in such a mouth and will usually enjoy whatever enforcement value that national law will have on that occasion. (1994a: 136)

Karen Alter also took the view that the legal doctrines of EC law supremacy and direct effect were essential to the increasing political power of the ECJ. The support by national courts was critical: it made ECJ rulings enforceable, emboldened the ECJ, and lessened the political threat of non-compliance. The real "linchpins" of the EU legal system were the national courts, whereas the ECJ's docket with the Commission and the Member States remained rather empty (see Alter 1998: 227). Unsatisfied with conventional legal doctrine debates, Alter added an inter-court competition explanation:

> The inter-court competition explanation claims that different courts have different interests *vis-à-vis* EC law, and that national courts use EC law in bureaucratic struggles between levels of the judiciary and between the judiciary and political bodies, thereby inadvertently facilitating the process of legal integration. (1998a: 241)

Especially lower courts "found few costs and numerous benefits in making their own referrals to the ECJ and in applying EC law" (Alter 1996: 466).

> For a lower court, the ECJ was akin to a second parent where parental approval wards off sanction. When a lower court did not like what it thought one parent

(a higher national court) would say, or it did not agree with what one parent said, it would ask the other parent (the ECJ). Having the other parent's approval decreased the likelihood of sanctions for challenging legal precedence or government policy. If the lower court, however, did not think that it would like what that other parent might say, it could follow the 'don't ask and the ECJ can't tell' policy and not make a referral. (Alter 1996: 466–467)

Within the competitive dynamic between higher and lower courts, the latter were empowered, so Alter claimed, by the ECJ doctrines and became "the motors of EC legal integration into the national order, and legal expansion through their referrals to the ECJ" (1996: 467). Alter's most compelling example for this thesis is the British gender equality policy in the 1980s, which experienced a boost caused by industrial tribunals, being at "the lowest rung of the judicial hierarchy" (Alter and Vargas 2000: 460).

According to Jonathan Golub, national judges may use preliminary references as a "sword" to foster integration or to force policy change on a reluctant national government. Or, by "strategically" withholding references, they can shield national policy from ECJ interference. Golub concluded from empirical evidence for Great Britain – especially for environmental policy – that there are domestic political factors, such as a prevailing political climate of Euro-pessimism, which create strong disincentives for national judges to make preliminary references (1996: 377–381).

Lisa Conant postulated, without providing sufficient evidence, that the "overwhelming" majority of national court rulings on European law take place outside the preliminary reference structure.[8] She claimed that, "[n]ational courts are most often applying European law ... without any formal interaction with the ECJ" (2003: 81). In addition, she assumed that the likely "negative" effect of independent and decentralized judicial review by national courts is the unintended divergent interpretation of European law across jurisdictions (2003: 83). However, Conant held that "[e]vidence on national judicial behavior suggests that opportunities to generate pressure [on administration, AJO] through persistent litigation remain limited" (2003: 74). According to her, EC law is generally applied case by case without causing major changes in legislation or policy (2003: 80).

The division of powers between the ECJ and the courts of the Member States within the preliminary reference structure is characterized in two contradictory ways: Gareth Davies saw a monological "conversation" taking place, where the ECJ folds application into interpretation and leaves the national courts "emasculated and infantilised" (2004a: 15 and 19). Others noticed a more dialogical "conversation" (Slaughter et al. 1998). In Koen Lenaerts' words, the ECJ "recruited" the national

---

8 The "new" Member States Austria, Finland, and Sweden, were an exception: a study for Austria confirmed this. Bedanna Bapuly and Gerhard Kohlegger (for the period from January 1995 to June 2002) found that the highest Austrian courts (OGH, VfGH, VwGH) referred 194 cases to the ECJ but ruled autonomously in 286 cases (2003: 27–28).

courts and "accepted an extensive role for national judges in the scheme of judicial oversight of Member State compliance with Community law" (1992: 4).

Tallberg distinguished between a centralized and a decentralized compliance system, the latter being the national judiciary: in pushing forward with the internal market in the late 1980s, the European Commission and the ECJ gradually shifted the EU's center of gravity in enforcement toward decentralized supervision through national courts. The policy initiatives launched by the Commission in the framework of managing the internal market and the activism of the ECJ to boost national courts as enforcers of its rulings bear witness to this shift (1999: 194–206).

Most authors agree that the application of EC law by national courts can *in principle* lead to its legal implementation. Indeed, the behavior of national courts as a bridge between the EU and the citizens of the Member States is a central variable in explaining the implementation of ECJ rulings. National courts refer preliminary cases to the Court of Justice. The ensuing rulings have to be accepted by the national courts to solve the case at hand. If the national courts do not refer cases to the ECJ, the latter cannot develop its dogmatic principles. If the national courts do not accept the ECJ doctrines and do not apply them in a proper way, implementation cannot take place. However, if national courts refer cases and apply the ECJ rulings, other domestic actors, such as the administration and the legislator, may – with a multiplication of cases and increasing judicial uncertainty – be forced to consider implementing the rulings.

What role did the national courts play regarding the *Kohll/Decker* jurisprudence in the three Member States of France, the UK and Germany, and beyond? Were they able to influence the implementation of the ECJ decisions? If yes, to what extent? My hypothesis here is the following:

Working hypothesis 4   If national courts in an EU Member State accept and apply the doctrines elaborated by the ECJ, the implementation of the rulings will take place much more quickly and smoothly than in Member States where court activism is absent.[9]

Fine-Tuning (Extending and Restricting) Doctrines by the ECJ

For EU Member States, ECJ rulings very often create a high degree of legal uncertainty as to how to implement them. As Miguel Poiares Maduro pointed out, "the language used by courts may sometimes lead them [the legal community, AJO] to say more than they wanted to say or to be interpreted more broadly than they expected to be interpreted" (2004: 47). Legal uncertainty, though, is relative. According to Tallberg, "[t]he ECJ's infringement judgments ... fulfill the managerial function of reducing the legal uncertainty of EU rules, by clarifying

---

9   According to Hjalte Rasmussen judicial activism "connotes regular judicial policy-making in pursuance of policy-objectives which usurp the rule and policy-making powers of other branches of government" (1998: 27).

the treaties and providing precedents for future disputes" (2002: 618). Conant claimed that "[u]ncertainty about the extension of legal principles across cases precludes rapid policy reform" (2003: 52). This estimation notwithstanding, several authors have pointed to the fact that precisely the legal uncertainty is decisive in understanding ECJ rulings and the implementation of it. Susanne K. Schmidt for instance claimed that the Court consciously establishes fuzzy new principles of law. In a longer stream of cases, the ECJ can see the reactions and the acceptance of national courts, judicial commentators and politics in general, and can, if necessary, modify its jurisprudence (2004: 36):

> Da die Auswirkungen einzelner Urteile für andere Sachverhalte oft unsicher
> bleiben – die Implikationen eines Urteils müssen erst auf andere Fälle ...
> übersetzt werden – wird die Akzeptanz erleichtert. Wie groß die Betroffenheit
> von einem Urteil ist, entscheidet sich oft erst nachdem weitere in vergleichbaren
> Fällen ergangen sind und die Rechtsprechung bereits etabliert ist. (2004: 37)[10]

Albert Bleckmann considered the "nachträgliche Konsensfähigkeit" [ex post ability to achieve a consensus, AJO] of an ECJ ruling to be necessary (1983: 81). Ulrich Everling stated similarly that whenever the European Court of Justice enters new terrain, its ruling is often times framed in a general way. The Court specifies, supplements, restricts and corrects the ruling in the following, after having absorbed the legal discussion and problems encountered in practice (see Everling 2000: 224).

As a recent development in the field of free movement of services, Vassilis Hatzopoulos noticed a "fragmented and apparently incoherent case law" of the ECJ, which "might be the result of the current tendency of the Court to give specific answers to specific questions, rather than to deliver generally applicable rules" (2000: 52–55). Depending on the facts of each case it adopted a different approach.

Dorte Sindbjerg Martinsen depicted "a Court that applies a systematic method of 'gap-filling,' where the line of a legal principle is gradually being drawn and extended to a new policy field." According to Martinsen, "[t]he full scope and consequence of the legal deduction is revealed from case to case and, in the case of healthcare, evidently remains in a formative process" (2005b: 1036).

According to T.C. Hartley, there is an observable pattern in the institutionalization of legal principles by the ECJ:

---

10 "Since the consequences of single rulings for different cases are often uncertain – the implications of a ruling first have to be translated to other cases – their acceptance is facilitated. The applicability of a ruling is often times decided after further decisions in similar cases are delivered and as soon as the jurisprudence is established" (translation of the author).

> A common tactic [of the ECJ, AJO] is to introduce a new doctrine gradually:
> in the first case that comes before it, the Court will establish the doctrine as
> a general principle, but suggest that it is subject to various qualifications; the
> Court may even find some reason why it should not be applied to the particular
> facts of the case. The principle, however, is now established. If there are not too
> many protests, it will be re-affirmed in later cases; the qualifications can then be
> whittled away and the full extent of the doctrine revealed. (2003: 81–82)

Gerald Rosenberg had found much earlier that judges are gradualists and
"small changes must be argued for before big ones" (1991: 31).

Martinsen cited the two *Pierik* decisions in the 1970s by the ECJ as evidence
that "a judicial doctrine in formation ultimately must be politically supported,
and that, if individual litigation proceeds excessively in terms of financial and
political implications, the member states will seek to mobilise joint action against
the Court's interpretative course" (2005b: 1038). The ECJ had held in these two
cases that treatment abroad had to be authorized when the foreign treatment had
been recognized as necessary and effective, even if it was not on offer in the health
package of the state of insurance. As a reaction, the Council unanimously amended
the concerned Regulation 1408/71, and inhibited the "regime-shopping" effects of
the *Pierik* rulings (2005b: 1037–1039).

The judicial uncertainty created by an ECJ ruling is in principle similar to the
one caused by an EU directive. Nevertheless, the degree and the kind of uncertainty
are different. Usually, the room for maneuvering in the case of a directive is more
circumscribed than it is in a Court ruling, where the case at hand is quite clear, but
the broader implications are disputed. Whereas a directive is typically formulated in
a general way and binds all Member States, a Court ruling often relies on a general
principle and applies it to a specific country and a specific case. The academic
discussion on a formal binding effect of ECJ decisions *inter partes* or *erga omnes*
is still contested. In any case there is an informal "intellectual binding effect."
EU Member States, however, can always claim that their system is different from
the involved country's system and that the decision does not apply to them. It is
difficult to determine whether Member States deliberately adopt these arguments
as a pretext to prevent or slow down the application of a ruling or whether they
do so because they are really concerned about legal uncertainty and ambiguity.
The judicial uncertainty created by ECJ rulings is usually resolved by extending
the Court's argument to other countries and circumstances. Navigating a line of
rulings in one area, the ECJ specifies its correct application and thus dissolves
such uncertainty.

For interinstitutional disputes between the European Parliament and the
Council of Ministers, Margaret McCown found that "the dynamics of precedent-
based decision-making [by the ECJ, AJO] come to constrain even quite hostile
actors" (2003: 978). The ECJ precedent shapes the future behavior of actors before
the Court. To win a case they now advance much of the precedent's arguments
instead of fighting against the original case:

Litigants respond quite defensively to ECJ decisions: rather than devoting immense resources to challenging entire decisions, they tend to advance qualifying arguments in which they simply try to distinguish their case from a disliked precedent. In doing this, however, they are left implicitly acceding to the precedents. (McCown 2003: 980)

Building on McCown's argument, I argue that not only the regulatory and procedural force of ECJ precedent shapes the behavior of Member States, but that the on-going development of the content of a ruling through the Court also shapes the implementation behavior of Member States. The follow-up rulings build on a newly established doctrine and tailor it to the systems of other EU countries. This on-going development, that is the fine-tuning of the jurisprudence (restriction and extension of the material doctrines) by the ECJ, is an important intervening variable that contributes to the willingness of Member States to implement Court rulings.[11]

When the European Court of Justice decided the *Kohll* and *Decker* cases it entered new terrain. The design of internal social security systems was exclusively in the hands of the EU countries. The intrusion into this domain through the principles of the passive free movement of services and the free movement of goods started a new "negotiation process" between the ECJ and Member States on how their competency would be circumscribed. The reactions to the rulings were therefore often very hostile, as will be seen in Chapters 6 through 8. The conditions for implementing the jurisprudence were far from favorable. To some extent the follow-up jurisprudence to *Kohll* and *Decker* took these reactions into account. Did the fine-tuning of the *Kohll/Decker* jurisprudence contribute to its implementation, and if yes, how? This leads me to the following hypothesis:

Working hypothesis 5   The development of the material doctrines embedded in the *Kohll/Decker* jurisprudence in further ECJ decisions facilitated its implementation in the EU Member States.

De-territorialization, Internal De-structuring and Financial Destabilization?

A last set of questions addresses possible effects of de-territorialization, internal de-structuring and financial destabilization caused by the *Kohll/Decker* jurisprudence. Whereas de-territorialization looks at the impact of ECJ rulings on the territorial principle of health care systems, de-structuring deals with the effects on their internal functioning. Financial destabilization effects are the third kind of effects

---

11   I thank Reinhard Slepcevic for pointing out to me that the unfolding of the jurisprudence by the ECJ should be understood as an intervening rather than an explanatory variable.

addressed. All three together allow me to assess the overall impact of these ECJ rulings on domestic social security systems.

De-territorialization: Abolishing or Weakening of the Principle of Territoriality?

Maurizio Ferrera defined the principle of territoriality as "the inclusion in a given territorial community, and entitlement to its sharing arrangements" (2005: 126). According to Peter Altmaier, the principle of territoriality consists of two aspects: First, the national sovereignty to determine whether and to what extent benefits are provided abroad. Second, the justification and regulation of benefits on a national level only apply to domestic cases without an equivalent for foreign cases (Altmaier 1995: 73).

In former times "[t]he 'principle of territoriality' strictly reserved control over the most relevant aspects of social security in the hands of national governments" (Ferrera 2003: 15). In the case of health care they exercised spatial control over the consumption of benefits, as well as many other aspects. National governments controlled the quality and standards of health care, as well as the planning and managing of service capacity within constrained budgets. This territorial closure of health care systems has been challenged by both endogenous and exogenous pressures (Ferrera 2003: 16). The exogenous pressure of interest for this study is supposed to come from European integration in general and the ECJ in particular. Ferrera saw the "trend" that the activist rulings of the ECJ perforated the external frontiers of domestic health care systems (2005: 237). As early as 1995, Altmaier observed critical comments from the judicial and political arenas, especially in Germany, in which the ECJ was charged with a "*Durchbrechung* oder gar *Aushöhlung* des im nationalen Sozialversicherungsrecht verankerten *Territorialitätsprinzips*" (71).[12] Stephan Leibfried and Paul Pierson went even further and claimed in influential articles in 1995, 2000, and 2005, that the "closed shop" – the domestic health care system – had been opened (Leibfried and Pierson 1995, 2000, Leibfried 2005). However, they did not explain to what extent this had taken place. According to Leibfried, national governments simply lost their exclusive control (2005: 268). This relaxing of the boundaries of domestic social security systems is referred to as "de-territorialization."

Prior to the *Kohll/Decker* jurisprudence domestic regulations in all three EU countries made use of a strict territorial principle for providing health care. In the German Social Code Book V on statutory health insurance, Paragraph 16(1)(1) suspended health care benefit claims when an insured person stayed abroad. The French Social Security Code in Articles L. 332–3 and R. 332–2, the French Public Health Code in Article L. 6211–2–1, and the UK NHS Act from 1977 in Section 5(2)(b) also enshrined a strict territorial principle. These provisions were certainly modified by the European Coordination Regulations 1408/71 and 574/72

---

12   A "breach or even the erosion of the principle of territoriality enshrined in national social security law" (translation of the author).

for the social security of migrant workers, which were eventually extended to all persons. Nevertheless, these European regulations were meant to only coordinate the domestic provisions of Member States without affecting their territoriality. This is best proved by the continued territorial closure of providing health care in Germany, France, and the UK. Altmaier therefore noted that the norms elaborated by the ECJ do not completely abolish the principle of territoriality. Rather, they limit themselves to selective modifications and breaches (see Altmaier 1995: 86).

It is difficult to operationalize territorialization and de-territorialization because no country has a completely closed system. All of them allow more or less far-reaching exceptions. Also, the different degrees of the strength of the principle of territoriality are difficult to distinguish. That it is hard to operationalize the fuzzy concept of (de-) territorialization should not keep us, however, from comparing domestic health care systems before and after the implementation of the *Kohll/ Decker* jurisprudence.

In order to determine whether an institutional policy change concerning the principle of territoriality and the predominant provision of health care is major or minor, I draw on a heuristic developed by Peter A. Hall (1993). He identified three distinctive subtypes of policy changes according to the magnitude of the changes involved: a "first order change" affects the level of a basic instrument of policy, a "second order change" the technique or the policy instrument, and a "third order change" the overarching goals of a policy (Hall 1993: 278–279). Applied to implementing the *Kohll/Decker* jurisprudence in the EU Member States, a "first order change" would consist of simplifying the authorization scheme or of increasing the rate of reimbursement for a treatment purchased abroad. A "second order change" would be a modification of the way health care is provided, for example the introduction of an additional reimbursement scheme, or the perforation of territoriality, which is enshrined in domestic health care systems, for example further exceptions from the general principle. The outright abandoning of the principle of territoriality or a radical shift from providing in-kind benefits to reimbursing the costs would be considered changes of the "third order."

De-territorialization is understood here as the (gradual) weakening or tearing apart of the closure practices of domestic social security systems. The principle of territoriality in providing health care benefits is unquestionably a core element of domestic social security systems which EU Member States may weaken or abolish. If the core principle or important parts of it are changed we could speak of de-territorialization. I am able to determine the extent and the shape of such changes by looking at the resulting legislative and administrative changes.

Leibfried, Pierson, Ferrera, and other authors who speculated about de-territorialization, usually relied on the material principles elaborated by the ECJ in its decisions: domestic restrictions on when and how to receive treatment or medical goods abroad were violating basic freedoms, the passive free movement of services, the free movement of goods, and the free movement of workers. Therefore, the territorial restrictions of the health care systems were to be weakened or abolished. However, these authors did not link concrete legislative changes to the ECJ jurisprudence.

Some authors, like Ulrich Becker, disagreed with this assessment. They found that in legislative terms health care systems across the EU continued to be strictly closed (2003: 2272).

If we believe in the assessment of those authors who advocate de-territorialization, we can state the following hypothesis:

Working hypothesis 6   The implementation of the *Kohll/Decker* jurisprudence has led to the partial or complete abolition of the territorial foundation of the domestic social (health care) systems.

De-structuring Dynamics: Is there a Spillover to Internal Structures?

The question of de-territorialization looks at the opening of the domestic health care systems, caused by ECJ rulings. If the closed health care systems were pried open to some extent, did internal de-structuring of domestic health care systems accompany this? According to Ferrera, the *Kohll/Decker* jurisprudence unleashed "a destructuring potential that ... may lead to significant changes in the institutional configuration of this sector [that is the health care sector, AJO] of the welfare state, especially in certain countries" (2003: 22). He expected that "[g]iven the wide variation in structural profiles [of individual welfare states, AJO], we should expect that the potential de-structuring (and re-configuration) of European welfare systems will take place in different forms and degrees of intensity" (2003: 32). Ferrera classified EU Member States as follows:

> The impact of the recent ECJ case law is likely to be more direct on those systems which are based on a plurality of occupational funds (Belgium, France, Luxembourg, Austria, Germany and the Netherlands), especially if these funds operate through ex post re-imbursement as in the first three countries of the group. The impact should remain more limited in those countries which have a national health service (the UK, Ireland, the Nordic and Southern European countries). But even in such systems we might expect some de-stabilising consequences. The idea that reimbursement is always due in case of territorial 'exit' may undermine cost containment strategies introduced at the national or sub-national level; it may challenge the logic of functioning of national health services resting on in-kind provisions (especially their rationing policies). (2003: 33)

Similarly, Maximilian Fuchs expected that "only in such cases where purely cost reimbursement takes place ... changes can be detected that arise as a consequence of the settled case law of the Court of Justice" (2002: 552). Does the empirical evidence allow us to classify the internal de-structuring dynamics in the EU Member States in that way? If this classification does not hold, are there alternative ways to classify the developments in these countries?

A de-structuring of domestic social security systems takes place when adjustments due to ECJ rulings change the very functioning of the system. Some German insurance funds for instance feared that a range of internal control mechanisms, for example budgets, health delivery plans, and rationing restrictions, would be challenged by the *Kohll/Decker* jurisprudence, and that this would happen even when patients did not make use of their newly won mobility. The extent to which domestic laws and administrative practices were changed due to the ECJ decisions allows me to determine whether such internal de-structuring occurred. If the EU countries did not change their laws and practices substantially in reaction to the ECJ's jurisprudence but simply incorporated the new elements into their systems without further repercussions, then national welfare states may not have been harmed. But if, in addition to opening the national health care containers, national laws and practices were amended substantially because core features of the systems were changed, then the ECJ jurisprudence has significantly de-structured national welfare states. In order to answer this question I place the changes of laws and administrative practices and their consequences in the broader context of welfare state reforms, or more precisely health care reforms (see Chapter 11). In sum, I examine the following hypothesis:

Working hypothesis 7 The *Kohll/Decker* jurisprudence has de-structured the workings of social security systems. EU Member States could not limit the effects to patient mobility abroad. In order to comply they had to change the internal mechanisms of their social security systems.

Financial Destabilization:
Did Patients take Advantage of the Newly Gained Mobility?

Last but not least, I analyze financial destabilization effects attributed to the *Kohll/Decker* jurisprudence. Governments and insurance funds have argued that the destruction of the territorial closure of their health systems and that the internal de-structuring dynamics of ECJ rulings would cause a significant loss of control over receipts and expenditures, and would ultimately destabilize the domestic statutory health care systems financially. Following this line of arguments, I examine also the last hypothesis:

Working hypothesis 8 The *Kohll/Decker* jurisprudence caused Member States significant financial losses.

Chapter 3
Conceptualizing the ECJ's Integration Function

The reception and perception of the ECJ has changed over time. Legal scholarship "discovered" the political role of the ECJ in the 1980s.[1] Scholarly research in general and political scientists in particular paid limited attention to the political impact and the dynamics of ECJ rulings: however this scientific neglect came to an abrupt end in the 1990s. Preoccupation with the Court became fashionable.[2] This change in perception was caused by a new political and social environment and the new conditions under which the ECJ operated (see Weiler 1994a). Today the importance of the ECJ "as an actor and of law as a context in which to situate political analysis of the Community has become widely accepted" (Weiler 1994a: 131–132). The "discovery" of the ECJ by political scientists in the 1990s has generated a vivid discourse of proponents of different political science approaches such as neofunctionalism, (neo)realism, and intergovernmentalism, a debate that has reached out to the legal approaches. This controversy has led to a steady increase of literature on the ECJ, legal integration and integration through law.[3]

In general terms, the evolution of the EU legal system is conceptualized such that law is either immune against developments from outside the legal system, or else it is dependent on these developments. The most important legal and political science approaches concerning the ECJ are compiled in Table 3.1.

---

1   Among the first to write about the political role of the ECJ were Weiler (1982), Cappelletti et al. (1986), and Rasmussen (1986). For the literature on courts and politics in Europe, see for example Rehder (2007).

2   An extract of the abundant literature in the 1990s are the following influential books and articles: Weiler (1991), Burley and Mattli (1993), Alter and Meunier-Aitsahalia (1994), Weiler (1994a, 1994b), Alter (1996, 1998b), Mattli and Slaughter (1998), Rasmussen (1998), Stone Sweet and Brunell (1998), Leibfried and Pierson (2000), Stone Sweet (2000), Shapiro and Stone Sweet (2002), and Stone Sweet (2004).

3   Legal integration refers to the expansion and penetration of Community law into the national legal and political systems of the EU Member States, whereas integration through law means the function and potential which legal institutions and mechanisms have had and may have in the process of integration.

Table 3.1 Different perspectives on the evolution and operation of the EU legal system

	Approach	Representatives	General characteristics	Role of the ECJ
Legal approaches	Legalism	• Some legal scholars specializing in EU law, like Rasmussen • Some (ex-)ECJ judges	• Most important are the internal logic of law and legal reasoning: "Rule of law"; • Law is an objective and apolitical power and self-interest is irrelevant; • There are no ideological and sociopolitical influences or constraints on the Court's jurisdiction.	• Important role; • Independent actor; • No judicial activism and policy-making at all, or only teleological policy-making.
	Contextualism	• Some legal scholars specializing in EU law • Weiler, Snyder	• There is a reciprocal relationship between law and politics/policy.	• Policy-maker; • Independent actor; • Judicial activism, but also self-restraint.
Political science theories	(Neo)Realism	• Scheingold	• Primacy of national politics over community law; • Judicial interpretation is a translation of treaty provisions and rules (formulated by EU Member States) into operational language, devoid of political content and consequence.	• Technical and subservient; • "Validator of decisions."
	Intergovernmentalism, Rational choice (Game theory)	• Garrett, Kelemen, Schulz • Kilroy	• Intergovernmental analysis and realist premises.	• Neither servant nor master; • Responsive strategic agent of EU Member governments who seeks to push forward integration but who is bound by Member States' preferences.
	Neofunctionalist theories	• Mattli, Slaughter • Leibfried, Pierson (moderate) • Stone Sweet, Brunell, Caporaso • Alter (lower national courts and ECJ)	• Law functions as a mask for policy implications of ECJ jurisprudence and as a shield against political attacks; • Legal integration is driven by societal demand.	• Policy-maker; • Independent actor; • Judicial activism.

Legal Approaches

There are two types of legal approaches that assess the evolution and operation of the EU legal system differently: legalism and contextualism. "Legalist" scholars – according to Anne-Marie Burley and Walter Mattli "the vast majority of European legal scholars specializing in EC law" (1993: 45) – claimed that only legal logic and reasoning can explain legal integration. Legalists rejected the idea that ideological and socio-political factors have had an influence on the jurisprudence of the Court. The ECJ and legal integration were conceptualized in a political vacuum (Burley and Mattli 1993: 45). "Contextualist" scholars analyzed "the reciprocal relationship between the legal and political spheres in European integration" (Burley and Mattli 1993: 46). In contrast to authors who argued in a purely legal fashion, contextualists did acknowledge ECJ activism. Both approaches, with their focus on legal considerations, cannot explain why the implementation processes and outcomes of EU Member States vary.

Political Science Approaches

In contrast to legal theories, all political science approaches see law as contingent upon politics. Political science theories are more skeptical and split about the role of the ECJ in the integration process. (Neo-)realist theorists for instance reduced the ECJ to a "technical serviant [sic!],"[4] denied its role as a policy-maker altogether and stressed the primacy of national politics over community law (see for example Scheingold 1971). For all these reasons (neo)realism in general paid little attention to the ECJ (see Burley and Mattli 1993: 48–49). From a "rationalist" game theoretical point of view, the ECJ was strategically interacting with domestic governments. Geoffrey Garrett, Daniel Kelemen and Heiner Schulz built three "testable" hypotheses around this strategic interaction. Unfortunately based on very few ECJ decisions, their findings were as follows:

> First, the greater the clarity of EU treaties, case precedent, and legal norms in support of an adverse judgement, the greater the likelihood that the ECJ will rule against litigant governments. Second, the greater the costs of an ECJ ruling to important domestic constituencies or to the government itself, the greater the likelihood that the litigant government will not abide by the decision. Third, the greater the costs of a ruling and the greater the number of EU member governments affected by it, the greater the likelihood that they will respond collectively to rein in EU activism – with new secondary legislation revisions of the EU treaty base. (1998: 174)

---

4 Weiler used this notion in order to reproach scholars for seeing predominantly the instrumental function of law (1982: 39).

In 1993, Anne-Marie Burley and Walter Mattli tried to revive the neofunctionalist approach acknowledging the power of the ECJ to promote integration through its own agenda. According to them, the ECJ was an "unsung hero" of the integration process (1993: 41). They explained legal integration with functional and political spillover effects (1993: 65–69). In the neofunctionalist perspective there is no necessary congruence between ECJ rulings and interests of EU Member States. The ECJ (lower) national courts, and individual litigants follow their own interests and hence are a driving force behind the process of integration (Mattli and Slaughter 1998: 180–181). The ECJ functioned both as a shield and a mask, but only as long as its credibility and neutrality was unchallenged.

Most of the above presented conceptualizations focused on "legal integration"/ "integration of law" which has to be distinguished from "integration through law." Legal integration describes the gradual/incremental construction of an EU legal system that privileges EU law over national law. In this case,

> ... law is examined as an *object* of integration itself, the focus being on the problems created by the interaction of several initially distinct legal systems under the umbrella of a central authority. (Cappelletti et al. 1986: 15)

"Integration through law" characterizes the instrumental function of legal institutions and mechanisms on economic, political, and social integration. Here,

> ... law is examined as an *instrument*, the focus being on the function and potential which legal institutions and mechanisms have had and may yet have in the process of integration – economic, political, cultural etc. (Cappelletti et al. 1986: 15).

I focus on EU law as an instrument in the integration process of health care systems.

It is the role of the ECJ as a policy-maker which is of interest to this study. It is important to account for the ECJ's role for two reasons: First, one has to understand the role of the ECJ as a policy-maker to determine how the development of the jurisprudence by the Court affects the Member States. If the ECJ had no activist role, we should expect that the impact of its jurisprudence would be rather "easy to digest" by the EU countries. But if it is an activist court, implementation of its jurisprudence should be more cumbersome. Secondly, we need to know how the *Kohll/Decker* jurisprudence fits into the commonly used periodization of the ECJ's unfolding of its function for European integration. In my analysis, I should either confirm the established periodization, nuance it, or modify it.

The ECJ's Function in the Institutional Setting of the EU

In the founding Treaties of the European Community, the ECJ was charged with ensuring that "in the interpretation and application of this Treaty the law is observed" (former Article 164, today Article 220 EC Treaty).[5] Over time the ECJ has transformed the treaties into the quasi-European constitution and has become the constitutional court of the European Community. It resolves legal disputes among the institutions of the European Community, between Member States and supranational institutions, and among Member States themselves. Also, in the overwhelming majority of cases, it provides authoritative interpretations of European law to judges of national courts through preliminary references, in which European law is applied to the facts at hand. The latter competency will be the focus of this study.

The ECJ has gradually constitutionalized the Treaties by articulating several important structural doctrines. First, the Treaties (any Community norm) are supreme and derogate domestic law including the domestic constitution (see Case 6/64, *Costa/ENEL*). Second, European law is directly applicable in Member States (see Case 26/62, *van Gend & Loos*). In addition, the ECJ created the doctrines of state liability (see C-6/90 and C-9/90, *Francovich* and *Bonifaci*), and of the direct effect of directives (see Case 8/81, *Becker*), and so on.[6]

In an important ruling in 1986, after having succeeded in constitutionalizing the Treaties, the ECJ held that "the European Economic Community is a Community based on the rule of law, inasmuch as neither its Member States nor its institutions can avoid a review of the question whether the measures adopted by them are in conformity with the basic constitutional charter, the Treaty" (Case 294/83: para. 23). Therefore, the ECJ is in a permanently tense relationship with the Member States and the other institutions of the European Community.

On the one hand, the EU Member States need the ECJ in order to establish their interests vis-à-vis other Member States or Community institutions. On the other hand, the Court constrains their freedom of action. In Article 234 proceedings, national courts rely on the legal preliminary ruling of the ECJ, which concerns the validity and interpretation of Community law. In the majority of cases the compatibility of domestic with European law was and is directly and indirectly challenged (see Everling 1983: 101–102).

---

5   The ECJ is located in Luxembourg. It is composed of 27 Judges and eight Advocate Generals who are appointed for a renewable term of six years. The jurisdiction of the ECJ comprises references for preliminary rulings, actions for failure to fulfil obligations, actions for annulment, actions for failure to act, appeals, and reviews: For detailed information on the ECJ see for instance Rasmussen (1998), Slaughter et al. (1998), and De Búrca and Weiler (2001).

6   For further principles and the corresponding ECJ rulings, see Bapuly and Kohlegger (2003: 3).

In its role as *The Guardian* of the Treaty the European Commission has a symbiotic relationship with the ECJ as it ensures respect for Community law. In infringement proceedings the Commission brings violations of European law before the ECJ.

A discussion of the relationship of the Court to the other Community institutions is not necessary, as I am focusing on preliminary references.

The General Function of the ECJ as a Policy-maker

Hjalte Rasmussen distinguished among the terms "judicial law-making," "judicial policy-making," and "judicial activism." Judicial law-making is done by all courts. Judicial policy-making is usually a "legitimate element of judicial business," but when done on "thin legal ice" can become problematic. Judicial activism "connotes regular judicial policy-making in pursuance of policy-objectives which usurp the rule and policy-making powers of other branches of government, specifically if judicial choice-making over a procrasted period of time is at odds with election-day results" (Rasmussen 1998: 26–27). The concept of "judicial self-restraint" according to Rasmussen is "commonly used to designate the situation in which judges defer their judgements to some extent … to the political branches of government" (1986: 33). For the purpose of this study, it is important to locate the ECJ's rulings between the two poles of judicial policy-making/activism and judicial self-restraint. Do we perceive a rise and fall of ECJ activism over time? What are the established periodizations of Court activism and self-restraint? How does the *Kohll/Decker* jurisprudence fit into this picture? What does the analysis of these decisions tell us about the role of the ECJ?

In the early 1990s, Gerald Rosenberg studied whether or not the Supreme Court of the United States has brought about social change. He analyzed litigation in the areas of civil rights, abortion, women's rights, the environment, reapportionment, and criminal rights, and contrasted two distinctive logics: a "dynamic court view" and a "constrained court view." The dynamic view sees the Supreme Court as an effective producer of social reform, whereas the constrained view perceives it as an ineffective instrument (Rosenberg 1991: 1–36). Rosenberg sided with the constrained court perspective: "U.S. courts can *almost never* be effective producers of significant social reform. At best, they can second the social reform acts of the other branches of government" (1991: 338). Is this assessment transferable to the ECJ? Do ECJ rulings lead to change in the Member States?

The most common assessment of the development of the role of the ECJ as a policy-maker refers to two main phases: an early phase of judicial activism and a later more self-restrained period. Rasmussen asserted that the ECJ engaged in activist pro-federalist policy-making from the early 1970s until the late 1980s, and went far beyond the limits of the legislation of the European Community, overstretched its mandate and public tolerance, and thus "transgressed the borderline to the Community's judicial function" (1986: 508). Rasmussen points to the most commonly offered rationale:

> [T]he judges became convinced that the political processes of the Community were unlikely to result in the promised land of a European union. And that they then decided to substitute judicial to political decision. (1998: 30)

The constitutionalization of the legal and political order of the European Community marked the beginning of this first phase. Imposing a new constitutional regime by the Court on the Member States from the early 1960s onwards was a "quiet revolution" accompanied by "benign neglect" from researchers (see Weiler 1994a, b). Toward the end of the first activist phase, the ECJ pointed more and more to disparities between domestic laws and the proper functioning of a Common European Market. Koen Lenaerts argued that the EU Member States

> were led to prefer political legislation, even at the risk of being pushed into the minority on a vote concluding Council deliberations in which they had participated, to a kind of 'creeping legislation' through the judicial process, to which they were completely external. (1992: 16)

According to Lenaert's assessment, the final result of this strong judicial impetus was the Single European Act and the new Article 100A (today 94) EC Treaty, which gave competence to the Community to harmonize domestic laws in order to create the internal market. In the post-Maastricht period, the ECJ could look back on a satisfactory level of public satisfaction with its performance, however, without being able to create diffuse support, which would be necessary to support the Court even when its decisions are disagreeable. According to James Gibson and Gregory Caldeira's diagnosis, the ECJ rested therefore on a "precarious bedrock of support":

> To the extent that the ECJ is required to make a series of controversial decisions that attract the attention of the mass public, it may well find itself with only a small reservoir of goodwill within the mass public. (1998: 90)

Getting involved in policy-making, the ECJ generated more and more opposition and

> [j]ust as the tools to evaluate its policy-making role were being sharpened, the Court, however, has given signs of retreat from its predominant role. Most famously it reversed its case law in the field of free movement of goods in *Keck* [decided in 1993, AJO]; it further stepped back from its threat to use EC competition law as the measuring rod for national economic legislation and,

more recently, it refused to be used by the Commission as a short cut to the dismantling of national electricity monopolies. (Schepel 2000: 2)[7]

Beginning with the late 1980s, according to Rasmussen, "judgements ideologically marked by self restraint are now handed down at impressively short intervals" (1998: 28). The concrete examples Rasmussen provided were: the *Barber* cases, *Marschall*, *Johnson II*, *Keck* (1998: 294, footnote 588). He therefore summarized that partially "self restraint has in some measure taken over where activism used to be the name of the game" (1998: 292). In this context Norbert Reich suspected "that the internal market has been completed, at least in large parts, as of the end of 1992, and that therefore the legitimacy for judicial activism which is always problematic can be put to doubt" (1994: 482).

The periodization in an early-activist and a later-self-restraint phase, however, is contentious. Ulrich Everling suggested a more wavelike pattern of jurisprudence – with certain anomalies – that moves with the fluctuations of political developments of the European Community (2000: 224).

This book shows that to dichotomize an early activist versus a present self-restrained period is too simplistic and does not reflect the complex reality of ECJ jurisprudence. In its function as a constitutional court the ECJ very much depends on its rulings being accepted by Member States. In order to achieve acceptance and implementation, the ECJ has to be responsive to the objections of the Member States in its rulings. I incorporate this often neglected aspect.

The ECJ as a Policy-maker in Social (Health Care) Policy

Although research on legal integration and integration through law has steadily increased, studies of the impact of ECJ decisions on (social) policy are still hard to come by and often speculative. I now examine briefly these accounts which focused on the influence of ECJ jurisprudence on social (health care) policy. In this literature there is great disagreement over the impact and the meaning of ECJ decisions in the domain of social law. One explanation could be that not even the ECJ has systematized its own approach, but rather develops it as it goes along. Every interpreter of the jurisprudence of the ECJ, especially in the area of social security then runs the risk of reading too much into the decisions and deriving general principles from the rulings that have to be revised next time around.[8] In order to simplify matters, the existing literature can be divided according to whether it is pro or con the policy-making role of the ECJ in social (health care) policy.

---

7 Norbert Reich considered the ECJ rulings Keck, Meng and Audi, which were all decided in November 1993, to be part of a "November revolution," in which the predominant pattern of law-making and law reform incited by ECJ rulings has been revisited (1994: 482–483).

8 On this problem, see especially Kingreen (2003: 368).

A Major Role for the ECJ

On the pro side, Stephan Leibfried and Paul Pierson from political science attribute a major role to ECJ decisions in social policy developments. In a series of publications on the policy-making qualities of the ECJ, they stated that its recent case law based on internal market rules changed the exclusive nature of national welfare states and gradually led to an erosion of national welfare state sovereignty and autonomy (Leibfried and Pierson 1995, 2000, Leibfried 2005). This erosion process was to take place through "positive" initiatives aimed at developing uniform social standards at the supranational level and also – causing a far more important impact – through "negative" reforms.[9] Leibfried and Pierson identified the Court as one significant actor in the erosion of national welfare state sovereignty and a center of social policy-making (2000: 288). According to them, the net effect of innovative court decisions was "to limit national capacities to contain transfers by territory and to shape welfare state reform trajectories" (2000: 278). From a legal perspective, Klaus Sieveking also acknowledged the important role of the Court. He claimed that the ECJ had given impulses of integration that had modified law on a European and on a national level (1997: 194). Klaus-Dieter Borchardt similarly agreed with the important role of the ECJ as an "Ersatz"-legislator in social and labor law (1995: 62). Peter Clever conceded the policy-making role when he complained about the considerable power of the ECJ in framing labor law, discrimination law, and social security matters with respect to third country nationals. According to him, the ECJ rulings overshot the mark and paralyzed the development of domestic social policy (1994).

According to Rasmussen, the *Kohll/Decker* jurisprudence belongs to the "still occurring, occasional flashes of activism" (1998: 350). Dorte Sindbjerg Martinsen claimed that "[j]udicial activism alone has applied the principle of the free movement of services to the policy field of healthcare, and thereby further energized the process [through which a European health care dimension has been established and patient mobility has been extended, AJO]" (2005b: 1035).

> That Europe ever came to regulate national healthcare has not occurred as an output of rational political decision-making, but rather as a 'side effect' of how the European Court of Justice gradually conferred a 'supreme' status to the free movement provisions in the EU legal construct and in this way interfered in virtually all areas of national law and policy. Since 1998, however, the impact of these 'side-effects' on national healthcare policies has reached a turning-point, making irrevocably clear that the policy domain of healthcare is hardly an 'island beyond the reach of Community law'. (Martinsen 2005b: 1035)

---

9   Leibfried understood "negative" reforms as "the ECJ's imposition of market compatibility requirements ... that restrict, but also redefine the social policies of member states" (2005: 245).

Martinsen tried to demonstrate that the ECJ had been "a Court that historically has been politically restrained, but which recently – in the absence of political voice – has been capable of acting both cautiously and ambitiously at one and the same time, thus extending the rights of the European patient" (2005b: 1036).

A Minor Role for the ECJ

On the con side, Thorsten Kingreen was rather critical about the impact of ECJ decisions. He claimed that the Court practiced self-restraint in the application of the basic freedoms to social security (2003: 546). Therefore, the political responsibility remained largely with Member States (2003: 583). Maximilian Fuchs noticed that the impact of Court decisions on health care was very limited because the majority of Member States had a national health system, which according to his interpretation in 2002 did not fall under the ambit of these decisions (552). Lisa Conant brought forward a "justice-contained" argument and supported this reasoning with a cross-sectoral comparison of the role of law in the European and the domestic policy-making processes (2003). She looked for policy responses in different policy fields, one of them social benefits. Here, Conant identified three prevailing domestic strategies of national governments: first, a lack of formal institutional support combined with possible financial burdens on Member States led to a conscious containment of compliance; second, ECJ rulings were actively overruled through European legislation; and third, preemptive European and national legislation was enacted (2003: 178). Conant did not only speak of contained justice, but of "reversed" justice. She concluded:

> Contained compliance has been pervasive for all social benefits and constitutes the dominant response to ECJ decisions on social and tax advantages. Member States have gone beyond such passive evasion in the area of social security, overruling ECJ decisions on the exportability of particular benefits with unanimous European legislation and pre-empting ECJ interference with domestic legislation. (2003: 187)

Her assessment, however, pertains mainly to third country nationals' access to social benefits. Also, her justice-contained argument about social benefits is based on little evidence that is not fully convincing and makes further investigation necessary.[10]

The literature discussed above draws a rather confusing and ambivalent picture of the impact of ECJ rulings on social policy in general and patient mobility in particular. The detailed analysis of the *Kohll/Decker* jurisprudence in this book clarifies the situation and adds some nuances.

---

10   For example, for the French case Conant relied primarily on Roger (1993).

Conclusion

I have shown how differently political and legal scientists conceive the role of the European Court of Justice, and how this affects its power to frame an issue in general and particularly in social (health care) policy. The assessments of the ECJ policy-making role in social policy vary considerably. One side regards the Court as the decisive or at least an important source of change for domestic social security systems. The other side considers the role and impact of the ECJ rulings to be negligible. In the following chapters, I deal with the *Kohll/Decker* jurisprudence. This allows me to reassess the previous conceptualizations of the Court's role.

Chapter 4

ECJ Jurisprudence on Patient Mobility

In order to show the impact of ECJ rulings on national social policy, I examine a line of cases about the exportability of health care benefits. This line started with *Kohll* and *Decker* in 1998, and was followed by *Vanbraekel* and *Geraets-Smits/Peerbooms* in 2001, *Müller-Fauré/van Riet* and *Inizan* in 2003, *Leichtle* in 2004, *Keller* in 2005, *Watts* and *Acereda Herrera* in 2006, and most recently, *Stamatelaki* in 2007. These rulings taken together will be referred to in short as the "*Kohll/Decker* jurisprudence."

First, I describe the provisions of Article 22 of Regulation 1408/71/EEC. Then, I summarize the ECJ rulings of the *Kohll/Decker* jurisprudence in which this European secondary law was challenged and patient mobility promoted.[1] I cite extensively from the original rulings, not to torture the reader but to emphasize the spirit and complexity of the rulings.

The Legal Basis: Provisions of Article 22 Regulation 1408/71/EEC[2]

The core elements of the European Single Market were and are the four fundamental freedoms: the free movement of goods, persons, services and capital (see Articles 3(1)(c) and 14(2) EC Treaty). The European Community's first real success in social policy was in labor mobility provisions. In order to achieve its economical objectives, the Community needed to coordinate social security systems. Several crucial regulations were issued: the first regulations were already established in 1958, Regulations 3 and 4 on the Social Security of Migrant Workers, based on Article 42 EC Treaty.[3] In 1971–72, Regulation 1408/71 and Regulation 574/72 concerning administrative procedure replaced these regulations.[4]

---

1 *Secondary* law consists of provisions or instruments, for example regulations and directives, enacted by the EU institutions. It is contrasted with *primary* law, which is found in the Treaties.

2 Regulation 883/2004 is going to replace 1408/71. It is not yet applicable, though, as no procedure regulation has been decided on yet and several important annexes are missing.

3 "The Council shall, acting in accordance with the procedure referred to in Article 251, adopt such measures in the field of social security as are necessary to provide freedom of movement for workers; to this end, it shall make arrangements to secure for migrant workers and their dependents" (Article 42 EC Treaty).

4 Regulation (EEC) No 1408/71 of the Council of 14 June 1971 applies social security schemes to employed persons and their families moving within the Community, Official

These regulations were focused on coordinating, rather than on harmonizing, domestic social security law. The diversity of national social systems was to be preserved. The original aim of Regulations 3, 4, 1408/71 and 574/72 was to protect migrant workers from disadvantages arising from crossing national borders, that is from leaving one social security system and moving into another one. Regulations 1408/71 and 574/72 were meant to facilitate the free movement of persons covered by social insurance and to ease the provision of cross-border medical services. Before the *Kohll* and *Decker* rulings of 1998, Article 22(1) of Regulation 1408/71 determined that an insured person and family members staying or residing in another Member State were entitled to receive in-kind benefits according to the legislation of this Member State as if they were insured there, at the expense of their home country insurance institution.[5] This entitlement concerned in-kind benefits which became medically necessary during a stay in another EU Member State. The nature of the benefits and the expected length of stay had to be taken into account. The typical cases addressed here were vacations and further short term stays in other Member States.

For planned treatment abroad, Article 22(2)(c) of Regulation 1408/71 determined that authorization for such a treatment

> may not be refused where the treatment in question is among the benefits provided for by the legislation of the Member State on whose territory the person concerned resides and where he cannot be given such treatment within the time normally necessary for obtaining the treatment in question in the Member State of residence taking account of his current state of health and the probable course of the disease.

If authorization was granted, the treatment was provided according to the legislation of the Member State where the treatment took place, and at the expense of the insurance institution in the Member State of insurance.

Journal L 149, July 5, 1971, p. 0002–0050; Regulation (EEC) No 574/72 of the Council of March 21, 1972 determines the procedure for implementing Regulation (EEC) No 1408/71, Official Journal L 074, March 27, 1972, p. 0001–0083; Regulation (EC) No 631/2004 adapted rights and simplified procedures; on Regulations 3, 4, 1408/71 and 574/1972 see for instance Cornelissen (1996), Ruellan (1998), Schulte/Barwig (1999), Börzel/Risse (2002), Fuchs (2005), and Spiegel (2006).

5   Regulation (EC) No 631/2004 replaced former Subparagraph 1(a) of Article 22 Regulation 1408/71. It extended entitlements already in place for pensioners to all other patient groups. All patients are now entitled to health care "whose condition requires benefits in kind which become necessary on medical grounds during a stay in the territory of another Member State, taking into account the nature of the benefits and the expected length of the stay."

Medically Necessary Treatment while Staying Abroad: E111/EHIC

If medical benefits were necessary during a short-term visit in another EU country, the E111 form since 1993, in application of Article 22 Regulation 1408/71, covered all in-kind benefits, both out-patient and in-patient.[6] The type of treatment and the expected duration of the stay had to be taken into consideration. The patient had to submit the E111 paper form to the foreign service provider (the physician or the hospital) who had to check its validity. In 2004, the European Health Insurance Card (EHIC) replaced the E111 form (see European Commission 2003b).[7]

Authorization for Planned Treatment Abroad: E112 Procedure

If a patient needed a specific treatment in an EU/EEA country and Switzerland, the E112 procedure applied.[8] The competent health insurance institution, after consultation with its own physician, had to authorize the treatment. The E112 procedure is used only under very special conditions when the treatment cannot be provided in the EU Member State itself in the appropriate time frame. In the foreign country, the E112 form has to be converted in a document appropriate for such claim under that Member State's insurance regime (see Decision 153).

The ECJ decisions, which will be discussed below, challenged this established structure and paved the way for an additional modus of receiving medical benefits in another EU Member State based on the free movement of services and goods. I now examine the "*Kohll/Decker* jurisprudence". This line of rulings started with *Kohll* (C-158/96) and *Decker* (C-120/95) in 1998, and was followed chronologically by *Vanbraekel* (C-368/98) and *Geraets-Smits/Peerbooms* (C-157/99) in 2001, *Müller-Fauré/van Riet* (C-385/99) and *Inizan* (C-56/01) in 2003, *Leichtle* (C-8/02) in 2004, *Keller* (C-145/03) in 2005, *Watts* (C-372/04) and *Acereda Herrera* (C-466/04) in 2006, and *Stamatelaki* (C-444/05) in 2007.

Stone Sweet and others examined the relationships "between the arguments contained in the observations filed by the Commission and the Member States, for each case, and the Court's ultimate decision" (2004: 186). This effort aimed at answering the question of whether these observations presage or influence the

---

6   Decision No 153 of October 7, 1993 on the model forms necessary for the application of Council Regulation No (EEC) 1408/71 and (EEC) No 574/72 (E 001, E 103 to E 127) (Text with EEA relevance) (94/604/EC), Official Journal L 244, September 19, 1994, p. 0022–0122.

7   The Administrative Commission on Social Security for Migrant Workers has prepared a series of standardized forms in order to deal with different cases of cross-border social security matters. This Commission is made up of representatives of the ministries of social affairs, employment and health of the Member States and the European Commission. It assures the correct application of Regulations 1408/71 and 574/72. For detailed information on the Administrative Commission, see Bokeloh (2001).

8   The European Economic Area (EEA) was founded in 1994. It comprises the EU Member States and the three EFTA Member States: Iceland, Liechtenstein, and Norway.

Court's rulings. I have undertaken a similar effort for the cases *Kohll* and *Decker*. I have coded the observations in these two cases as "successful" or "unsuccessful" of predicting the final decision. The results of the examination are included in the following section. However, I refrained from iterating this for the follow-up rulings, mainly for two reasons: firstly, many preliminary questions entail more than one question; *Watts* for instance comprises seven questions. In addition, sometimes there was congruence only in a part of the questions. Therefore, it was impossible to code the observations in "successful" and "unsuccessful." Secondly, the follow-up rulings are sometimes of such technical detail that it is not always possible to determine doubtlessly the (non-)congruence of observations and rulings.

Kohll and *Decker*: Revolution or Evolution[9]

In April 1998, the *Kohll* and *Decker* rulings were finally delivered. They had been expected by legal scholars for a long time and redrew the borders between national and European social security law, based on the basic freedoms of providing services and goods. The Luxembourg High Court, the *Cour de Cassation*, had referred *Kohll* to the ECJ already in April 1996. A lower court, the *Conseil Arbitral des Assurances Sociales*, had referred *Decker* in April 1995.

Raymond Kohll, a Luxembourg citizen, was refused authorization by his Luxembourg health insurance for an orthodontist out-patient treatment in Germany for his daughter. His request was rejected because the treatment was not deemed urgent and could have been carried out in Luxembourg. Nicolas Decker was refused reimbursement by his Luxembourg health insurance for a pair of glasses he had bought in Belgium using a prescription from a Luxembourg ophthalmologist. The justification here was that Decker had not sought prior authorization as demanded by the Health Insurance Code of Luxembourg at that time.

In the *Kohll* and *Decker* proceedings before the ECJ (1995–1997), all EU Member States agreed in their written observations – 13 had submitted such an observation – that either the freedom to provide services did not apply to national social protection systems or that, if it applied, prior authorization procedures for health care consumption abroad were justified.[10] Member States

---

9 Case C-158/96, *Raymond Kohll vs. Union des Caisses de Maladie* [1998] ECR I–1931; Case C-120/95, *Nicolas Decker vs. Caisse de Maladie des Employés Privés* [1998] ECR I–1831. On the rulings *Kohll* and *Decker*, literature is abundant. Only an extract of this literature can be provided here: Becker (1998), Eichenhofer (1999), Gobrecht (1999b), van der Mei (1999), Hatzopoulos (2000), Künkele (2000), Kessler (2001), Hatzopoulos (2002), Jorens (2002), Kessler (2002), Becker (2003), Bloemheuvel (2003), Brouwer et al. (2003), Jorens and Schulte (2003), Schulte (2003), Zerna (2003), Jorens et al. (2005), Martinsen (2005b), and Sieveking (2007).

10 For the written observation, see Article 23 of the statute of the ECJ: "Within two months of this notification [by the Registrar, AJO], the parties, the Member States, the

adopted two slightly different lines of defence. On the one hand, the French and German governments claimed that an uncoordinated opening of the markets for pharmaceuticals, medical equipment, and medical care would seriously endanger the very structure of the national systems of social security (see ECJ, Rapport d'audience, *Kohll*: paras. 53–60, 64–72, and *Decker*: paras. 29–46, 53–64).[11] The French government postulated that the equilibrium of all Luxembourg-style social security systems, such as its own, would be at stake, if the principle of territoriality was to be breached (see ECJ, Rapport d'audience, *Kohll*: para. 68). On the other hand, the UK government tried to differentiate its National Health Service from social security systems. It stated that Articles 49 and 50 EC Treaty did not apply to systems which are financed by public funds (para. 85). In addition, according to the UK, maintaining prior authorization schemes was justified for the financial stability of the domestic social protection regimes (para. 87).

The European Commission argued in the *Decker* proceedings that the free movement of goods precluded national restrictions (see ECJ, Rapport d'audience, *Decker*: para. 89). In *Kohll* it stated that prior authorization procedures violated the freedom to provide services in general, but that for reasons of general interest, restrictions were justified (see ECJ, Rapport d'audience, *Kohll*: para. 104).

In its *Kohll* ruling, the ECJ observed, first, that, "according to settled case-law, Community law does not detract from the powers of the Member States to organise their social security systems" (para. 17). However, EU Member States "must nevertheless comply with Community law when exercising those powers" (para. 19). Second, the ECJ determined that a national regulation, which made the reimbursement of dental treatment abroad dependent on the prior authorization of the competent insurance institution, as it was in place in Luxembourg, did violate the (passive) free movement of services, Articles 49 and 50 EC Treaty, and was neither justified by the control of health expenditures nor by the balancing of the budget of the social protection systems (paras. 35, 42 and 54). Even though the Luxembourg *Cour de Cassation* asked two rather general preliminary questions, the ECJ only responded to the very specific Luxembourg case at hand regarding dental treatment. In its preliminary *Decker* ruling, the ECJ held that requiring prior authorization for the purchase of medical products abroad violated the free movement of goods guaranteed in Articles 28 and 30 EC Treaty (para. 36) without justification in the two respects just mentioned for *Kohll* (para. 40).

None of the thirteen written Member State's observations could presage *Kohll* and *Decker*. All Member States agreed that either free movement of services and

---

Commission and, where appropriate, the European Parliament, the Council and the European Central Bank, shall be entitled to submit statements of case or written observations to the Court." For the oral observation, see Article 104 Paragraph 4 of the rules of procedure of the ECJ.

11 In addition to the usually very detailed opinion of the advocate general and the actual ECJ ruling, the report for the hearing can be a highly valuable document to analyze the political preferences of Member States.

goods could not be applied to social protection systems, or they perceived national restrictions as justified. The European Commission's observations could presage the ruling in *Decker* but only partly in *Kohll*. Thus, in these two rulings, the ECJ clearly did not defer its decisions to the preferences of Member States.

According to Yves Jorens, *Kohll* and *Decker* were not revolutionary; rather they were "a logical consequence of the dynamic development of European Community law and, in particular, the fundamental freedoms whereby national law, aided not least by the ECJ, is interpreted in an increasingly narrow manner" (2002: 93). Even if not considered revolutionary, *Kohll* and *Decker* – in addition to Regulation 1408/71 – created a second avenue of cross-border care (see Jorens 2002: 110): patients could now seek medical treatment in another EU Member State without depending on the discretion of their domestic insurance institutions. These two cases held that ambulatory treatment and eyeglasses could be purchased abroad, in social security systems organized like Luxembourg's that provide health care through cash reimbursement. The implications for national health systems and health insurance systems based on delivering primarily in-kind benefits, as well as the consequences for other types of benefits such as hospital care, were unclear. Initially, most Member States refrained from implementing the jurisprudence because of this uncertainty. This means they did not change administrative practices and the law in the social codes (see for example Palm et al. 2000). However, of more importance was that they saw the jurisprudence – as a whole – as an unjustified intrusion into their exclusive right to determine the fundamental principles of the organization of their social protection systems.

Before *Kohll* and *Decker*, the belief was widespread that the fundamental freedoms – with the exception of the free movement of persons – did not affect national social law (see Eichenhofer 1999: 102). Now, the ECJ promoted cross-border patient mobility based on the free movement of services and goods. The central question the Court had to answer was the compatibility of national rules with these two basic freedoms. The rulings also challenged Article 22 of Regulation 1408/71 that required a mandatory prior authorization of the insurance funds before the insured persons could acquire their social provisions abroad and thus restricted free access to health care Europe-wide. Eberhard Eichenhofer concluded that the European coordination law ceased to comprehensively regulate the conditions for cross-border benefit claims; the ECJ had found the simple system of European coordination law lacking (1999: 118–119).

In the *Kohll* and *Decker* rulings "the ECJ used EU law ... to increase substantially a patient's options for receiving non-emergency health care in another member state at the expense of his or her social health care system" (Nickless 2002: 57). Thus, the free movement of services (Articles 49 and 50 EC Treaty) and the free movement of goods (Articles 28 to 30 EC Treaty), in addition to the free movement of workers became the gateway for the ECJ to probe national mechanisms that restrict people's access to medical treatment in other EU Member States.

Kohll and *Decker* brought a new dimension to European health care policy-making; the two rulings were only a first step. They prompted more questions than they could answer and led to considerable administrative, political and legal uncertainty. The two rulings were aimed at Luxembourg's health insurance, which provides health care through cash reimbursement. The patients demand health care benefits on the market. They advance the costs for the treatment and receive partial or full reimbursement from their health insurance. The consequences of *Kohll* and *Decker* for similar systems were quite clear. However, the consequences for health insurance systems based on delivering in-kind benefits, for national health care systems, and for other types of benefits such as in-patient care were disputed. Here, a major difference between ECJ rulings and national court decisions emerges. The ECJ usually decides in a preliminary ruling only on the compatibility of one national legal system with European law. However, since its rulings can be applied to the whole Community, they have to be "translated" into other national legal systems. This poses a considerable problem for the ECJ who can only insufficiently analyze the consequences for these different systems in its proceedings (Steinmeyer pointed to this deficiency, 1995: 97).

The legal uncertainty created by *Kohll* and *Decker* was (partly) relieved in subsequent rulings (to be discussed). *Vanbraekel* and *Geraets-Smits/Peerbooms*, both from July 2001, brought the first nuances to *Kohll* and *Decker*.

The Follow-up Jurisprudence: Extending and Narrowing Doctrines

The ECJ determined in *Kohll* and *Decker* that the free movement of services and goods precludes national rules in Luxembourg-style health systems which subject reimbursement of ambulatory treatment and health care products to prior authorization. In the follow-up cases, these doctrines were extended to other types of health care systems, to other states, and to additional areas, and, more importantly, simultaneously narrowed.

After *Kohll* and *Decker* were decided in 1998, most EU Member States carried on their efforts to persuade the ECJ of the peculiar non-economic nature of their social protection systems and of the dangers of an unrestricted application of the basic freedoms. This can be seen in the proceedings before the Court in the pending follow-up cases *Vanbraekel* and *Geraets-Smits/Peerbooms*. However, the unanimous rejection of the *Kohll/Decker* principles altogether started to crumble slowly. Two groups of countries can be discerned. Whereas France, Belgium and Austria conceded that health care services were of an economic nature, others continued to deny this (see Opinion of Ruiz-Jarabo Colomer, *Geraets-Smits/ Peerbooms*: para. 32). All Member States agreed that in any case prior authorization procedures were justified.

Vanbraekel and *Geraets-Smits/Peerbooms* were finally decided in 2001. Despite the efforts of Member States in the proceedings, the ECJ found again that arguments, which stressed the non-economic nature of health care services and denied the application of the free movement of services to social protection systems, could not be upheld (see ECJ, *Geraets-Smits/Peerbooms*: paras. 48–52). However, the ECJ partially accommodated Member State concerns in these two cases.

Vanbraekel: Reimbursement up to the Level of the Home State[12]

The preliminary reference case *Vanbraekel* was referred to the ECJ in October 1998 by the Belgian *Cour du travail de Mons*, a court of second instance. It concerned Mrs. Jeanne Descamps affiliated with the Belgian *Alliance nationale des mutualités chrétiennes* (ANMC). She was refused authorization for an orthopedic surgery at a French hospital. Despite being refused authorization Mrs. Descamps underwent the orthopedic operation in France in 1990; her Belgian insurer then refused to reimburse the costs. In the course of the national proceedings, however, it turned out that the original refusal of authorization was not justified. Therefore, the Belgian higher labor court held that "the medical costs at issue ... must be paid by the ANMC in accordance with Article 22 of Regulation 1408/71 and Articles 59 and 60 of the Treaty [today 49 and 50 EC Treaty]" (*Vanbraekel*: para. 28). The amount to be reimbursed remained disputed: 38,608.99 FRF according to the formula laid down in French legislation, or 49,935.44 FRF according to the Belgian legislation. Article 22(1)(c)(i) of Regulation 1408/71 determined that a patient who had obtained prior authorization to travel abroad for treatment was entitled to

> benefits in kind provided on behalf of the competent institution by the institution of the place of stay or residence in accordance with the provisions of the legislation which it administers, as though he were insured with it.

In this case, however, the costs of the benefits in the treatment provided by the French hospital were lower than those offered by the Belgian insurer for the same treatment in Belgium. Therefore, the referring court asked:

> Where, in the context of proceedings before it, a national court has acknowledged that hospital treatment in a Member State other than that of the competent institution was necessary, although the prior authorisation provided for in Article 22 of Regulation No 1408/71 was refused:
>
> (a) Must the costs of hospital treatment be reimbursed in accordance with the scheme of the State of the competent institution or in accordance with that organised by the State on whose territory the hospital treatment has taken place? (*Vanbraekel*: para. 19)

---

12   Case C-368/98, *Abdon Vanbraekel and Others vs. Alliance nationale des mutualités chrétiennes (ANMC)* [2001] ECR I-5363; specifically on the *Vanbraekel* case, see Hatzopoulos (2002).

In its ruling in July 2001, the ECJ reiterated its position in *Kohll* that Articles 49 and 50 EC Treaty also apply to national social security rules. In the case at hand,

> there is no doubt that the fact that a person has a lower level of cover when he receives hospital treatment in another Member State than when he undergoes the same treatment in the Member State in which he is insured may deter, or even prevent, that person from applying to providers of medical services established in other Member States and constitutes, both for insured persons and for service providers, a barrier to freedom to provide services (*Vanbraekel*: para. 45). [Therefore] Article 59 of the EC Treaty [today 49, AJO] is to be interpreted as meaning that, if the reimbursement of costs incurred on hospital services provided in a Member State of stay, calculated under the rules in force in that State, is less than the amount which application of the legislation in force in the Member State of registration would afford to a person receiving hospital treatment in that State, additional reimbursement covering that difference must be granted to the insured person by the competent institution. (*Vanbraekel*: para. 53)

The *Vanbraekel* ruling brought additional elements into the *Kohll/Decker* jurisprudence. First, Articles 49 and 50 EC Treaty precluded national legislation which inhibited the reimbursement of costs incurred in a hospital if an authorization was made *ex post*. Second, Article 22 of Regulation 1408/71 was interpreted as granting to patients (patients who had first been refused authorization, but who were then granted authorization *ex post*) a reimbursement of costs up to the (higher) level of the home state.

Geraets-Smits/Peerbooms: Extension to Hospitals and In-kind Benefit Systems[13]

Geraets-Smits/Peerbooms was referred to the ECJ in April 1999 by the Dutch first-instance court *Arrondissementsrechtbank te Roermond*. The importance of *Geraets-Smits/Peerbooms* and the ensuing *Müller-Fauré/van Riet* case can already be gathered from the fact that these rulings were 109 and 110 paragraphs long respectively, whereas *Kohll* and *Decker* only encompassed 55 and 47 paragraphs.[14]

---

13 Case C-157/99, *B.S.M. Geraets-Smits vs. Stichting Ziekenfonds VGZ and H.T.M. Peerbooms vs. Stichting CZ Groep Zorgverzekeringen* [2001] ECR I–5473; selected articles on the *Geraets-Smits/Peerbooms* case are Bieback (2001), Kessler (2001), Hatzopoulos (2002), and Brouwer et al. (2003).

14 Not only was the sheer number of paragraphs higher in these cases, but also the length of these paragraphs was on average longer. Here, all the lengths of the ECJ decisions for a comparison: *Kohll*: 55 paras., *Decker*: 47 paras., *Vanbraekel*: 57 paras., *Geraets-Smits/ Peerbooms*: 109 paras., *Müller-Fauré/van Riet*: 110 paras., *Inizan*: 61 paras., *Leichtle*: 60 paras., *Keller*: 72 paras., *Watts*: 149 paras., *Acereda Herrera*: 53 paras., and *Stamatelaki*: 39 paras.

Accordingly, Francis Kessler pointed to the unusual length of the ruling which indicates the "intention pédagogique" [pedagogical intention, AJO] of the Court in this case (2001: 2).

Geraets-Smits and Peerbooms were two patients who sought in-patient treatment in Germany and Austria with institutions which had no contract with their insurance fund, after their Dutch insurer had not authorized such treatment.[15] The two claimants sued to get their costs reimbursed from their Dutch insurance fund.

Geraets-Smits/Peerbooms added two important elements to the existing jurisprudence. First, a national system of prior authorization for hospital care was not per se violating European law; for the hospital sector, where planning is required, such a system was deemed both "necessary and reasonable" (para. 80). The ECJ thus reacted to substantiated Member State concerns, as can be seen in the following remarks:

> Looking at the system set up by the ZFW [the Dutch Sickness Fund Act, AJO], it is clear that, if insured persons were at liberty, regardless of the circumstances, to use the services of hospitals with which their sickness insurance fund had no contractual arrangements, whether they were situated in the Netherlands or in another Member State, all the planning which goes into the contractual system in an effort to guarantee a rationalised, stable, balanced and accessible supply of hospital services would be jeopardised at a stroke. (*Geraets-Smits/Peerbooms*: para. 81)

However, second, the ECJ regulated the hospital sector as well: prior authorization may not be refused if an identical or equally effective treatment cannot be obtained without "undue delay" from an institution under contract with the competent sickness fund (see *Geraets-Smits/Peerbooms*: paras. 103–104):

> Furthermore, in order to determine whether equally effective treatment can be obtained without undue delay from an establishment having contractual arrangements with the insured person's fund, the national authorities are required to have regard to all the circumstances of each specific case and to take due account not only of the patient's medical condition at the time when authorisation is sought but also of his past record. (*Geraets-Smits/Peerbooms*: para. 104)

---

15   In general, two types of health care providers must be distinguished. There are providers (physicians, hospitals) who have concluded a contract with the statutory health insurance institutions. In this case, the patient usually does not have to pay the treatment costs and the applied tariffs are directly refunded by the health care institution to the service provider. The other type of service provider does not have such a contract. In this case, the patient is treated as a private patient and has to pay the bill that is issued by the service provider.

Here, the ECJ "unquestionably determined that systems based on the benefits in kind principle do fundamentally fall within the ambit of freedom to provide services" (Fuchs 2002: 541) and are thus also affected by the developing exportability of domestic health benefits.

With *Vanbraekel* and *Geraets-Smits/Peerbooms* it became clear that prior authorization could be justified for medical provision in hospitals. Prior authorization for in-patient care did not necessarily violate Articles 49 and 50, if specific conditions existed. *Geraets-Smits/Peerbooms* referred primarily to the Dutch system, although according to the Court's reading,

> [i]t must be accepted that a medical service provided in one Member State and paid for by the patient should not cease to fall within the scope of the freedom to provide services guaranteed by the Treaty merely because reimbursement of the costs of the treatment involved is applied for under another Member State's sickness insurance legislation which is essentially of the type which provides for benefits in kind. (para. 55)

Nonetheless, some states still wondered how the decision would impact on their health care system. In addition, *Geraets-Smits/Peerbooms* concerned in-patient care, and theoretically left open whether out-patient care in EU Member States with in-kind benefit systems had to be treated like in those operating with cash benefits. Because of the still undecided questions, for the time being, the UK and Germany did not implement the rulings, but only conceded negligible changes.

Two and a half months after the ECJ preliminary ruling, the *Arrondissementsrechtbank te Roermond* rejected both Ms. Geraets-Smits and Mr. Peerbooms' claims.[16]

Like the foregoing cases, *Vanbraekel* and *Geraets-Smits/Peerbooms* did not clarify the full scope of the ECJ patient mobility doctrines. To close this gap, a related case was already in the pipeline.

Müller-Fauré/van Riet:
Extension to Out-Patient Care in In-kind Benefit Systems[17]

The Dutch higher social security court *Centrale Raad van Beroep* referred *Müller-Fauré/van Riet* to the ECJ in October 1999. Mrs. Müller-Fauré, a Dutch national, underwent dental treatment in Germany. Back in the Netherlands the

---

16   The Advocate General Ruiz-Jarabo Colomer pointed to this in *Müller-Fauré/van Riet* (footnote 38).

17   Case C-385/99, *V.G. Müller-Fauré vs. Onderlinge Waarborgmaatschappij OZ Zorgverzekeringen UA and E.E.M. van Riet vs. Onderlinge Waarborgmaatschappij ZAO Zorgverzekeringen* [2003] ECR I-4509; on *Müller-Fauré/van Riet* see for instance van der Mei (2004), Davies (2004b), and Jorens (2004).

reimbursement of her costs was refused. Ms. van Riet was on a waiting list for an arthroscopy with her insurance fund and was refused authorization for being treated in Belgium.

Müller-Fauré/van Riet confirmed the view that health care systems based on in-kind delivery were affected by the *Kohll/Decker* jurisprudence. In addition, *Müller-Fauré/van Riet* made it clear that these rulings also applied to EU Member States with a national health service. The ECJ held that

> Articles 59 and 60 [today Articles 49 and 50, AJO] of the Treaty do preclude the same legislation [that is reimbursement conditional upon prior authorization, AJO] in so far as it makes the assumption of the costs of non-hospital care provided in another Member State by a person or establishment with whom or which the insured person's sickness fund has not concluded an agreement conditional upon prior authorisation by the fund, even when the national legislation concerned sets up a system of benefits in kind under which insured persons are entitled not to reimbursement of costs incurred for medical treatment, but to the treatment itself which is provided free of charge. (para. 109)

In *Müller-Fauré/van Riet*, the ECJ confirmed that cross-border out-patient care did not require prior authorization; for in-patient care the Court allowed prior authorization. In addition, the ECJ gave guidance to the insurance institutions about the meaning of the phrase "without undue delay." To satisfy this condition,

> the national authorities are required to have regard to all the circumstances of each specific case and to take due account not only of the patient's medical condition at the time when authorization is sought and, where appropriate, of the degree of pain or the nature of the patient's disability which might, for example, make it impossible or extremely difficult for him to carry out a professional activity, but also of his medical history. (*Müller-Fauré/van Riet*: para. 90)

In this case the ECJ referred to systems of other EU Member States and stated generally that "a medical service does not cease to be a provision of services because it is paid for by a national health service or by a system providing benefits in kind" (*Müller-Fauré/van Riet*: para. 103). The UK Administrative Court of the Queen's Bench Division of the High Court reasoned from this wording that the attempt by the UK government to draw a distinction between systems such as the Dutch and its own NHS had been rejected by the ECJ (Administrative Court 2003, *Watts*: para. 107).

Inizan: Authorization is Obligatory if "Undue Delay"[18]

In November 2000, the *Tribunal des Affaires de Sécurité Sociale de Nanterre*, a French court of first instance, referred the *Inizan* case to the ECJ. In 1999, the *Caisse Primaire d'Assurance Maladie (CPAM) des Hauts-de-Seine* had refused to reimburse the costs of a hospital treatment in Germany to Patrizia Inizan. The CPAM had held that the requirements of Article 22(2) of Regulation 1408/71 were not met, namely that it could provide the treatment "within the time normally necessary for obtaining the treatment in question in the Member State of residence [in this case France, AJO] taking account of his current state of health and the probable course of the disease" (Article 22(2) Regulation 1408/71, according to the version in force at the time). The *Tribunal* asked the ECJ two questions. First of all, may the reimbursement of health care costs incurred in another EU Member State be made subject to a prior authorization, as determined in Article 22 of Regulation 1408/71, without violating Articles 49 and 50 EC Treaty? Secondly, is Article R. 332–2 of the French Social Security Code compatible with Articles 49 and 50 EC Treaty?

In its ruling of October 2003, the ECJ pointed again to its previous jurisprudence: national systems that rely on prior authorization for allowing the reimbursement of medical costs incurred in another Member State are indeed violating Article 49 EC Treaty (*Inizan*: para. 18). Article 22 of Regulation 1408/71, however, was not invalidated (*Inizan*: para. 26). Referring to *Geraets-Smits/Peerbooms* and *Müller-Fauré/van Riet* the ECJ affirmed that prior authorization for in-patient health care was necessary, reasonable, and justified (*Inizan*: para. 56).

The ECJ may not decide per se whether a specific national law is inconsistent with European law. Nonetheless, it did provide the French court with criteria in order to interpret European law correctly. It clearly indicated that the contested Article R. 332–2 was violating the free movement of services (*Inizan*: para. 54). For in-patient care, however, restrictions were justified under certain conditions: when the same or equally effective treatment could be offered in France without undue delay (*Inizan*: para. 59); when prior authorization is based on objective, non-discriminatory criteria known in advance; when the procedural system is "easily accessible and capable of ensuring that a request for authorisation will be dealt with objectively and impartially within a reasonable time;" and when it is possible to challenge a rejection of reimbursement in judicial or quasi-judicial proceedings (*Inizan*: para. 57). According to the ECJ, Article R. 332–2 only met these requirements in part.

---

18   Case C-56/01, *Patricia Inizan vs. Caisse primaire d'assurance maladie des Hauts-de-Seine* [2003] ECR I–12403; specifically on *Inizan*, see Jorens (2004).

Leichtle: Extension to Health Cure Costs[19]

In November 2001, the *Verwaltungsgericht Sigmaringen*, a German administrative court of first instance, referred two questions of *Leichtle against Bundesanstalt für Arbeit* to the ECJ for a preliminary ruling based on Articles 49 and 50 EC Treaty. This case was special as it concerned the civil servants health insurance scheme, not the statutory health insurance for workers. Nevertheless, the case clearly belongs to the *Kohll/Decker* jurisprudence since it concerns the application of Articles 49 and 50 EC Treaty to cross-border health cures. The *Bundesanstalt für Arbeit* had refused to authorize assistance for a health cure that Mr. Ludwig Leichtle, a civil servant of the *Bundesanstalt*, intended to obtain in Italy. Without waiting for the result of his appeal and, therefore, without prior authorization he went to Italy for his health cure. The referring German court asked the ECJ: First, are

> Articles 49 EC and 50 EC to be interpreted as precluding rules of national law ... under which the costs of a health cure taken in another Member State are reimbursable only where it is absolutely essential that the cure be taken outside the Federal Republic of Germany because it thus offers greatly increased prospects of success, where that is established in a report drawn up by a medical officer or a medical consultant and where the spa concerned is listed in the Register of Spas? (*Leichtle*: para. 26)

Second, the *Verwaltungsgericht Sigmaringen* asked,

> whether Articles 49 EC and 50 EC are to be interpreted as meaning that they preclude the application of national rules under which reimbursement of expenditure incurred on board, lodging, travel, visitors' tax and the making of a final medical report in connection with a health cure taken in another member state is precluded where the person concerned has not awaited the conclusion of the procedure for obtaining prior recognition of eligibility for assistance provided for in those rules or of any subsequent court proceedings before commencing the cure in question? (*Leichtle*: para. 52)

In its reference, the *Verwaltungsgericht* argued with indications from *Kohll* and *Geraets-Smits/Peerbooms*, but it still thought that there was "no settled national case-law on the question" (*Leichtle*: para. 25).

In answering the first question the ECJ again confirmed its jurisprudence and applied it to health cures:

> Articles 49 EC and 50 EC are to be interpreted as meaning that they preclude rules of a Member State, such as those at issue in the main proceedings, under

---

19   Case C-8/02, *Ludwig Leichtle vs. Bundesanstalt für Arbeit* [2004] ECR I–2641; on *Leichtle* see for instance Jorens (2004) and Kingreen (2005).

which reimbursement of expenditure incurred on board, lodging, travel, visitors' tax and the making of a final medical report in connection with a health cure taken in another Member State is conditional on obtaining prior recognition of eligibility, which is given only where it is established, in a report drawn up by a medical officer or a medical consultant, that the proposed cure is absolutely necessary owing to the greatly increased prospects of success in that other Member State. (*Leichtle*: para. 51)

The ECJ answered the second question with reference to *Vanbraekel*:

both the practical effect and the spirit of that provision [Article 22(1)(c) Regulation 1408/71, AJO] required that if the request of an insured person for authorisation on the basis of that provision has been refused by the competent institution and it is subsequently established by a court decision that that refusal was unfounded, that person is entitled to be reimbursed directly by the competent institution by an amount equivalent to that which it would ordinarily have borne if authorisation had been properly granted in the first place. (*Leichtle*: para. 55)

The *Leichtle* case brought two new findings to the existing jurisprudence: First, health cure costs, like transportation and lodging costs, which are not directly part of a health benefit, may still be reimbursed. Second, a social insurance fund cannot refuse reimbursement with the argument that a preliminary authorization had not been given before the treatment.

Keller: Binding Decisions for Home State Institutions[20]

In November 2001, *Keller* was referred to the ECJ by the *Juzgado de lo Social no 20 de Madrid*, a Spanish first-instance social court. Ms. Annette Keller, a German national residing in Spain, had first received an E111 form to travel to Germany for family reasons, and then an E112 prior authorization form to treat a malignant tumor that was detected while she was in a German hospital where she continued to receive treatment. The physicians in the German hospital referred Ms. Keller to the private Zurich University Clinic in Switzerland, the only clinic in Europe which could treat her condition. The competent Spanish social security institution, the *Instituto Nacional de la Salud*, refused to reimburse her the costs for the hospital treatment since "reimbursement of the costs of medical treatment provided in a non-member country required prior authorization on its part" (ECJ, *Keller*: para. 19). The *Juzgado de lo Social* wanted to know from the ECJ in its preliminary questions, first, "whether the competent Spanish institution is bound by the diagnosis and choice of treatment of the doctors authorised by the German institution concerned"; and second, whether

---

20 Case C-145/03, *Heirs of Annette Keller vs. Instituto Nacional de la Seguridad Social (INSS), Instituto Nacional de Gestión Sanitaria (Ingesa)* [2005] ECR I–2529.

there is an obligation to reimburse the costs of Ms Keller's hospital treatment in the Zurich University Clinic, in view of the fact that it was confirmed that, under the legislation applicable in Germany, where Ms Keller was staying when the hospital treatment became necessary, she would have had those costs paid in full if she had been affiliated to *AOK Rheinland* [Rhineland Local General Sickness Fund, AJO]. (*Keller*: para. 24–25)

In April 2005, the ECJ decided, first, that

where the competent institution has consented, by issuing a Form E111 or Form E 112, to one of its insured persons receiving medical treatment in a Member State other than the competent Member State, it is bound by the findings as regards the need for urgent vitally necessary treatment made during the period of validity of the form by doctors authorised by the institution of the Member State of stay, and by the decision of those doctors, taken during that period on the basis of those findings and the current state of medical knowledge, to transfer the patient to a hospital establishment in another State, even if that State is a non-member country. (*Keller*: para. 72)

Secondly, it held that

the cost of the treatment provided in that State must be borne by the institution of the Member State of stay in accordance with the legislation administered by that institution, under the same conditions as those applicable to insured persons covered by that legislation. (*Keller*: para. 72)

The *Keller* case was debated in the Grand Chamber of the ECJ, which proves its significance.[21] However, considering the very special nature of the case, its impact is likely to be rather minor.

Watts: Extension to National Health Systems[22]

The Court of Appeal for England and Wales referred the *Watts* case to the ECJ in July 2004. Again, this case was of great importance since the decision was taken in the Grand Chamber of the ECJ; moreover, the ECJ ruling has an unprecedented 149 paragraphs.

In 2002, Yvonne Watts, a 72-year-old UK national suffering from osteoarthritis in both hips, applied under the E112 scheme for surgery abroad. Her competent

---

21   The ECJ usually sits in chambers of three or five judges. It may also sit in a grand chamber of 13 judges either in particular cases that are prescribed by the statute of the ECJ or in exceptionally important cases.

22   Case C-372/04, *The Queen on the application of Yvonne Watts against 1) Bedford Primary Care Trust 2) Secretary of State for Health* [2006] ECR I–4325.

Bedford Primary Care Trust (PCT) put her on a waiting list as a routine case and refused authorization for treatment abroad. According to the PCT, the conditions for sending her abroad using form E112 under Article 22 of Regulation 1408/71 did not obtain and the necessary treatment could be provided in the UK "without undue delay" (ECJ, Report for the hearing, *Watts*: para. 26–28). In the review proceedings the Bedford PCT again refused to send her abroad but reduced Mrs. Watts' waiting time to three to four months; she was listed for surgery in either April or May 2003 (see Administrative Court 2003, *Watts*: paras. 22–26). Despite this ruling, Yvonne Watts had her hips replaced in France in March of 2003. The Administrative Court of the Queen's Bench Division of the High Court dismissed the judicial review of the refusal and the lawsuit for the reimbursement of her costs because Mrs. Watts failed on the facts. The English judge concluded that

> [i]n my judgement, in this case, having regard to all the circumstances, the period of delay which was tolerable before it reached the level of what is 'undue' was a period very much less than the year with which the claimant was originally faced but, on the other hand, a period significantly (though probably not substantially) greater than the period of delay until April or May 2003 with which she was faced on 4 February 2003. On that simple ground, as it seems to me, the claimant's case breaks down. (Administrative Court 2003, *Watts*: para. 174)

But the Administrative Court also decided that the necessary treatment for Mrs. Watts was within the scope of Article 49 EC Treaty "despite the fact that reimbursement of the costs of the treatment received was applied for under the NHS" (ECJ, Report for the hearing, *Watts*: para. 35). Mrs. Watts therefore "succeeded in demonstrating that the Secretary of State's understanding of the law is wrong" (Administrative Court 2003, *Watts*: para. 175), and won on all the legal arguments in relation to Article 49 (para. 207). Both parties appealed against this decision to the Court of Appeal for England and Wales. The Secretary of State for Health appealed on the ground that NHS patients were not entitled to rely on Article 49 EC Treaty and that the case was exclusively regulated by Article 22 of Regulation 1408/71 (see ECJ, Report for the hearing, *Watts*: para. 36–37). Mrs. Watts appealed because she did not get reimbursed for her treatment abroad. In his Administrative Court opinion the judge declared Mrs. Watts had "won a mighty battle with the Secretary of State on a matter of great public importance." Nevertheless, as she lost on the facts, he wrote, Mrs. Watts would not enjoy the fruits of this victory: "Her exertions will enure for the benefits of those who come after her" (para. 210). In its ruling in February 2004, the Court of Appeal decided quite contrary to the Administrative Court that the ECJ jurisprudence of the time did not directly concern a state-funded national health service like the NHS (see Court of Appeal, *Watts*: para. 88) and, therefore, together with the issue of defining "undue delay," referred seven questions to the ECJ. In the first and most important question the Court of Appeal asked whether in light of the ECJ jurisprudence

Geraets-Smits/Peerbooms, *Müller-Fauré* and *Inizan*, UK nationals are entitled in principle to receive hospital treatment in other EU Member States. The Court specifically asked whether the state-funded UK NHS has to be distinguished from the health care system of the Netherlands. The UK government proposed to answer with "yes" as it was strongly opposed to the application of the ECJ jurisprudence on its own NHS (see ECJ, Report for the hearing, *Watts*: paras. 46 and 67). The other questions by the Court of Appeal concerned mainly the conditions under which prior authorization for hospital treatment in other Member States could be refused.

In its preliminary ruling from May 2006, the ECJ decided that the obligation to reimburse the costs of in-patient treatment provided in another Member State also applied to the UK National Health Service, "regardless of the way in which the national system with which that person is registered and from which reimbursement of the cost of those services is subsequently sought operates" (*Watts*: para. 90). According to the Court it was irrelevant whether hospital treatment in the NHS was a service within the meaning of Article 49 EC Treaty (*Watts*: para. 91). In general, the restrictions in UK legislation of treatment abroad were considered an obstacle to the free movement of services (*Watts*: para. 98). The restriction of an obligatory prior authorization scheme for in-patient treatment abroad was justified, though, if the NHS could establish that its waiting time "does not exceed the period which is acceptable on the basis of an objective medical assessment of the clinical needs of the person concerned in the light of all of the factors characterising his medical condition" (*Watts*: para. 79). The sheer existence of waiting lists that are necessary to plan and manage in-patient health care on the basis of general clinical priorities cannot justify the rejection of prior authorization "without carrying out in the individual case in question an objective medical assessment of the patient's medical condition, the history and probable course of his illness, the degree of pain he is in and/or the nature of his disability" (*Watts*: para. 119).

The *Watts* ruling added one essential element to the *Kohll/Decker* jurisprudence: for the first time in this patient mobility line of cases, the ECJ explicitly ruled on a national health service and found that national provisions which inhibited patients' travel abroad were violating the fundamental principle of the passive free movement of services.

Acereda Herrera:
No Coverage of Travel, Accommodation and Subsistence Expenses[23]

Still, the ECJ had not yet clarified whether travel expenses also had to be reimbursed. It tackled this issue, though, in the case of *Acereda Herrera against Servicio Cántabro de Salud*. An appeals court, the *Tribunal Superior de Justicia de Cantabria*, referred this case to the Court in October 2004. In January 2003, Mr.

---

23   Case C-466/04, *Manuel Acereda Herrera vs. Servicio Cántabro de Salud* [2006] ECR I-5341.

Manuel Acereda Herrera, a Spanish resident, had received an E112 authorization to travel to France for treatment. The *Servicio Cántabro de Salud* refused to pay for his travel, accommodation and subsistence costs and the costs incurred by a family member who accompanied him. The *Tribunal,* then, had an important question for the ECJ: does the right to be reimbursed also include travel, accommodation and subsistence costs? In June 2006, the ECJ answered the most important question of the preliminary reference:

> Article 22(1)(c) and (2) and Article 36 of Council Regulation (EEC) No 1408/71 ... must be interpreted as meaning that authorisation by the competent institution for an insured person to go to another Member State in order there to receive hospital treatment appropriate to his medical condition does not confer on such a person the right to be reimbursed by the competent institution for the costs of travel, accommodation and subsistence which that person and any person accompanying him incurred in the territory of that latter Member State, with the exception of the costs of accommodation and meals in hospital for the insured person himself. (*Acereda Herrera*: para. 53)

Stamatelaki: No Differentiation between Public and Private Hospitals[24]

In the last case so far in this line of rulings, the ECJ declared national legislation not conform to EC law that allows the reimbursement of costs in public and private hospitals domestically, but restricts it in private hospitals abroad to children under 14 years of age (*Stamatelaki*: para. 38). In the earlier rulings, the Court had excluded hospital care *de facto* from its patient mobility doctrine (see above). In *Stamatelaki*, the ECJ specified that restrictions in the in-patient sector had to be proportionate as well (see especially para. 34).

Cornerstones of the Patient Mobility Doctrines and Conclusion

The patient mobility doctrines elaborated in *Kohll* and *Decker* and the follow-up cases consist of two cornerstones: First, prior authorization systems in out-patient care violate the (passive) free movement of service. Second, the ECJ has recognized three overriding reasons which justify national legislation that is a barrier to the freedom to provide hospital services. The first overriding reason is the risk of seriously undermining the financial basis of a social security system (*Kohll*: para. 41, *Geraets-Smits/Peerbooms*: para. 72, *Müller-Fauré/van Riet*: para. 73, *Watts*: para. 103). Second, an overriding reason is the objective of maintaining a high quality balanced medical and hospital service open to all (*Kohll*: para. 50, *Geraets-Smits/Peerbooms*: para. 73, *Müller-Fauré/van Riet*: para. 67, *Watts*: para.

---

24 Case C-444/05, *Aikaterini Stamatelaki vs. NPDD Organismos Asfaliseos Eleftheron Epangelmation (OAEE)* [2007] ECR I–3185.

104). And the third overriding reason is the maintenance of treatment capacity or medical competence on national territory (*Kohll*: para. 51, *Geraets-Smits/ Peerbooms*: para. 74, *Müller-Fauré/van Riet*: para. 67, *Watts*: para. 105).

Each of the cases making up the *Kohll/Decker* jurisprudence discussed in this chapter reaffirmed, refined and amplified the preceding cases. Each case clarified some aspects and at the same time raised new questions. This is why I consider them a "line" of cases. In Table 4.1, I provide an overview of the above described cases and the principles they prompted.

Kohll and *Decker* concerned specifically Luxembourg and the other two EU Member States with health care systems structured as cash reimbursement systems: France and Belgium. The ECJ applied the free movement of services and the free movement of goods to the out-patient health care sector only, more specifically to eyeglasses purchased in another EU country and orthodontic treatment. *Vanbraekel* essentially clarified that the amount to be reimbursed had to be up to the (higher) level of the state of insurance. In *Geraets-Smits/Peerbooms* the ECJ admitted that there were viable justifications to exclude in-patient care from the free movement of services. In *Müller-Fauré/van Riet*, the free movement of services in the out-patient sector was extended to Member States operating their health care systems in the in-kind benefit modus: Germany, Austria, and the Netherlands. There were already significant hints, on which a UK judge relied on, that the principle also applied to national health systems. *Inizan* detailed the application of Article 22(2) Regulation 1408/71 and Articles 49 and 50 EC Treaty in that it held that if a treatment cannot be provided without undue delay, then referring patients abroad may not be refused. *Leichtle* clarified that health cures were also within the scope of that jurisprudence. In *Keller*, the ECJ determined that prior authorization to travel abroad included the referral to other countries if necessary. In *Watts*, the Court explicitly extended the principle of free movement of services to countries having a national health system, that is to all the other EU countries. In *Acereda Herrera*, travel, accommodation and subsistence expenses were excluded from the scope of the *Kohll/Decker* jurisprudence. And in *Stamatelaki*, the last in this line of cases, a restriction of reimbursement in private hospitals abroad was declared not conform to EC law.

Regarding the question of whether an EU Member State was affected by an ECJ ruling, I situate my analysis between *inter partes* and *erga omnes* effects. I assume that a country falls under the scope of the *Kohll/Decker* jurisprudence as soon as one ruling for a Member State with a similar health care system has been delivered.

In the following Chapters 5 through 8, I elaborate on how the *Kohll/Decker* jurisprudence was implemented in all EU Member States, paying closer attention to its implementation in three select countries: Germany, France, and the United Kingdom.

Table 4.1 ECJ introduction of new material doctrine and relevance for EU Member States

ECJ ruling	Basic new material doctrines and their specifications introduced in the course of the jurisprudence	EU Member States to which the jurisprudence was directly relevant
Kohll and *Decker*	• To require prior authorzation in the ambulatory sector in cash benefit systems is an unjustified restriction of the free movement of services (Articles 49/50 EC) and the free movement of goods (Articles 28/30 EC).	Luxembourg, France, Belgium
Vanbraekel	• Specifies Article 22 of Regulation 1408/71: if prior authorzation has been wrongfully refused, the patient is entitled to be reimbursed directly by the insurance institution by an amount equivalent to that which would have been granted by the legislation of the state of residence if authorzation had been given in the first place; • interprets Article 49 EC: if the reimbursement of medical costs incurred in a hospital in the Member State of treatment is less than the amount in the state of insurance, additional reimbursement covering the difference must be granted.	All EU Member States
Geraets-Smits/ Peerbooms	• A system of prior authorzation for the hospital sector may be justified; • however, a system relying on prior authorzation has to meet certain criteria: national authorities have to take into account: all circumstances of each specific case, patient's medical condition, and past record.	The Netherlands, Germany (Austria was at that time already in line with ECJ requirements)
Müller-Fauré/van Riet	• Extends the free movement of services to health care systems relying on benefits in-kind in ambulatory care; • specifies what the ECJ meant by "undue delay": national authorities have to take into account: circumstances of each specific case, patient's medical condition, degree of pain, nature of the patient's disability, and medical history.	All social security systems based on cash reimbursement and in-kind benefits
Inizan	• Specifies Article 22(2) Regulation 1408/71 and Articles 49/50 EC: if treatment cannot be provided "without undue delay" referring patients abroad may not be refused.	All EU Member States
Leichtle	• Articles 49/50 EC apply also to health cure costs.	All EU Member States
Keller	• Specifies Article 22(1) Regulation 1408/71: the responsible institution in the state of insurance is bound by decisions of medical bodies in the state of treatment in case of prior authorzation through forms E111 or E112.	All EU Member States
Watts	• Extends the free movement of services to national health systems.	National health systems
Acereda Herrera	• Specifies Article 22 Regulation 1408/71: a right to be reimbursed for costs of travel, accommodation and subsistence is not conferred through prior authorzation with an E112 form.	All EU Member States
Stamatelaki	• No differentiation between public and private hospitals.	All EU Member States

Chapter 5

Implementing the *Kohll/Decker* Jurisprudence: The Overall Picture in EU Member States

EU Member States should incorporate the requirements laid down in ECJ rulings into their national laws and administrative practices. It is impossible to analyze implementation in all Member States in detail. Therefore, I chose three country cases standing for the three different types of social security systems in the EU. To get a general idea of the implementation of the *Kohll/Decker* jurisprudence, I start with an overview of the reactions of twelve "old" Member States and their first implementation steps. Following this, I will describe and analyze the implementation in the countries I have selected for a more detailed analysis: Germany, France, and the United Kingdom.

Member State Preoccupation with the *Kohll/Decker* Jurisprudence over Time

Table 5.1 reveals that the rulings in the cases of *Kohll* and *Decker* received a great deal of attention, especially from Member States running a social security system, and to a lesser degree from national health systems. Seven EU Member States gave a written or oral observation on *Decker*, six on *Kohll*.[1] The follow-up rulings *Vanbraekel* (11 observations), *Geraets-Smits/Peerbooms* (11), and *Müller-Fauré/van Riet* (10) caused even more interest and preoccupation among the "old" Member States.[2] Starting with *Inizan* (7), the preoccupation began to

---

1 The proceedings before the ECJ are divided into a written and an optional oral stage: In the written stage, the national court submits a preliminary reference to the ECJ. The reference is then translated into all official EU languages. A notice is published in the Official Journal of the EU which states the names of the parties and the content of the questions. The ECJ Registry notifies the reference to the parties to the proceedings, the Member States, the EU institutions, the EEA States and the EFTA Surveillance Authority. The parties, the institutions and the States have two months to submit written observations to the ECJ which are summarized in the optional report for the hearing. In these observations, the parties, the institutions and the States present their opinion on the case. In the optional oral stage, the ECJ Judges and Advocate Generals may interrogate the parties in a public hearing in which the institutions and the Member States may also submit their oral observations.

2 The two EEA Member States Norway and Iceland commented on *Geraets-Smits/Peerbooms* and *Müller-Fauré/van Riet*.

decrease (*Leichtle* (2), *Keller* (3)). Member State interest increased again with *Watts* (7).[3] Finally, five Member States commented on *Acereda Herrera* and three on *Stamatelaki*.[4]

Five findings can be gathered from Table 5.1: First, all "old" EU Member States, without exception, commented either in a written or oral observation at one point or the other on the *Kohll/Decker* jurisprudence in the proceedings before the Court. Table 5.1 illustrates this extraordinary preoccupation with the patient mobility case law: in total 80 observations in eleven cases.[5] *Kohll* and *Decker* received a great deal of attention especially from Member States running a social security system, and to a lesser degree from national health systems. The interest in the follow-up cases was more equally distributed. Second, as soon as the jurisprudence stabilized around certain cornerstones (see Chapter 4), interest decreased. It increased again with *Watts*, which was concerned with national health systems. Third, the national health systems were reluctant to deal with *Kohll* and *Decker*, but got more involved in the course of the follow-up jurisprudence. Fourth, *Müller-Fauré/van Riet* in 2003 determined in detail the requirements necessary to comply with the jurisprudence for the three Member States running a social security system based on in-kind benefits: Austria, Germany, and the Netherlands. These countries, therefore, virtually stopped commenting. Fifth, the Belgian and French governments continued to comment on *Keller, Watts*, and *Acereda Herrera*, although these rulings predominantly affected national health systems.

In the years following *Kohll* and *Decker*, an intense debate at political, administrative, and academic levels, both nationally and supranationally, took place on how these rulings had to be interpreted and what their expected impact would be. These controversial debates will be highlighted briefly in the following paragraphs.

---

3   From the "new" EU Member States Malte and Poland submitted observations on *Watts*.

4   Cyprus and Poland also commented on *Acereda Herrera*.

5   In his chapter on Sex Equality Law (with Rachel Cichowski) Stone Sweet counted only 142 Member State observations for 88 rulings (2004: 187).

Table 5.1 Written or oral observations on the *Kohll/Decker* jurisprudence by member state

Case	Date of ruling	Referring Court	Social security systems based on benefits in kind			Social security systems based on cash reimbursement			National health systems								
			DE	AT	NL	FR	BE	LU	DK	FI	EL	IR	IT	P	ES	SE	UK
Decker C-120/95	28.04.1998	Conseil arbitral des assurances sociales (LU)															
Kohll C-158/96	28.04.1998	Cour de Cassation (LU)															
Vanbraekel C-368/98	12.07.2001	Cour du travail de Mons (BE)															
Geraets-Smits/ Peerbooms C-157/99	12.07.2001	Arrondissements-rechtbank te Roermond (NL)															
Müller-Fauré/van Riet C-385/99	13.05.2003	Centrale Raad van Beroep (NL)															
Inizan C-56/01	23.10.2003	Tribunal des Affaires de sécurité sociale de Nanterre (FR)															
Leichtle C-8/02	18.03.2004	Verwaltungsgericht Sigmaringen (DE)															
Keller C-145/03	12.04.2005	Juzgado de lo Social no 20 de Madrid (ES)															

Table 5.1 continued

| Case | Date of ruling | Referring Court | Social security systems based on benefits in kind | | | Social security systems based on cash reimbursement | | | | | National health systems | | | | | | |
			DE	AT	NL	FR	BE	LU	DK	FI	EL	IR	IT	P	ES	SE	UK
Watts C-372/04	16.05.2006	Court of Appeal (England and Wales) (UK)															
Acereda Herrera C-466/04	15.06.2006	Tribunal Superior de Justicia de Cantabria (ES)															
Stamatelaki C-444/05	19.04.2007	Diikitiko Protodikio Athinon (EL)															

Notes: The hatched cases stand for having commented with a written or oral observation in the specific case. In the rulings *Geraets-Smits/Peerbooms* and *Müller-Fauré/van Riet*, Norway and Iceland submitted observations. In *Watts*, Malta and Poland submitted observations. In *Acereda Herrera*, Cyprus and Poland submitted observations. AT = Austria, BE = Belgium, DK = Denmark, FI = Finland, FR = France, DE = Germany, EL = Greece, IR = Ireland, IT = Italy, LU = Luxembourg, NL = Netherlands, P = Portugal, ES = Spain, SE = Sweden, UK = United Kingdom.

The Legal Arena

In the scholarly legal debate, the rulings *Kohll* and *Decker* were not perceived as a novelty but rather "une suite logique dans le développement dynamique du droit communautaire européen" (Jorens 2004: 380).[6] Anne Pieter van der Mei found it even "remarkable that it took so long before the questions on the compatibility of prior authorisation rules … were submitted to the Court" (1999: 14). Paul Belcher similarly wrote in an overview for the Dutch Council for Health and Social Service that

> [w]hile the rulings may be considered a revolution from a healthcare perspective, given the potential increases in patient mobility, they could be seen merely as an evolution from the perspective of EC law development. Indeed, many legal specialists have voiced surprise that it has taken so long for the European Court to rule on the incompatibility of prior authorisation rules with the principles governing the free movement of good (sic!) and services. (1999: 69)

Bernd Schulte also agrees with those who found the disturbance that was caused by *Kohll* and *Decker* surprising, perceiving those rulings as an evolution of European law and not as a revolution (2003: 170, 2005: 46). Regardless of this assessment, many legal scholars ascribed a considerable (doctrinal and financial) impact on national systems to them.

The Political Arena

Although the legal profession anticipated *Kohll* and *Decker* for many years, these rulings were considered an "explosive issue" in 1998 in the political arena (Gobrecht 1999b: 17). They provoked a major stir in many EU Member States and prompted vivid debates in the Council of Ministers and in the Administrative Commission on Social Security for Migrant Workers. Some politicians called for political action at the EU-level to overrule or blockade these rulings. However, no joint action followed. According to Willy Palm et al., the government's responses concerning the implementation of *Kohll* and *Decker* were "defensive and disorganised" (2000: 98). They also noted that "[e]ven though the Member States consulted each other, formally or informally, on the measures or stance to be taken following the rulings, in terms of public opinion the strategy taken was very much a conspiracy of silence and rejection" (Palm et al. 2000: 78). All in all, most Member State politicians rejected the jurisprudence as well as the application of it to their health system.

---

6 "A logical consequence of the dynamic development of European Community law" (translation of the author).

The Political Science Arena

Standing "on the shoulders of doctrinal writers" (Arnull 2008: 425), political scientists highlighted the groundbreaking potentials of the rulings *Kohll* and *Decker*. In the quasi-absence of "positive" social policy integration at the EU-level, "innovative" ECJ rulings were considered to significantly change the internal institutional configuration of domestic social protection systems and to gradually weaken or tear apart the exclusive national spatial demarcation lines and closure practices (see for example Ferrera 2005, Leibfried 2005, Martinsen 2005a). Stephan Leibfried, Maurizio Ferrera and others assumed that the ECJ rulings would provoke enormous political and financial costs. However, these assessments focused on the legal doctrines elaborated by the ECJ and not on the actual implementation of these doctrines. Therefore, Leibfried added that the real influence of ECJ rulings on social protection systems still remained "opaque and continuously contested" (2005: 265).

Before engaging in a deeper analysis of the implementation in Germany, France, and the UK, I will provide an overview of the immediate reactions in the other "old" Member States and their first implementation measures. According to the European Commission, Member States with a reimbursement system implemented *Kohll* and *Decker* in a "patchy" way, while other countries considered them not to be applicable to their systems (Commission Staff Working Paper 2003c). Is this assessment correct?

I will first look at Austria, the only EU Member State in conformity with the jurisprudence from the outset. Subsequently, I will address those countries that provide health care via cash reimbursement, then those providing benefits in kind, and finally the national health systems. Except for Austria, the information presented below comes mainly from individual country reports, which have been produced in the framework of the European Observatory on Social Security for Migrant Workers, a report produced for the DG Employment and Social Affairs from 2000 written by Willy Palm et al., and three general reports from 2005, 2006, and 2008 written by Yves Jorens and József Hajdú in the framework of the network "Training and Reporting on European Social Security."[7]

---

7   For the Austrian case I rely primarily on a report that I have written for the World Bank (Obermaier 2009). In 1998, the European Commission organized a series of seminars on the implementation of Regulation 1408/71. In the wake of these seminars the European Observatory on Social Security for Migrant Workers was founded by the Commission, under the coordination of the Max-Planck Institute for Foreign and International Law in Munich. Its main role was to provide the Commission with systematic information from the Member States on the application of the coordination regulations on social security for migrant workers in order to be able to identify common problems and solutions. In all Member States national reports were elaborated by national experts which then served as the basis for a common European report. The ECJ jurisprudence was an important part of these reports. As a successor of the observatory the European Commission initiated the so-called trESS-network (Training and Reporting on European Social Security) (http://www.

Implementation by Country

Austria

In Austria, *Kohll* and *Decker* did not cause much of a reaction. The Austrian statutory health insurance, in contrast to many other EU Member States, does not suspend the right to health care while an insured person stays abroad. When health care is received in another country, the point of reference for the reimbursement of treatment costs is Paragraph 131(1) General Social Security Act (*Allgemeines Sozialversicherungsgesetz*, ASVG). This paragraph states that if an insured person does not see the contractual partners of her health insurance institution according to Paragraph 338 ASVG or the facilities affiliated directly to her health insurance institution, then she has the right to a reimbursement of 80 percent of the amount the health insurance institution would have had to pay for a treatment by a physician who has a permanent contract with that institution. According to Paragraph 131(2) ASVG, the reimbursement of expenses can be excluded if the insured has seen an "in-network" facility for the same insurance case.[8] The same rules applied to the other Austrian social security sub-schemes.[9] According to the Austrian health care law, a foreign physician was thus treated like any other Austrian "out-of-network" physician. The cut of 20 percent was justified with the additional administrative burden caused by bills from out-of-network physicians. An individual calculation of the bills from out-of-network physicians considerably increased administrative expenditures compared with the computer-based billing of in-network physicians. In 2000, the Austrian Supreme Constitutional Court upheld this differential treatment and did not regard the principle of equality violated.[10]

Kohll and *Decker* did not pose difficulties for Austria as they were no novelty (see Marhold 1998: 40). The Austrian social protection system was in line with European requirements; it already provided reimbursement for health care benefits received abroad. Neither national legislation nor administrative procedures needed to be changed.

The Austrian experience with the ASVG reimbursement provisions and the other sub-schemes could have been instructive for other EU Member States. These

---

tress-network.org). Supervised by the University of Ghent, this network aims at identifying national problems with the implementation of European law and bringing those persons together who are concerned with the implementation of European law.

8   In general, physicians and health care facilities work either out-of-network, that is they do not have a formal contract with a health care institution, or in-network, that is they have a contract.

9   Paragraph 59 of the Civil Servants Health Insurance Act (*Beamten-Kranken und Unfallversicherungsgesetz*, B-KUVG); Paragraph 96 of the Social Security Act for the Self-employed (*Gewerbliches Sozialversicherungsgesetz*, GSVG); and Paragraph 80 of the Farmers Health Insurance Act (*Bauern-Sozialversicherungsgesetz*, BSVG).

10   Austrian Supreme Constitutional Court, March 18, 2000, G 24/98, V 38/98.

provisions were not endangering the statutory health care system because they were primarily used for cheaper treatments, for example dental care. Patient mobility did not cause additional expenditures for the health insurance institutions. The amount remained the same whether used to reimburse for treatments in or outside the country.

In a statement to the European Commission, for 1997/98 Austria reported a stable number of 58,030 persons per year, making up 1.0517 percent of all persons covered by the national insurance scheme in Austria who have been (partially) reimbursed without prior authorization mainly for non-hospital services received abroad.[11] The overall costs for this category amounted to €3,445,470 per year (see European Commission 2003c: 29). The exact number of patients seeking health care abroad outside the EU regulations and Austrian reimbursement provisions, however, remains unknown.

The Netherlands

A working group initiated by the Ministry for Health and Sports elaborated the Netherlands' approach toward *Kohll* and *Decker*. This working group organized two interministerial conferences and comprised the Ministry, the umbrella organization for insurance funds, the Central Tariff Authority, several Dutch insurers, and the Interministerial Commission for European law (see Bloemheuvel 2003: 70–71). The common position of this working group was that the Dutch social security system based on in-kind benefits did not violate European law. Claims for reimbursement for treatment by non-contracted providers could be made independent of whether the treatment took place inside or outside the Netherlands. Nevertheless, the working group formulated several recommendations to change the existing legislation and practices, for instance, to change the exclusion of reimbursement in the Dutch law on access to private "Krankheitskostenversicherungen" [insurances for sickness costs, AJO] (Bloemheuvel 2003: 88–92).

Belgium

Belgium had suspension regulations for health care if an insured person sojourned abroad. In response to *Kohll* and *Decker*, it modified this legal basis in 1999/2000 and amended its implementing circulars for Article 22 of Regulation 1408/71 in 1998/1999 (Van Hoogenbemt 2001: 24–28).

Luxembourg

Whereas Palm and others observed that after *Kohll* and *Decker*, medical devices, pharmaceuticals and out-patient treatment were reimbursed without prior

---

11   Due to a lack of statistical information, the Austrian government estimated these figures from the available data provided by individual regional health insurers.

authorization in Luxembourg (2000: 84–85), Jorens and Hajdú noticed in their general trESS-report in 2005 that

> the sickness institutions did not basically change their position. They continued to reject prior authorization for ambulatory medical treatment abroad (for example, treatment from an orthodontist in Germany) or they refused to reimburse costs linked to in-patient medical treatment abroad without prior authorization. (57)[12]

The impact, if any, of the *Kohll/Decker* jurisprudence on Luxembourg seems to have been predominantly court-driven (see Kerschen 2003: 7).

Denmark

Jorens and Hajdú observed that "Denmark has taken the lead in implementing this case law [the *Kohll/Decker* jurisprudence, AJO], it being one of the few Member States that – perhaps not perfectly – applies it" (2005: 58). The legal consequences were discussed in an inter-ministerial working group which was set up in the wake of *Kohll* and *Decker*, composed of the Ministry of Health, the Ministry of Foreign Affairs, the Ministry of Social Affairs, and the Ministry of Justice (see Abrahamson and Roseberry 2003: 21). Denmark changed its National Health Security Act in May 2000 and, in June, the Ministry of Health issued a decree establishing new rules and regulations (Abrahamson and Roseberry 2003: 64). It provided for the reimbursement of dental care, psychotherapy and chiropractic treatment, as well as general and medical specialist treatment for the 1.5 percent of Danish insured persons who opted for a special arrangement (see Jorens and Hajdú 2005: 58). Unlike domestic service providers, foreign providers do not have to conclude an agreement under the Danish sickness insurance legislation (see Abrahamson and Roseberry 2003: 21–22). The practical effects of the new rules with regard to goods were thought to be

> fairly limited, since the only health-related goods for which reimbursement is available from the Danish public health insurance are glasses for children under 16 years old and nutritional preparations. Costs for health-care related goods that are provided free of charge in Denmark or not otherwise reimbursed by the Danish national health insurance are not reimbursed when purchased abroad. (Abrahamson and Roseberry 2003: 64)

An indirect impact of *Geraets-Smits/Peerbooms* on Denmark was that, since 2002, Danish patients could freely choose a private hospital or clinic in Denmark or abroad "if the municipality where the patient resides cannot offer treatment

---

12 Unfortunately, the individual national trESS-reports, unlike the reports within the framework of the Observatory on Social Security for Migrant Workers, have not been disclosed. Therefore, I had to rely on the general report as the only source of information.

within two months after the referral is received at the public hospital which would normally treat the patient" (Abrahamson and Roseberry 2003: 22). An additional condition was that the foreign hospital needed to have a contract with a Danish public hospital (Abrahamson and Roseberry 2003: 22).

In the wake of *Watts*, the Danish government pointed to its waiting lists and denied any practical effect of this ECJ ruling (see Jorens and Hajdú 2006: 92–93). Since October 2007, the maximum waiting time for treatment has been lowered to one month. If the public health system cannot provide the treatment within this time frame, "the patient is entitled to treatment in the private sector or at a hospital in another Member State" (Jorens and Hajdú 2008: 44).

Finland

In reaction to *Kohll* and *Decker*, the Finnish guidelines of the Social Insurance Institution on cost reimbursement were changed. Out-patient treatment received abroad was reimbursed at Finnish rates without prior authorization. Legislation on health benefits, though, was not amended (see Sakslin 2003: 15–16). In 2005, the Finnish Health Insurance Act was amended, allowing for the reimbursement of treatment received abroad (see Jorens and Hajdú 2005: 58).

Greece

The Greek government did not change its legislation and administrative practices after *Kohll* and *Decker* (see Palm et al. 2000: 84). The Social Security Institute (*Idryma Koinonikon Asfaliseon*, IKA), which covers the majority of employed persons, did not consider the jurisprudence as legally binding and, therefore, regarded *Kohll* as not having any impact (see Kremalis 2003: 43).

Ireland

Mel Cousins observed in 2003 that the Irish government had not yet modified its legislation. He noted the absence of a relevant Irish case before the ECJ and complained about the low level of public awareness:

> There has yet to be an Irish case challenging a refusal to give authorisation for a service available in another EU state. It is suspected that this is due to the low level of public awareness of a right to seek treatment in another EU state where it is necessary and is not available without undue delay in the Member State. (Cousins 2003: 20)

However, Séamus Brennan, at the time the Minister for Social Affairs, announced in June 2005 that the Treatment Benefits Scheme would start to offer the choice for patients to be treated in another EU Member State and to be directly reimbursed by the Department of Social and Family Affairs.[13] The Statutory Instrument 185 of 2005 made these changes concerning dental and optical treatments, contact lenses, and hearing aids:

> In the cases where people choose to have the treatment in another EU Member State, the Department of Social Affairs will pay an amount equivalent to the rate paid for treatments carried out in Ireland or the amount actually paid for the treatment, whichever is the lower ... For services received abroad under the new arrangements, the patient pays the practitioner in full, and afterwards sends the application form ... to the Department. (Irish Department of Social and Family Affairs 2005)

Italy

Italy did not make any changes in legislation or administrative practice in its National Health Service (NHS). The *Corte di Cassazione*, however, became active and stated in several cases that

> if an Italian national has health problems and cannot be referred to the NHS either because the treatment needed does not exist in Italy or cannot be provided as a result of the length of waiting lists, s/he can seek treatment abroad without waiting for the USL's authorisation [the Italian NHS is divided at the regional level in several Local Sanitary Units, *Unità Sanitarie Locali*, USL, AJO] and the same USL has to reimburse the whole cost. (Ales 2003: 58)

Portugal

In the national report on Portugal from 2003, *Kohll* and *Decker* were not even mentioned (see Guibentif 2003).

Spain

For the time being, the *Kohll/Decker* jurisprudence has had no impact on the Spanish national social security system (see Sánchez-Rodas Navarro 2003: 26–29, Jorens and Hajdú 2006: 90).

Sweden

The Swedish government was not concerned by *Kohll* and *Decker* (see Palm et al. 2000). Ann Numhauser reported that "[t]he Kohll and Decker cases ... did not

---

13   This scheme is based on Pay-Related Social Insurance contributions and covers dental and optical treatments, contact lenses, and hearing aids. Over 700,000 people benefited in 2004 from this scheme.

provoke much public debate in Sweden and so far has not led to any considerable changes in the restrictive Swedish attitude" (2003: 23).

However, as Jorens and Hajdú pointed out in their trESS-report, the Supreme Administrative Court found in three rulings in 2004 that persons who had received medical services abroad and demanded reimbursement from Sweden "should be reimbursed, to the extent that the medical service would have been covered by the Swedish national health system" (2006: 91). They added that a proposal has been made in Sweden to stop "the generous application" in these rulings (Jorens and Hajdú 2006: 91).

Conclusion

I have summarized the above described administrative and legislative changes in Table 5.2. It is impossible, however, to follow the implementation in all 15 "old" EU Member States in detail. Therefore, the information presented in Table 5.2 remains incomplete.

The overview shows that the interpretation of the ECJ jurisprudence and the conclusions drawn from it varied considerably. The prevailing first reaction to *Kohll* and *Decker* was simply to perpetuate the status quo. This pattern exists, for instance, in Portugal, Spain, and Sweden. However, in some EU Member States like Denmark, legislative and administrative changes were made. There is no uniform reaction by type of health care system. All three groups of countries reveal both good and bad compliance. The national health systems, though, seem to fare worse regarding compliance than the other types.

This first look at EU Member States does not provide sufficient knowledge to understand the extent to which *Kohll* and *Decker* were implemented and what the driving forces were. To gain deeper insight into all that happened at the Member State level, I need to develop my three case studies on Germany, France and the UK. In all three studies, First, I provide a short description of the central principles of the health care system as well as the attitudes/policies toward cross-border health care before *Kohll* and *Decker*; second, I determine the overall degree of misfit with the jurisprudence for each country; and third, I describe chronologically the first reactions of the main actors and the following implementation. For these in-depth analyses I consider the impact of several crucial actors: insurance funds, domestic administrations and governments, national courts, the ECJ and the European Commission. Finally, in the respective conclusions, I explain the different implementation strategies, the driving forces behind the implementation, the de-territorialization, internal de-structuring and financial destabilization effects, and the role of the implementation of the jurisprudence within overall domestic health care reforms.

Table 5.2 Administrative and legislative changes made to comply with the
***Kohll* and *Decker* jurisprudence in 12 "old" EU member states**

Group of countries	EU Member State	Effected administrative and legislative changes
Social security systems based on cash reimbursement	Belgium	Modification of the Circular for Article 22 of Regulation 1408/71 in 1998/99; Modification of the Suspension Regulation in 1999/2000.
	Luxembourg	None.
Social security systems based on benefits in kind	Austria	None. Already in line with the jurisprudence.
	The Netherlands	None.
National health systems	Denmark	Modification of the National Health Security Act in 2000; Introduction of an Order establishing new rules and regulations in 2000; Free choice of private hospital since 2002.
	Finland	Modification of reimbursement guidelines; Modification of the Finnish Health Insurance Act in 2005.
	Greece	None.
	Ireland	Modification of reimbursement for dental and optical treatment received abroad, as well as for contact lenses and hearing aids.
	Italy	None.
	Portugal	None.
	Spain	None.
	Sweden	None.

Chapter 6

The Case of France

The French statutory health insurance system consists of the General Scheme (*Régime Général*), which covers 83.5 percent of the population, the Scheme for Non-Agricultural Self-Employed (CANAM), and the Agricultural Scheme (MSA), that together cover 12.5 percent, as well as Special Schemes (4 percent).[1] The *Régime Général* comprises 129 local funds – *Caisses Primaires d'Assurance Maladie (CPAM)* – that affiliate members and reimburse the costs of treatment, 16 regional funds that are responsible for accidents at work and work-related illnesses, and a National Fund – the *Caisse Nationale d'Assurance Maladie des Travailleurs Salariés* (CNAMTS) – that has a supervisory role (see Sandier et al. 2004: 23–24). In 1999, the Universal Health Coverage Act (*Couverture Maladie Universelle*, CMU), extended statutory health insurance coverage to all French residents. Insured persons have to advance the costs for a medical treatment that they receive from a provider they can choose freely. The competent statutory insurance institution refunds fully or in part the costs for the treatment received (*avance de frais*, principle of cash benefits). The part not reimbursed by the statutory insurance institution may be covered by a complementary voluntary insurance with a mutual non-profit insurance association, a private for-profit insurance company or provident institutions which cover about 92 percent of the population (see Sandier et al. 2004: 43–46).[2] Insured persons are reimbursed according to tariffs, which are first set in agreements between the health insurance funds and the representatives of the medical professions and then approved by the government. Practitioners who are not part of the agreement can charge more than the agreed fees, however, reimbursement then takes place on an extremely low level (*tarif d'autorité* according to Article L. 162–5–10 Social Security Code).[3] Another central principle of the French statutory health insurance system is the principle of solidarity. The health insurance contribution is geared to the income of the insured person with strong elements of social compensation between the different societal groups.

---

1 The *Caisse Nationale d'Assurance Maladie* (CNAM) provided this information.

2 Sandier et al. explain these complementary institutions as follows: "The mutual insurance associations are non-profit bodies, legally and financially supervised by the state through the Mutual Insurance Code; the insurance companies are commercial enterprises governed by the Insurance Code; and the provident institutions are run jointly by unions of employees and employers and governed by the Social Security Code" (2004: 44).

3 For example, in 2002, the *CPAM de Gironde* reimbursed a consultation of a contracted physician with €20 and a consultation of a non-contracted physician with €0.49.

In general, the French political system is characterized by a strong executive branch and central administration with strong hierarchical structures. This is also true for health care. The French state interferes heavily in the administration of the health insurance system; therefore, we can speak of its limited autonomy (see Döhler and Hassenteufel 1995: 806–810). The Ministry of Health regulates the financing and organization of health care. However, the regions and departments also have an important say, leaving the Ministry with a limited steering capacity (see Lepperhoff 2004: 83–84). According to Article 34 of the French constitution, law determines only the fundamental principles of social security (see Lascombe 1999: 184). Therefore, the government can decide on health issues without consulting the Parliament. Another important feature is that the government and the insurance funds are closely interwoven (see Lepperhoff 2004: 86).

Cross-border Provisions: Breach of Principle (Territoriality)

Prior to the implementation of the *Kohll/Decker* jurisprudence, the French Social Security Code (*Code de la Sécurité Sociale*, CSS) rested upon the strict territorial principle of Article L. 332–3. The rights of patients who received health care treatment abroad were suspended if there had been no other provisions. However, there were exceptions for unexpected urgent health care and when there was no possibility to receive a particular treatment in France. Article R. 332–2 CSS regulated these cases. In case of an unexpected sickness abroad the responsible insurance fund could reimburse the costs incurred up to the amount that would have been granted in France. Patients who could not receive appropriate treatment in France itself could be authorized to travel abroad. According to French non-codified practice three demands had to be met: First, the treatment had to conform to the state of medical knowledge and had to be published in an international scientific journal. Second, the condition of the patient undeniably had to require treatment. And third, no French physician could deliver the treatment with a comparable result and in the time required (see Fillon 2001: 6). Article R. 332–2 CSS did not distinguish between EU and non-EU cases.

Degree of Misfit: Medium

The French health care system relies on the principle of reimbursement of incurred health care costs. To apply this principle to foreign cases also seems comparatively simple. The policy misfit concerned especially the principle of territoriality in Article L. 332–3 CSS which was not in line with the requirements of the *Kohll/Decker* jurisprudence. In addition, France was too restrictive in authorizing patients to travel abroad for treatment (see Palm et al. 2000: 53–54). The conditions for prior authorization provided for in Article R. 332–2 CSS did not satisfy the mode determined by the ECJ. In the politics/polity dimension there was no misfit. In the absence of waiting lists the incentives for French patients to travel abroad for treatment were low, and therefore the expected financial costs were also supposed to be low. The overall misfit of the French health system with the requirements of the *Kohll/Decker* jurisprudence was medium (see Table 6.1).

Table 6.1 Overall misfit in France

Degree of legal misfit	(Expected) Financial costs	Politics/polity misfit	Degree of overall misfit
Medium	*Low*	*None*	*Medium*
• Strict principle of territoriality; • Restrictive application of the prior authorization scheme of Regulation 1408/71.	• No waiting lists; • Low numbers of patients traveling abroad.		

Step-by-Step Administrative and Legislative Implementation

The French government represented by the Ministry of Foreign Affairs argued in the proceedings before the ECJ that unrestricted patient mobility would result in "de mettre gravement en cause les possibilités de survie des régimes de sécurité sociale fondés sur le principe de solidarité" (Rapport d'audience, *Kohll*: 67).[4] France was particularly concerned with the expected outcome of the decision, that is with a gradual abolishment of the territoriality principle. This can be gathered from the following statement submitted to the ECJ:

> C'est l'équilibre général de tous les systèmes d'assurance maladie comparables au système luxembourgeois qui serait rompu par la suppression, de proche en proche, de la règle de territorialité. (Rapport d'audience, *Kohll*: 17)[5]

Immediate Reaction: Temporizing

On June 29, 1998, two months after *Kohll* and *Decker*, the French *Ministère de l'Emploi et de la Solidarité* issued a ministerial letter in which it explained its position

---

4 This would "seriously question the survival possibilities of social security systems that are based on the principle of solidarity" (translation of the author).

5 "The general equilibrium of all social health systems comparable to the Luxembourg-system would be disturbed by the step-by-step suppression of the rule of territoriality" (translation of the author).

on these decisions. The Ministry announced a careful examination of the meaning and consequences of the rulings. At the same time, it instructed the insurance funds to strictly apply the national rules (namely Articles L. 332–3 and R. 332–2–1/ 2, *Code la Sécurité Sociale*) until a national decision was made to implement the jurisprudence in an appropriate and concerted manner (see *Ministère de l'Emploi et de la Solidarité* 1998). The Ministry wished to discuss the practical and dogmatic consequences of the rulings first and prevent the insurance funds from rushing ahead in an unconcerted manner and apply the jurisprudence in diverse ways (see Interview F3).[6] The insurance funds respected this ministerial instruction as can be seen, for example, from later upcoming national court rulings.[7]

To discuss the problems of implementing *Kohll* and *Decker*, the Ministry immediately appointed a working group under the social security director at the time, Briet. This "Briet Working Group" focused on several important topics for which four sub-groups were installed: "*professionnels de santé*," "*hospitalisation*," "*laboratoires d'analyse de biologie médicale*," and "*dispositifs médicaux*." It comprised the Ministry of Health, the Specialized Services, and the *Caisse Nationale d'Assurance Maladie* (see Interview F3). The outcomes of these working groups were then transmitted to the cabinet that, however, wanted to stick to the status quo for the time being (see Interview F3). Despite the general awareness of *Kohll* and *Decker* the debates inside the Ministry were drawn out and the forthcoming instructions promised in the ministerial letter were postponed for many years.

What are the reasons for this delay? The financial impact of the ECJ decisions was less threatening and supposedly manageable because the actual number of people traveling abroad for health care was believed to be negligible (see Interview F3). In a November 1998 working meeting for the German EU presidency, the French participants considered the expected quantitative effects of *Kohll* and *Decker* to be minor in the short and medium term (see Gobrecht 1999b: 16–17). However, the administration perceived the rulings to be a potential danger for the entire French social security system. It believed that the "*conventionnement*" (contract) with French doctors could not be easily extended to foreign providers (see Interview F3). The "*conventionnement*" was an internal instrument for the government to limit health expenditures by sanctioning health care professionals. Doctors from abroad without a "*conventionnement*," so it was feared, could have endangered this steering instrument. In addition, technical application problems were expected, for example with the reimbursement of products that were unknown in France (see Interview F3). A high-ranking official of the *Direction de la Sécurité Sociale/Division des Affaires Communautaires et Internationales* (DSS/DACI) affirmed that the Ministry was not in principle against opening up the formerly closed French social security system (see Interview F3). However,

---

6   A list of all conducted interviews is provided in the Bibliography. I have numbered the interviews according to country and date.

7   The *CPAM Strasbourg*, for instance, referred in the *Pfrimmer* case explicitly to the ministerial letter (see *Tribunal des Affaires de Sécurité Sociale* 2000a).

the administration wanted to first assess the potential risks and then come up with a feasible solution. For several years to come, no concrete steps were taken.

In its first session in January 1999 the French *Assemblée Nationale* dealt with the issue of the reimbursement of health care costs incurred in another EU Member State.[8] In this session, then RPR MP André Berthol observed that "les caisses de maladie semblent encore réticentes à accepter cette logique [de la libre circulation des services, AJO]" (*Assemblée Nationale* 1999).[9] Berthol asked Bernard Kouchner, then *Secrétaire d'Etat à la Santé et à l'Action Sociale*, which measures were planned to apply *Kohll* and *Decker*. Kouchner responded that without doubt French legislation was affected by this jurisprudence since it was very much like the Luxembourg legislation. He pointed to the grave consequences that *Kohll* and *Decker* could have for the entire French social security system, especially the handling of the medical expenditures. Kouchner referred to the impossibility to extend French regulations to foreign health care providers. According to him the question was still under consideration in France and in the EU. For the moment the existing French legislation was to be applied (*Assemblée Nationale* 1999).

The European Commission Intervenes: Things Start to Move

Beginning in the mid-1990s, the European Commission received many individual complaints that France either refused to reimburse health care provided in another Member State or to authorize going abroad. After the *Kohll* and *Decker* decisions, the Commission received many inquiries from citizens who wanted to know more about their new rights according to this jurisprudence (see Interview EC1). Although considerable reflection took place in the French government and administration, no concrete steps were taken. In this period of non-activity, the European Commission received a complaint from a person insured by a French insurance fund in 1999. This insured person was refused reimbursement according to French tariffs for the costs of a pair of eyeglasses bought in Germany because she lacked authorization by her insurance (see European Commission 2001: 30). This case fit perfectly to *Decker*. Consequently, in October 1999, the Commission sent a Letter of Formal Notice to the French government stating that this refusal to reimburse directly contradicted *Decker*.[10] In its response from

---

8 The *Assemblée Nationale* in general plays a "very limited role in the formulation of French positions on EC legislation" (Menon 2000: 90).

9 "The health insurance funds seem to be still reluctant to accept the logic of the free movement of services" (translation of the author).

10 For detailed information on the monitoring function of the Commission, see its Communication (2003a). In the first stage of an infringement procedure the Commission sends a Letter of Formal Notice to the respective Member State. This procedure "lacks an official character" (Falkner et al. 2005: 207). The Commission is rather secretive about this step and does not make it public (see Interview EC1). For a detailed description of the different stages of an infringement procedure, see Falkner et al. (2005: 205–215).

January 27, 2000, the French *Ministère de l'Emploi et de la Solidarité* claimed
that the immediate and unprepared application of the ECJ decisions would
endanger the efficiency of domestic health care systems concerning health care
personnel and health care expenses. A hurried application of *Kohll* and *Decker*
would disorganize the domestic health care systems (see European Commission
2000: 2–3).[11] The Commission was not satisfied with this response. Therefore, in
October 2000, it sent a Reasoned Opinion to that French ministry.[12] In this second
stage of the infringement proceeding, the European Commission simply repeated
and confirmed its position that the French legislation was not in conformity
with European law and violated the principle of free movement of goods (see
European Commission 2000: 3). The Commission considered the French position
unfounded. The (limited) application of *Decker*, namely reimbursing the costs for
eyeglasses purchased in another Member State, in no way risked disorganizing
domestic health care systems, according to the Commission. In March of 2001,
the French *Ministère de l'Emploi et de la Solidarité* succumbed to the pressure
from the Commission. The DSS/DACI issued a circular in which it invalidated
the initial ministerial letter from June 29, 1998, and informed the insurance
funds about the new French position concerning *Decker*: optical products
purchased abroad had to be reimbursed according to French reimbursement rules
(see Circular DSS/DACI/2001/120).[13] With this circular the French ministry
followed the ECJ in *Decker* and the interpretation of the European Commission.
Nevertheless, Elisabeth Guigou, now Minister *de l'Emploi et de la Solidarité* of
the *Parti Socialiste* declared that the general reservations about *Kohll* and *Decker*
and their effect on French national health politics and the control of health care
expenditures were still valid and that French legislation and its regulations remained
unchanged. According to her, the concession to the European Commission, that
is the reimbursement of optical products, did not destabilize the French system of

---

11   The Letter of Formal Notice has not been made public. Fortunately, in the
Reasoned Opinion the Commission elucidates its preceding communication with the French
government in detail.

12   If the Letter of Formal Notice is not satisfying for the Commission, it sends
an official and publicized Reasoned Opinion in the second stage of the infringement
procedure.

13   In general, French administrative authorities issue circulars in order to inform their
services. Very often circulars bring a new law or decree to the attention of those actors who
have to apply it. A circular usually has the function of explaining a text without adding to
it. The circular DSS/DACI/2001/120 and the following circulars to be discussed have been
worked out by the *Division des Affaires Communautaires et Internationales* (DACI) in
collaboration with other units of the *Direction de la Sécurité Sociale* (DSS), the *Direction
de l'Hospitalisation et de l'Organisation des Soins* (DHOS), the *Direction Générale de la
Santé* (DGS) and the *Caisse Nationale de l'Assurance Maladie des Travailleurs Salariés*
(CNAMTS) (information by email of a high-ranking official of the DSS/DACI from
December 6, 2005, in possession of the author).

social security. Therefore, French insurance funds should from then on follow this ECJ jurisprudence. However, a very strict application of *Decker* was demanded in the circular: only optical products should be reimbursed, only products with a prescription in France, and only based on French tariffs (see *Union Régionale des Caisses d'Assurance Maladie* 2004: 30).

The concession of the French ministry to the European Commission was easy to make given the very low reimbursement for optical glasses and the minimal financial impact. At the same time, with this first step France signaled to the Commission that it was thinking about the jurisprudence and moving toward its implementation. In June 2002, the European Commission closed the infringement proceeding against France.

The First National Court Cases: The Pressure Mounts Further

In 2000, the first national court cases also started to shake up the administrative and governmental inactivity. These court activities will be treated below.

A number of French first-instance tribunals laid down decisions against individual CPAMs. For example, the *Tribunal des Affaires de Sécurité Sociale de Strasbourg* delivered three rulings against the *CPAM de Strasbourg* in June 2000: *Pfrimmer*, *Thébaud*, and *Vaquin*. In *Pfrimmer* it based its ruling on *Decker* and decided that the CPAM's refusal to reimburse the costs for eyeglasses purchased in Germany was "juridiquement infondée" [legally unfounded, AJO] (see *Tribunal des Affaires de Sécurité Sociale* 2000a).

The *Tribunal* decided similarly in *Thébaud* and *Vaquin*. Here, it based its decision on *Kohll* and *Decker* and ruled that optical products and dental prostheses purchased in another EU country had to be reimbursed by the *Caisse Primaire*. The CPAM appealed against these decisions before the *Cour d'Appel de Colmar*. This court rejected the appeals and confirmed all three rulings. The *Cour d'Appel* declared that neither the financing of the social security system nor public health considerations provided sufficient reasons to refuse the reimbursement (see *Cour d'Appel de Colmar* 2002a, b, 2003). In addition, in *Pfrimmer* the appeals court found that the ministerial instruction to ignore *Kohll* and *Decker* was wrong:

> Enfin, une directive donnée le 26 septembre 1998 par le Ministère de l'Emploi et de la Solidarité aux organismes gestionnaires de base de s'en tenir strictement à l'application de la réglementation nationale actuellement en vigueur ne saurait prévaloir sur une décision de la Cour de Justice des Communautés Européennes favorable à l'assurée sociale, qui doit en bénéficier immédiatement.[14]

---

14 "Finally, a directive given by the *Ministère de l'Emploi et de la Solidarité* the 26 September 1998 to the basic health care institutions to strictly stick to the application of the current national regulation in force cannot prevail over a decision of the ECJ which is in favor of a socially insured person and who has to benefit from it immediately" (translation of the author).

In March 2002, the French *Cour de Cassation*, referring explicitly to *Vanbraekel*, ruled in *Robert Magnan vs. CPAM Hauts-de-Seine*: Immediately necessary health care received in a UK private hospital outside the structure of the national health system had to be covered by the French insurance fund in charge (2002).[15] *Magnan* was highly important: this can be gathered from the fact that it was published in the official bulletin and portrayed in the Annual Report of the *Cour de Cassation*. The *Cour de Cassation* could have referred the case to the ECJ. It refrained, though, because it was convinced of the European requirements and obliged the *CPAM Hauts-de-Seine* to reimburse the health care costs of Robert Magnan based on Article 22 of Regulation 1408/71. Francis Kessler, although he was generally in favor of the implementation of the *Kohll/Decker* jurisprudence, criticized *Magnan*. He reproached the *Chambre Sociale* of the *Cour de Cassation* a "lecture plus qu'audacieuse et doublement extensive de l'arrêt Vanbraekel" [a more than audacious and double extensive reading of the ruling Vanbraekel, AJO]. According to him, *Magnan* transposed the imagined solution of the ECJ to a case to which the latter had not yet pronounced its opinion (2002: 650). Jean-Philippe Lhernould confirmed this view and said that the ruling was a step forward but at the same time too far-reaching as it went even further than *Vanbraekel* (see Interview F1). The expert of the French Ministry of Health, Jean-Claude Fillon, stated that the *Cour de Cassation* had simply systematically applied the ECJ jurisprudence to a different case, however in its scope (2002: 2). Two years later, in May 2004, the *Cour de Cassation* used almost identical formulations as in *Magnan* in *CPAM de Montpellier vs. Gérona*. It decided that the *Caisse Primaire* had to reimburse a patient who had received urgent hospital treatment in Spain (see *Cour de Cassation* 2004).

In September 2002, the *Cour de Cassation* ruled in *Caisse Nationale Militaire de Sécurité Sociale vs. Jozan* in reference to Articles 49 and 50 EC Treaty that an insured person who had been refused prior authorization to travel abroad for a surgical operation in Germany had no right to get reimbursed (see *Cour de Cassation* 2002).

Referring to the above cited national court cases Lhernould generally noted the willingness of French courts to respect ECJ jurisprudence (2003: 3). Although, according to Kessler, some French courts such as the *Cour d'Appel de Paris* still remained reluctant in following the *Cour de Cassation* (2003: 18), the extensive *Magnan* ruling was a quantum leap pushing for the implementation of the *Kohll/Decker* jurisprudence. The Ministry in reaction to *Magnan* issued a letter to the insurance funds approving the ruling (see Interview F3). The multiplication of court cases put more and more pressure on the administration and the government to come up with an instrument to end judicial uncertainty relating to patient mobility. I treat the subsequent steps of implementation below.

---

15   The *Cour de Cassation* is the supreme civil and criminal court in France. It reviews the decisions made by the tribunals and the court of appeals. The *Cour de Cassation* only judges the law and its application not the facts of the case.

The Ensuing Transitory Circular: A Promise of Full Compliance

With the Circular DSS/DACI/2003/286 from June 16, 2003, the ministerial letter from June 29, 1998, was again invalidated and the Circular DSS/DACI/2001/120 from March 1, 2001, completed. DSS/DACI/2003/286 was supposed to be a transitory text, in which first measures were taken to bring French practices and regulations in line with the evolution of ECJ decisions. In addition, it promised substantial reforms in the future to comply with European requirements. Circular DSS/DACI/2001/120 had slightly eased the outright rejection of the ECJ jurisprudence for optical products, and relied on a strict application of *Decker*. Circular DSS/DACI/2003/286 went far beyond this and even promised further steps to take into account the evolution of the ECJ jurisprudence. It changed French regulations with respect to medication, medical equipment, medical treatments, and the in-patient sector. Compliant with the ECJ jurisprudence, costs for medication prescribed or invoiced in another EU/EEA Member State had to be assumed henceforth by French insurance funds under the same conditions as those in France.[16] The prescription for the medication had to abide by French rules, the medication had to be listed with the domestically reimbursable medication, and the reimbursement had to be based on French tariffs. Medical equipment, similar to medication, had to be first allowed through a prescription, had to appear on a list, and was then reimbursed based on French tariffs. Foreign physicians were put on par with French physicians who had no contract with French statutory health insurance. Their treatment was reimbursed at an extremely low tariff (*tarif d'autorité*). In addition, the future working agenda was outlined in the circular: national and European negotiation on a list of reimbursable medication and medical equipment which is acknowledged everywhere; negotiation on contracts with foreign health care providers; permission of medical biological analyses by foreign laboratories; and preparation of a future circular on the criteria and conditions for authorizing in-patient care.

The ECJ Decision in Inizan

A few months later, in October 2003, the ECJ challenged in *Inizan*, which concerned France directly, Article R. 332–2 of the French Social Security Code (see Chapter 4). Not the *Cour de Cassation* but a court of first instance had referred this case to the ECJ. In the written *rapport d'audience* for the proceedings before the ECJ, the French government held that Article R. 332–2 was fulfilling European requirements (Rapport d'audience, *Inizan*: 12). *Inizan* basically confirmed previous ECJ jurisprudence.

The European Court of Justice cannot directly rule whether national legislation is in conformity with Community law pursuant to preliminary references; only

---

16 The regulations are thus valid for the EU Member States and the EEA Member States Norway, Iceland, and Liechtenstein, but not for Switzerland.

the national courts can reach such a conclusion (see Somsen 2000: 314–315). The ECJ can simply determine the validity and interpretation of Community law according to Article 234 EC Treaty. Nevertheless, it can provide the national courts with the criteria necessary to interpret European law correctly (see ECJ Case 45/75: para. 11, C-228/98: para. 36, *Inizan*: para. 51). In *Inizan*, the ECJ clearly indicated that the contentious provisions of R. 332–2 were violating the principle of free movement of services (para. 54). In the case of in-patient care, however, restrictions were deemed justified, but only if the same or equally effective treatment could be offered in France without undue delay (para. 59). In addition, the prior authorization procedure had to meet certain standards: it had to be based on objective, non-discriminatory criteria known in advance; it had to be "easily accessible and capable of ensuring that a request for authorisation will be dealt with objectively and impartially within a reasonable time"; and it had to be possible to challenge a rejection of reimbursement in judicial or quasi-judicial proceedings (para. 57). According to the ECJ, Article R. 332–2 clearly did not meet these requirements.

On the whole, *Inizan* does not seem to have been of great importance for implementing the *Kohll/Decker* jurisprudence in France.[17] *Inizan* was about in-patient health care where under certain conditions authorization schemes had been generally deemed valid. Also, the most important steps to bring French practices and laws in line with *Kohll* and *Decker* had already been initiated before *Inizan*. Nevertheless, the ECJ pressed for judicial certainty in authorization procedures for in-patient care, which was achieved in the 2005 decree that stipulated several obligations for the insurance funds, such as deadlines and appeal proceedings (see below).

The Ensuing Circular: Another Preliminary Measure

In March of 2004, yet another circular, DSS/DACI/2004/134, was issued as the intended completion of the preceding Circulars DSS/DACI/2001/120 and DSS/DACI/2003/286. Jean-François Mattei, then Minister of Health, drew on the first results of the Ministerial Working Group "Médicaments et dispositifs médicaux" and widened the reimbursement rights detailed in DSS/DACI/2004/134. This circular was a preliminary measure, though, because the responsible working group had not yet found the ultimate solution. Because of the technicality of the question and the low number of cases, it determined that insurance funds have to forward contested invoices for unidentifiable products to the national control

---

17   A high-ranking official of the DSS/DACI even goes so far as to claim that *Inizan* could have been counterproductive to the implementation, because according to his view, the ECJ had partly confirmed the existing French authorization procedure (see Interview F3).

body (*Service du Contrôle Médical*), and that the body then has to decide on the reimbursement.[18] This decision could then be used as a precedent in future cases.

Further Pressure from the European Commission and the ECJ

In March of 2004, the pressure from the European Commission and the ECJ on the French government mounted. The ECJ ruled in an action under Article 226 EC Treaty, launched by the Commission in December 2001, that the French Republic had failed to fulfill its obligations under Articles 43 and 49 EC Treaty "by requiring that bio-medical analysis laboratories established in other Member States have their place of business in France in order to obtain the requisite operating authorisation," and more importantly "by precluding any reimbursement of the costs of bio-medical analyses carried out by a bio-medical analysis laboratory established in another Member State" (ECJ, C-496/01: para. 1). According to a decree from November 4, 1976, only laboratories established in France had the authorization to provide their services. Having learned from the previous condemnation by the ECJ, the government modified Article L. 6211–2–1 of the *Code de la Santé Publique* (CSP) a few months later in August 2004 using the Law 2004–806: it laid down the procedure for EU/EEA biological medical analysis laboratories. In addition, the upcoming Decree 2005–386 took into account the interpretation of the Commission and the ECJ regarding foreign laboratories (see below). To provide their services, however, the foreign laboratories needed prior administrative authorization: the necessary procedural regulations R. 6211–46 to 56 were inserted with the Decree 2006–306 in the CSP in a new section dealing exclusively with EU/EEA laboratories. In December 2006, the government – pressed by the Commission – changed Article L. 6211–2–1 again according to Law 2006–1640, permitting EU/EEA laboratories to provide their services without prior administrative authorization.

The Decree 2005–386: Full Compliance

In July 2003, the *Assemblée Nationale* and the *Sénat* had authorized the French government to adapt the Social Security Code following the ECJ jurisprudence and to take the necessary steps in order to facilitate the use of health care abroad. Article 15 of the Law 2003–591 authorized the government to take all measures in order to facilitate the access of insured persons to health care in other EU Member States.

The first steps of the reform of the Social Security Code were the new Article L. 332–3 that was introduced with *Ordonnance* 2004–329 from April 15, 2004,

---

18   The *Service National du Contrôle Médical* is an independent organization under the umbrella of the CNAMTS.

and the Law 2004–810 from August 13, 2004.[19] The *ordonnance* distinguished for the first time between EU and non-EU cases. Article L. 332–3 announced that a forthcoming decree would make the necessary adaptations in Article R. 332–2.

In April 2005, French Prime Minister Jean-Pierre Raffarin issued the announced Decree 2005–386 that modified the *Code de la Sécurité Sociale* concerning the reimbursement of costs incurred for health care outside France.[20] The most important modification was the insertion of four new articles into the new Section 2 in the part of the legislation entitled "Soins dispensés hors de France" [Health care treatment received outside of France, AJO].

Article R. 332–2 basically remained the same with the exception that from then on it was valid for all foreign countries outside the EU/EEA. For the EU Member States and EEA Countries completely new provisions (R. 332–3 to 6) were inserted. According to R. 332–3, ambulatory health care costs incurred in another EU/EEA country now had to be reimbursed under the same conditions as if the treatment had been received in France, with the exception that a reimbursement must not exceed the actual costs incurred by the patient. R. 332–4 still required an authorization for in-patient health care. This authorization could be refused only under two circumstances: the treatment is not listed in French regulations as reimbursable; or, an identical or equally efficient treatment can be provided in France "*en temps opportun*" [without undue delay, AJO] considering the condition of the patient and the evolution of the condition. In addition, the detailed procedure for such an authorization was laid down: The insured had to address her claim to the insurance fund. The decision had to be taken by the medical control authority. In view of the degree of urgency and availability of health care, the decision had to be communicated within two weeks after having received the application; otherwise the insured person could assume that she was authorized to travel abroad. A negative response had to provide reasons and it had to facilitate an appeal before a tribunal. The new Article R. 332–5 allowed for contracts established between French social security institutions and EU/EEA providers for treatments not available in France. These contracts needed to be authorized by the ministry. Finally, R. 332–6 provided for the reimbursement

---

19   An *ordonnance* is a governmental act for a domain that is normally regulated by law. According to Article 38 of the French constitution, the government may ask the *Assemblée Nationale* to vote a *loi d'habilitation*, which allows the government to introduce an *ordonnance*.

20   A decree is a regulative act signed by the president or the prime minister in order to exercise their functions. Most of the political and administrative activities of the president and the prime minister are decrees. In the hierarchy of juridical norms, decrees are inferior to treaties, laws and general law principles, but are superior to ministerial orders. In the case at hand, it is a regulative decree signed by the prime minister that had to be submitted to the *Conseil d'État*. The *Conseil d'État* is advising the government. Projects for a "*décret en Conseil d'État*" have to be examined by the *Conseil d'État*. It states its opinion on the juridical regularity of the text, its form, and its administrative possibilities.

of analyses by foreign bio-medical laboratories, with the stipulation that French authorization was procured (see above).

The modalities of the application of Decree 2005–386 were determined one month later in the Circular DSS/DACI/2005/235 from May 19, 2005. This circular was the preliminary endpoint of a whole series of circulars; it invalidated the ministerial letter from June 29, 1998, and completed the preceding circulars. Circular DSS/DACI/2005/235 described the different stages of how the ECJ jurisprudence was integrated into French provisions: the three previous circulars had progressively opened French law, and they had redefined the conditions for the reimbursement of outlays for health products, in-patient and out-patient health care received in another EU/EEA Member State.

With the four articles inserted into the Social Security Code in the new section "Health care treatment received abroad," France took a considerable step toward conforming fully to the ECJ jurisprudence, with the single exception of requiring a French authorization for foreign laboratories in Article R. 332–6. This last incompatibility was changed in December 2006 (see above), so that France is now in full conformity with the *Kohll/Decker* jurisprudence.

The French government has consistently demanded that *Kohll* and *Decker* should be implemented by all Member States including those which, like the UK, relied on national health systems. According to the government, the jurisprudence should be implemented in a concerted way by all Member States and result in more harmonization (see Gobrecht 1999b: 16–17 and Interview F3). After it had implemented the jurisprudence, France seemed to be very interested in extending the *Kohll/Decker* jurisprudence to countries with a national health system such that all EU Member States would be affected. According to the French Ministry of Health, it was a matter of equity among Member States (see Interview F3). This strategy already surfaced in the *Watts* hearing in October of 2005. France was not directly concerned by this decision. However, it was the only country with a social security approach which commented on the case. The French government suggested in its written observation that Article 49 EC Treaty also apply to a national health service like the UK NHS (see ECJ, Report for the Hearing on *Watts*: para. 57).

Conclusion

It was clear from the start that *Kohll* and *Decker* could easily be transferred to the French health care system since it is quite similar to that of Luxembourg. Nevertheless, France took nine years to conform fully; its government adopted a rather obstructive strategy. According to its official position, it wanted to attain a uniform application in France and, equally important, among all EU Member States.

The government and administration monopolize the handling of ECJ decisions in France. They control that process with circulars, decrees, laws, and *ordonnances*, and thus run the implementation process almost exclusively. The hierarchical structure that connects the government with the insurance bodies, and which excludes the Parliament, allowed for slow and gradual implementation, a process that dovetailed governmental and administrative preferences. Step by step, through circulars that invalidated or added to preceding circulars, the French government adapted the system. Since the insurance funds have no discretion in applying these circulars, we must assume that they adapted their practices accordingly. Through two decrees in 2005 and 2006, decrees which changed prior legislation, France finally complied in great detail with all the requirements of this ECJ jurisprudence.

Why did it take France nine years to conform to these requirements? And why did it finally transpose the *Kohll/Decker* jurisprudence? The "non-culture du droit communautaire" [the non-culture of European law, AJO] (see Interview F1), that is, the pervasive gap in knowledge about EU law in France, is one part of the explanation for the implementation delay. Even the decisions by the *Cour de Cassation* – in which the *Kohll/Decker* jurisprudence was applied to France and which gave an important impetus to the government and administration to end judicial uncertainty – were thought to be flawed in their reasoning on EU law. The incompatibilities between the French social security system and the *Kohll/ Decker* jurisprudence were another major reason for the delay. French doctors have to sign "*conventionnements*," contracts between the insurance funds and the medical associations. This French precondition for reimbursement was thought impossible of extension to physicians abroad. Another problem concerned the level of reimbursement that was to be applied when refunding costs incurred abroad (see Interview F1).

Nine years passed – at first glance a long time – before France complied fully with the *Kohll/Decker* jurisprudence. Indeed, France apparently has a very bad overall record regarding its compliance with ECJ rulings. According to figures assembled by Derek Beach, the European Commission initiated 50 infringement proceedings against France between 1998 to 2001, all of them concerning non-compliance with an ECJ ruling after six months (2005: 116–117).[21] From the 47 second referrals to the ECJ under Article 228 EC Treaty between January 1997 and March 2007, ten were directed against France, putting it at the head of the EU pack in garnering second referrals.[22] Thus, it is logical to ask why France finally complied with this ECJ jurisprudence. Representatives of the DSS/DACI and the *Centre des Liaisons Européennes et Internationales de Sécurité Sociale*

---

21   However, infringement proceedings by the Commission are a problematic proxy for determining non-compliance with ECJ rulings. On this problem, see, for example, Börzel (2001: 804–808).

22   The second referrals have been assembled by the author with the help of the European Commission infringement decisions (2002 to 2007) and the Reports from the Commission on Monitoring the Application of Community Law (16th to 23rd Annual Report).

(CLEISS), even thought, after all, that France had been a "bon élève européen" [a good European pupil, AJO] regarding the *Kohll/Decker* jurisprudence (see Interviews F6, F4).[23]

The main reason for the implementation taking place was the combined and enduring pressure exerted by the European Commission through its infringement proceedings and by national courts through their rulings. This combination drove the French government step by step down the implementation path of the *Kohll/Decker* jurisprudence. First, the Commission took initiatives early on. Although the success of the first infringement proceeding was only a minor concession, the French position began to crumble more and more as the pressure continued. Secondly, the French national courts, especially the *Cour de Cassation* – frequently thought to be reluctant to refer cases to the ECJ (see Interview F1) – contributed considerably to the French government's change in position. With ever further decisions, the national courts put considerable and continuous pressure on the government to end judicial uncertainty.

In France, the territoriality principle enshrined in the *Code de la Sécurité Sociale* (CSS) eroded further with the legal transposition of the *Kohll/Decker* jurisprudence. Important new articles were inserted in the CSS, in which for the first time, non-EU/EEA and EU/EEA cases were treated differently. However, following the ECJ jurisprudence, unconditional reimbursement of costs incurred abroad was limited to out-patient health care. Therefore, de-territorialization remained confined. The ECJ decisions did not lead to the much feared internal de-structuring of the French social security system. France could comply with the ECJ jurisprudence without having to alter its domestic health care services structures. Financial destabilization was also limited because relatively few people traveled abroad for treatment and they did so primarily in cross-border regions.

The main health care reforms in France since the 1990s have taken place without being overly concerned with ECJ decisions. The reforms dealt primarily with cost containment, institutional and regional re-organization, and equity issues. So, the social security and hospital reforms of 1996 shifted the power from the national to the regional level. The Universal Health Coverage Act of 1999 aimed to increase the access to health care for people with low incomes. The 2004 reform of social security addressed primarily structural and financial aspects.[24] In short, French health care reforms followed their own domestic logic and were only peripherally concerned with ECJ decisions.

---

23 The CLEISS is the public French coordinating institution responsible for checking and paying claims and debts relating to European, international and bilateral social security agreements. In addition, its tasks are to collect and assemble statistical data, advise social security institutions in the implementation of the social security agreements, and translate relevant documents.

24 For a detailed discussion of French health care reforms, see, for example, Sandier et al. (2004: 115–132).

Chapter 7

The Case of Germany

The German Bismarck model of a statutory health care system (*Gesetzliche Krankenversicherung*, GKV) is based on a compulsory insurance principle and the principle of solidarity. The health insurance contribution is geared to the socio-economic status and the income of the insured person and the system is characterized by elements of social compensation between the different societal groups. Health insurance funds are public-law self-governing bodies and charged with the management and delivery of in-kind benefits. In order to do this, they negotiate contracts with predominantly private providers. Additional central principles are the autonomy of the health care system and a heterogeneous system of insurance funds.[1]

Cross-border Provisions:
Breaches of Principle (Territoriality and In-kind Benefits)

The German statutory health care system is characterized by the principle of territoriality, subject to domestic, supranational, international or bilateral exceptions (see Paragraph 30(2) of Social Code Book I, *Sozialgesetzbuch*, SGB). The duty to insure and the entitlement to insurance according to Paragraph 3 SGB IV extends to the territorial domain of the SGB. According to Paragraph 16(1)(1) SGB V – Statutory Health Insurance – benefit claims remained suspended as long as an insured person stayed abroad. As a matter of principle, health care benefits from care providers abroad could not be consumed at the expense of the responsible German insurance fund. Nevertheless, Paragraphs 17 and 18 SGB V made some exceptions to this rule: The former Paragraph 17 determined that insured persons employed abroad received health benefits from their employer who then had to claim the costs from the insurance fund. Paragraph 18 determined that an insurance fund could assume all or part of the costs of treatment abroad if a treatment according to the state of medical knowledge was only available abroad. Further breaches of the territoriality principle existed in the EU coordination regulations for the social security of migrant workers. Regulations 1408/71 and 574/72 basically concerned two cases: cases in which immediately necessary health care had to be provided abroad, and cases in which patients had to be authorized by their insurance fund to travel abroad for treatment.

---

1   For a detailed description of the basic structure of German statutory health insurance law see for instance Kingreen (2003: 461–481) and Busse/Riesberg (2004).

The general principle that health care services were provided through in-kind benefits (see paras. 27(1) and 2(2) SGB V) was breached in 1997: one could now choose cash reimbursement instead of in-kind benefits (see Article 1(1)(a) of Second Statutory Health Insurance Restructuring Act 1997: 1520). Only two percent of all insured in compulsory health insurance chose the reimbursement option (see Extended Committee of the Central Associations of Statutory Health Insurance Funds 1999: 22). For the compulsorily insured, this option was removed in 1999. Voluntarily insured persons, however, still have the possibility to opt for cash benefits.[2]

Degree of Misfit: High

Three dimensions measure the aggregated overall misfit in Germany with the *Kohll/Decker* jurisprudence: substantive legal misfit, politics/polity misfit, and the expected financial costs. The German health care system was characterized by two principles that contradicted the *Kohll/Decker* jurisprudence: territoriality and the provision of in-kind benefits, the latter only abrogated for the voluntarily insured. Desiderata established by *Geraets-Smits/Peerbooms* and *Müller-Fauré/ van Riet* concerning prior authorization for treatment abroad were already fulfilled by German law. Misfit in the politics/polity dimension could not be detected. Financial costs for Germany were expected to be low, as there was little incentive for patients to travel abroad. However, if we add up the misfits with the *Kohll/ Decker* jurisprudence in the policy and cost dimensions, we note a high overall misfit for Germany (see Table 7.1).[3]

One-Step Legislative Implementation

In the ECJ proceedings on *Kohll* and *Decker*, the German government had articulated the expectation that an uncoordinated opening of the markets for pharmaceuticals, medical equipment, and medical care would seriously endanger the structure of the national system of social security.[4]

---

2 For a discussion of this system breach, see von Wulffen (1997).

3 When aggregating the three dimensions of misfit, Falkner et al. argued that "no dimension of misfit can eradicate or soften adaptational pressure in another dimension" (2005: 32). Therefore, a high degree of misfit in one of the three dimensions needs to be rated as a high overall misfit.

4 See ECJ, Rapport d'audience, *Kohll*: paras. 55 and 60; and Rapport d'audience, *Decker*: para. 34.

Table 7.1 Overall misfit in Germany

Degree of legal misfit	(Expected) Financial costs	Politics/polity misfit	Degree of overall misfit
High	*Low*	*None*	*High*
• Strict principle of territoriality; • Restrictive application of the prior authorization scheme of Regulation 1408/71; • Cash reimbursement only for voluntarily insured.	• No waiting lists; • Low numbers of patients traveling abroad.		

Immediate Political Reaction: Strict Refusal of Transferability

When the ECJ adjudicated *Kohll* and *Decker* in 1998, they provoked strong reactions in Germany. Horst Seehofer, German Federal Minister of Health since May 1992, commented on *Kohll* and *Decker* in a press release on the very day they were issued:

> [Ich halte] die Entscheidungen des EuGH für äußerst problematisch. Welche konkreten Konsequenzen aus dem Urteil im nationalen und im europäischen Recht zu ziehen sind, bleibt einer sorgfältigen Prüfung vorbehalten. (Federal Ministry of Health 1998a)[5]

According to the Federal Ministry of Health, the two decisions were not applicable to the German in-kind benefit system, since the ECJ cases were about the Luxembourg system based on reimbursement. A binding effect for Germany was therefore denied (see Federal Ministry of Health 1998b).

In addition, in a letter to the Federal Insurance Authority (*Bundesversicherungsamt*, BVA) and the competent *Länder* ministries the Ministry of Health denied that this jurisprudence was transferable to Germany: The Ministry here relied on the

---

5 "I consider the decisions of the ECJ as extremely problematic. The concrete consequences of the ruling for national and European law will have to be examined thoroughly" (translation of the author). Kingreen considered this immediate rejection to be an attempt of "political immunization" of the German social security system (2003: 360).

reservations made in the ECJ rulings.[6] These reservations pertained to a threat to the ability to control the financial stability of the health care systems. The BVA passed this statement on to the Central Associations of the Insurance Funds and the regulatory institutions in the *Länder* (see Greß et al. 2003: 38). From this overall negative interpretation the Ministry of Health concluded that the legal position in Germany remained unaffected (see Federal Ministry of Health 1998b).[7]

According to officials of the Ministry of Health, the instruction to take a stand against *Kohll* and *Decker* came from the highest political level, namely minister Seehofer, who was openly opposed to the ECJ interfering in national health care systems. Such explicit instructions are atypical with respect to ECJ decisions; such issues are at a rather technical level and are usually handled by the responsible bureaucrats. Because of the vigorous rejection at the political level, the Ministry later found it difficult to revise its position (Interviews G1, G6).[8]

One reason why the Ministry of Health adopted such a negative position on the *Kohll/Decker* jurisprudence was simply to gain time. However, this was not the most important reason. Generally, it feared that the ECJ jurisprudence would cause intense political and legal pressure and would ultimately lead to structural changes for the domestic provision of health care. Already a few people claiming reimbursement of their costs incurred abroad were seen as causing major changes in the entire system. Statements of a Working Group on social insurance affirm this fear:

> Würde der EuGH das 'Decker/Kohll-Prinzip' auch auf Sachleistungssysteme anwenden und aussprechen, daß solche Systeme für im Ausland erbrachte Leistungen Kostenerstattungen zu gewähren haben, wäre innerstaatlich ein beträchtlicher politischer Druck möglich. Es steht zu befürchten, daß diesfalls gefordert werden würde, auch innerstaatlich Kostenerstattungen – die derzeit in reinen Sachleistungssystemen nicht vorgesehen sind – zuzulassen. (Working Group of the *Euroforum soziale Krankenversicherung* 1999: 8)[9]

After the German *Bundestag* elections in September 1998 and the consequent coalition between the Social Democrats and the Greens, the governmental position

---

6   The Federal Insurance Authority supervises the activities of the health insurance funds and the health professional institutions on the federal level.

7   For a description of the reaction of the German Ministry of Health, see Künkele (2000: 44–45).

8   A list of all conducted interviews is provided in the Bibliography. I have numbered the interviews according to country and date.

9   "If the ECJ applies the '*Decker/Kohll* principle' also to in-kind benefit systems and states that these have to allow cash reimbursement for in-kind benefits provided abroad, considerable political pressure would be possible nationally. It is feared that claims to allow cash reimbursement also nationally would be raised, which is not foreseen at the moment in systems relying solely on in-kind benefits" (translation of the author).

did not immediately change. The German administrative and governmental actors continued to deny the transferability of the *Kohll/Decker* jurisprudence to Germany. The Federal Ministry of Health did so, for example, in a preparatory meeting for the German EU Presidency in November 1998 in Bonn. EU Member States and the European Commission met at that occasion to discuss the implications of the *Kohll/Decker* jurisprudence. In the conference "The new Public Health Policy of the European Union" that took place in January 1999 in Potsdam the German viewpoint was iterated as follows:

> [T]hey [*Kohll* and *Decker*, AJO] solely concern the Luxembourg health system, based as it is on the principle of reimbursement. Therefore, the judgements are only transferable to systems that also operate on the costs reimbursement principle. (Gobrecht 1999a: 100)

The new government immediately reversed the 1997 reform that permitted the choice of cash benefits for all persons in the compulsory health insurance, thus fulfilling an election promise. This option was restricted in 1999 to the voluntarily insured and their co-insured family members. According to Manfred Zipperer, a former head of department in the Federal Ministry of Health, a transfer of the *Kohll/Decker* jurisprudence to Germany would have thwarted this step taken by the new government (1999: 31–32).

The Discordant Health Care Actors

While the Ministry of Health was fiercely opposed to the *Kohll/Decker* jurisprudence, according to Zipperer, the majority of care providers, patients' organizations and health insurance funds initially welcomed it (Zipperer 1999: 24). A first interpretation of the German insurance funds pointed to the transferability of the *Kohll/Decker* jurisprudence to Germany. They expected a stronger competition among care providers and ultimately financial relief (see *Frankfurter Allgemeine Zeitung* 1998). The *Allgemeine Ortskrankenkassen* (AOK), the largest German insurance fund association saw possible "positive effects" for health care consumers in Germany for dental prosthesis (see Gesundheitspolitischer Informationsdienst 1998: 114–115). Gert Nachtigal, then President of the Administrative Board of the AOK, stated right after the decisions that more competition was needed in the health sector and that instead of rising contributions some financial strain may be taken off the sickness insurance (see Gesundheitspolitischer Informationsdienst 1998: 115).

In May of 1998, the European Representation of the German Statutory Health Insurance in Brussels commented on *Kohll* and *Decker* in a statement to its members, asserting that, first, the two rulings were not seen as a surprise and, second, that they would have important consequences for the provision of in-kind benefits in Germany, not only for medical products but also for out-patient and in-patient care.[10] Important parallels were seen between Luxembourg and Germany regarding the provision of benefits through private physicians (see *Deutsche Sozialversicherung* 1998: 4–5)

The medical associations were split in their evaluation: The German Medical Association (*Bundesärztekammer*) pointed to the dangers emanating from *Kohll* and *Decker* for social security systems in general (see Gesundheitspolitischer Informationsdienst 1998: 117). The Association of Statutory Health Insurance Physicians (*Kassenärztliche Bundesvereinigung*, KBV) claimed that the decisions were not automatically transferable to the German in-kind benefit system and that their implications had to be examined first. Nevertheless, the KBV recognized the opportunity to attract foreign patients (see Gesundheitspolitischer Informationsdienst 1998: 117). The *NAV-Virchow-Bund*, an association of physicians, welcomed the ECJ decisions and hoped for pressure on the insurance funds and the federal government (see Gesundheitspolitischer Informationsdienst 1998: 118). The Association of Statutory Health Insurance Dentists (*Kassenzahnärztliche Bundesvereinigung*, KZBV) and the German Dental Association (*Bundeszahnärztekammer*) also welcomed the decisions. Both hoped for more freedom in the health care system and more personal responsibility on the part of patients (see Gesundheitspolitischer Informationsdienst 1998: 118).

Working Groups: The Long Way to Accepting the Transferability of the Rulings

In 1998/99, a Common Working Committee, which consisted of the German *Länder*, the Central Associations of Statutory Health Insurance Funds (*Spitzenverbände der gesetzlichen Krankenkassen*, SpiK), and the Federal Ministry of Health, discussed the implications of *Kohll* and *Decker* and the potentially required changes to the German social insurance law. The opinions of the Ministry and the Federal Insurance Authority were reflected in the report that followed from these discussions and that was approved by a conference of health ministers in June 1999. The report was to ensure uniform application of European law, as well as active involvement in developing initiatives at the European level (see Common Working Committee 1999: 4–5). The Working Committee distinguished the German system based on in-kind benefits from those systems operating with cash reimbursement. It concluded that in-kind benefit systems did not push their insured to purchase health benefits on the market. Therefore, the economical basic freedoms did not apply to these systems (see Common Working Committee 1999: 6).

---

10   The *Deutsche Sozialversicherung* has operated a common European representation in Brussels since 1993. It consists of the seven big German health insurance institutions, accidental insurance institutions, and pension insurance institutions. Its main goals are to inform the domestic umbrella institutions about all relevant European developments and to communicate with and influence the European institutions.

As the German social security system was based on the delivery of in-kind benefits, the Working Committee did not see it perturbed by *Kohll* and *Decker*. If the ECJ were to expand this jurisprudence to Germany, the Working Committee feared that the German ability to regulate the provision of health care would be at risk, as well as the quality of provision for out-patient and in-patient sectors (1999: 6–7). The Working Committee suggested that the present legal practice not be changed, that the territorial restriction for in-kind benefits be kept intact. Nevertheless, when the insured were entitled to receive cash benefits in domestic law, all territorial restrictions should be removed (see Common Working Committee 1999: 7).

In its own internal Working Group the Central Associations of Statutory Health Insurance Funds pleaded for handling *Kohll* and *Decker* strategically. They assumed that with increasing health care utilization in other European countries, national regulation capacities would lose effect partially or completely. The Working Group instead pleaded for a controlled regulation of cross-border health care utilization. This regulation was supposed to be achieved without effecting legislative changes. The Working Group thought that the existing possibilities from European regulations and the demand on the legislator to authorize contracts under private law with care providers from other EU countries would suffice. From the Working Group's point of view at that time, even if the ECJ had made an ulterior decision to grant extensive reimbursement for health care received abroad, the possibility to make contracts would have intercepted a significant part of this health care utilization (see Extended Committee of the Central Associations of Statutory Health Insurance Funds 1999: 15). The general conclusions of the Working Group of the Central Associations were two-fold. First, the territorial limitation of health care utilization in the form of in-kind benefits had to remain unaltered. However, when insured persons were entitled according to national law to receive reimbursement, the territorial limitation violated European law. At that time only two percent of all insured persons under compulsory health insurance were entitled to receive reimbursement. Therefore, the impact for Germany was considered to be minor. Secondly, the Working Group recommended that the possibilities of the insured to receive health care abroad should be improved. It had to be analyzed whether and when the insurance funds should be allowed to conclude contracts with foreign care providers analogous to the Netherlands (see Extended Committee of the Central Associations of Statutory Health Insurance Funds 1999: 22).[11]

In May of 2000, the ECJ Advocate Generals in *Vanbraekel*, Antonio Saggio, and *Geraets-Smits/Peerbooms*, Dámaso Ruiz-Jarabo Colomer, delivered their opinions. Relating to them, the Central Associations of Statutory Health Insurance Funds

---

11   These positions were reiterated in 2000 in a concerted statement by the Working Committee of the Central Associations of Statutory Health Insurance Funds in response to a questionnaire of the Federal Ministry of Health about the influence of the EU on the German health system.

reasoned that the basic freedoms would not be applied to social security systems based on in-kind benefits. Should they nonetheless be applied, they thought that one could rely on prior authorization. Therefore, they expected *Kohll* and *Decker* would only apply to voluntarily insured persons and those compulsorily insured persons who had chosen cash benefits instead of in-kind benefits before 1999 (see Working Committee of the Central Associations of Statutory Health Insurance Funds 2000: 3). To sum up, the Central Associations aimed at controlled cross-border health care utilization, therefore their instruments for regulating expenses, quality and capacity remained the same (see Working Committee of the Central Associations of Statutory Health Insurance Funds 2000: 8).

Although they generally supported the common position of the Working Committee of the Central Associations in rejecting *Kohll* and *Decker*, some insurance funds took a more ambivalent position. The Federal Association of Company Health Insurance Funds (*Bundesverband der Betriebskrankenkassen*) saw a potential business in cross-border health benefits for its members who were particularly concerned because they themselves participated substantially in international activities. Since 1998, the *Siemens* Company Health Insurance Fund (*Betriebskrankenkasse*, SBK) had wanted to accelerate the implementation of *Kohll* and *Decker* and make use of the new opportunities. As of August 1, 2001, all persons insured with the SBK who had opted for cash benefits according to Paragraph 13(2–3) SGB V were reimbursed for in- and out-patient care abroad without the need for prior authorization. This move was triggered by a paper of the Working Committee of the Central Associations of Statutory Health Insurance Funds in August 2000 that suggested applying *Kohll* and *Decker* to the voluntarily insured. The SBK did not advertise this new possibility, as these cases increased their costs. However, the SBK wanted to go beyond this first step and expand the chance to obtain health care abroad to all its patients, whether voluntarily or compulsorily insured, and whether for out-patient or for in-patient care. The Federal Insurance Authority, however, did not authorize the change in the SBK-statute in 2002.[12] Already in 2000 the SBK had taken legal action in the Social Court Munich and suggested a referral to the ECJ. However, this case was suspended in 2003 because the Social Court wanted to wait for the ECJ decision in *Bautz*.[13] Both sides did not reactivate the case later. The implementation of the *Kohll/Decker*

---

12   The SBK had changed its statute in March 2000 and inserted a Paragraph 22(a) which provided for reimbursement for health care costs incurred abroad. The Federal Insurance Authority refused authorization for this change in April 2000, whereupon the SBK marginally amended the statute. Again the Federal Insurance Authority refused its authorization in May of 2000. The SBK therefore took legal action against this decision in June of 2000 before the *Landessozialgericht* (LSG) Munich. The SBK explicitly incited the LSG to refer the case to the ECJ. The LSG Munich, though, wanted to await the pending ECJ case *Bautz* from Germany and suspended the case until a decision in *Bautz*.

13   Case C-454/02, *Karin Bautz vs. AOK Baden-Württemberg*, removed from the ECJ registry on June 8, 2004.

jurisprudence in the Statutory Health Insurance Modernization Act (see below) had cleared up the dispute in the meantime. As soon as this act came into force on January 1, 2004, the reimbursement for in-patient care had to be removed from the statute of the SBK (see Interview G5).

For competitive reasons, other insurance funds also tried to facilitate the consumption of benefits in EU Member States for its insured persons before the implementation of the *Kohll/Decker* jurisprudence. Already in 1999, the *Techniker Krankenkasse* (TK) did a survey on the experience of its members with treatment abroad and found that even a major increase in patient mobility would not destabilize statutory health insurance financially. The costs amounted to 25.6 Million Euro in 1999 and were therefore of minor importance. In addition, the costs for benefits in general increased stronger than those for benefits received abroad. Even if the demand of benefits provided abroad increased steeply, their financial significance would have only increased marginally. The TK therefore concluded:

> Eine erhebliche Gefährdung des finanziellen Gleichgewichts der GKV, die der EuGH als Rechtfertigungsgrund für eine Einschränkung des freien Waren- und Dienstleistungsverkehrs im Gesundheitswesen anerkennen würde, ist demnach durch grenzüberschreitende Leistungsinanspruchnahme nicht zu erwarten. (2001: 15)[14]

The Central Associations of Statutory Health Insurance Funds (SpiK) in their 2000 report relied on the opinion of the Advocate General in *Geraets-Smits/ Peerbooms* and were rather optimistic that Germany need not be concerned by the *Kohll* and *Decker* cases. They were playing for time. One of the main fears of the SpiK was that the principle of the delivery of in-kind benefits would erode and that cash reimbursement would become acceptable (see Working Committee of the Central Associations of Statutory Health Insurance Funds 2000: 14).

The First National Court Cases Arise

In 2001, the *Verwaltungsgericht Sigmaringen*, an administrative court of first instance, claimed that there was no settled national case law yet and referred its case to the ECJ with two questions on health cures (see *Leichtle* in Chapter 4).

In 2002, two German social courts each referred a case to the ECJ. The legal pressure mounted. In March, the Social Court *Augsburg* referred *Eva-Maria Weller vs. Deutsche Angestellten-Krankenkasse* (C-322/02) and asked whether Articles 16 and 18 of the SGB V of that time conflicted with Articles 49 and 50

---

14 "A considerable threat to the financial equilibrium of the statutory health insurance, that the ECJ would acknowledge as a justification for the restriction of the free movement of goods and services in the health sector, is therefore not to be expected from cross-border use of health care" (translation of the author).

EC Treaty. With this preliminary reference, the Social Court wanted to find out whether the German statutory sickness insurance scheme had to be treated like a system based on reimbursement.[15] In October 2002, the Federal Social Court (*Bundessozialgericht*, BSG) referred *Karin Bautz vs. AOK Baden-Württemberg* (C-454/02) to the ECJ for a preliminary ruling. The BSG wanted to know whether German provisions were violating European law that allowed insured persons to consult a doctor abroad only in the exceptional case, and that demanded prior authorization from the insurance fund. In 2003, the ECJ under consideration of *Müller-Fauré/van Riet* asked the German court to reconsider its request. According to the BSG, with *Müller-Fauré/van Riet* there was no longer a need to clarify European law. Therefore, its preliminary question was withdrawn – together with *Weller* – in May of 2004 and the case was referred back to the *Landessozialgericht* (see *Bundessozialgericht* 2004, para. 14). However, the German legislator had not waited for the court decisions, and had, much to the dismay of the insurance funds (see Interview G2), anticipated the rulings and changed legislation in 2003 (see below). Therefore, there is strong evidence that the national court cases were not instrumental for the implementation of the *Kohll/Decker* jurisprudence in Germany. Nonetheless, they were an additional factor to consider.

Geraets-Smits/Peerbooms: Continued Rejection

According to the Central Associations of Statutory Health Insurance Funds (SpiK), *Geraets-Smits/Peerboom* – issued in 2001 and stating that authorization procedures for hospital health care utilization abroad are in line with European requirements – confirmed the German position. Its reading of this ruling was as follows: "Der Europäische Gerichtshof ... hat jüngst bestätigt, dass ein Sachleistungssystem, wie es auch die deutsche Krankenversicherung prägt, europarechtskonform ist" (Working Committee of the Central Associations of Statutory Health Insurance Funds 2001).[16]

In a common circular the SpiK stated that the criteria for refusing prior authorization in the stationary sector, as elaborated in *Geraets-Smits/Peerbooms* and *Vanbraekel*, were met fully in German domestic law and did not create a new legal challenge for compulsory health insurance institutions (see Central Associations of Statutory Health Insurance Funds 2001).

In May 2002, the Working Committee of the SpiK drew attention to the possibility that the reservations for exporting health care expressed in *Geraets-Smits/Peerbooms* for in-patient health care might also be applicable to the out-patient sector.

---

15   After the legislative changes in Germany (see below), this reference was removed from the ECJ registry on May 17, 2004.

16   "The ECJ has confirmed recently that an in-kind benefit system such as the German health insurance conforms to European law" (translation of the author).

Until 2003, the official German governmental position remained unchanged. In his National Report for Germany in 2003 for the European Observatory on Social Security for Migrant Workers, Richard Giesen reported that the consequences for Germany after *Geraets-Smits/Peerbooms* and *Müller-Fauré/van Riet* were still unclear:

> The two decisions have opened the European market as far as ambulant treatment at a doctor's is concerned. Nevertheless, it is not clear if the decisions can apply to Germany, too. In Germany, the number of practitioners is regionally limited. This limitation system could justify a different point of view for Germany. On the other hand, the ECJ has made clear that a small number of cross-border health services cannot be regarded as a danger to national health systems. (2003: 6)

Müller-Fauré/van Riet: The Obstructive Position Starts to Crumble

Only when *Müller-Fauré/van Riet* (issued in May 2003) was decided did the Working Committee of the Central Associations officially concede: "Neu ist, dass Versicherte Leistungen außerhalb des Krankenhauses nunmehr direkt im EWR-Ausland in Anspruch nehmen können" (Concerted press release of the Working Committee of the Central Associations of Statutory Health Insurance Funds 2003).[17]

Those insurance funds that had already argued in favor of the *Kohll/Decker* jurisprudence, such as the *Techniker Krankenkasse* (TK), expressly welcomed *Müller-Fauré/van Riet*. The TK found its opinion confirmed: Reimbursement of costs had to be granted quite independently from the patient's choice of cash benefits or in-kind benefits, and it appealed to the German legislator to allow for reimbursement for all insured persons (see *Techniker Krankenkasse* 2003a).

In Germany, European jurisprudence usually need not be implemented via legislation into domestic law before it takes effect. If there is a settled ECJ jurisprudence and German law contravenes it, the settled jurisprudence automatically wins (see Interview G1). Therefore, German insurance funds started to abide by the rulings before the *Kohll/Decker* jurisprudence was incorporated into domestic law. The exact point in time cannot be determined; nevertheless, it seems that *Müller-Fauré/van Riet* marked the turning point for compliance. The insurance funds implemented this jurisprudence to a varying degree since they had considerable discretion in doing so. Two central aims of the incorporation were to reduce uncertainty and discretion, and to increase the transparency of the law for the individuals.

It is difficult to determine the exact point in time that the "paradigm shift" in the German Ministry of Health occurred. In 2002 and 2003, before the Statutory Health Insurance Modernization Act was drafted (see below), the Ministry consulted

---

17   "The new aspect is that insured persons now may claim services received outside of hospitals directly in EEA-countries" (translation of the author).

several insurance funds and discussed with them what needed to be incorporated into the law. The Ministry was waiting for the outcomes of the pending decisions of the ECJ. Over time the Ministry seems to have concluded that the *Kohll/Decker* jurisprudence could not destabilize the German health care system, but would probably provide a chance to decrease health care costs (see Interview G6). At the same time, the two ECJ decisions *Geraets-Smits/Peerbooms* and *Müller-Fauré/ van Riet* determined unquestionably that social security systems based on in-kind benefits also had to conform to the *Kohll/Decker* jurisprudence, clearing the way for a legal transposition of the jurisprudence.

After the 2002 *Bundestag* elections, the coalition between SPD and Bündnis 90/DIE GRÜNEN continued and expanded the responsibilities of the new Ministry for Health and Social Security (*Bundesministerium für Gesundheit und Soziale Sicherung*, BMGS). The red-green coalition presented a first draft of a bill on the Modernization of the Health System in June 2003 (see *Deutscher Bundestag* 2003a). In this draft the government coalition incorporated the ECJ jurisprudence and determined that voluntarily insured persons who had chosen cash benefits could make use of out-patient health care abroad and receive cash benefits. The opposition party – the CDU/CSU – criticized the draft bill as insufficient and asked for a revision. Under the heading "Beteiligungs- und Gestaltungsrechte für Patienten und Versicherte ausbauen" [extend rights of participation and organization of patients and insured persons, AJO] the CDU/CSU demanded that all insured should be able to choose cash benefits. Along with this claim, all insured should then be able to obtain out-patient health care in the EU/EEA with the right of reimbursement for the costs incurred (see *Deutscher Bundestag* 2003b: 7).

In several regional elections, the general political conditions had changed in favor of the CDU/CSU and FDP in the *Bundesrat* by May 2002. For major health reforms the approval of the opposition now became necessary in the *Bundesrat*. Therefore, the coalition government withdrew its first draft and negotiated with the opposition outside parliamentary legislative procedures. In September 2003, the SPD, Bündnis 90/DIE GRÜNEN, and the CDU/CSU presented a joint draft that extended the cash reimbursement principle for out-patient health care to all insured persons (see *Deutscher Bundestag* 2003d). This Statutory Health Insurance Modernization Act aimed at fundamentally reforming German compulsory health insurance. The main objectives were structural and financial reforms: strengthening of patient sovereignty; improvement of the efficiency and quality of health care; improvement of care delivery; reform of reimbursement procedures in the out-patient sector; reform of the delivery of medicine; change in organizational structure; provision with dentures; and change in the financial structure (see *Deutscher Bundestag* 2003d: 1–3). Here, the changes in the reimbursement procedure for the out-patient sector are of interest. The Act changed Paragraph 13 SGB V and inserted Paragraph 140(e) to make German law conform to the *Kohll/Decker* jurisprudence. In giving the reasons for the bill, the Parliament made it clear that the changes were aimed at implementing the ECJ jurisprudence (see *Deutscher Bundestag* 2003d: 80–82).

In the legislative process, virtually all insurance funds welcomed in principle the incorporation of the ECJ jurisprudence into German law.[18] In the course of mutual exchange in numerous working groups and meetings, the Central Associations of Statutory Health Insurance Funds (SpiK) had slowly altered their once rather obstructive attitude. In a position paper from 2004, the Working Committee of the SpiK claimed that with the new law, its demands to facilitate contracts with health care providers from the EU/EEA and to let the insured choose cash benefits were realized, and that now there was more legal certainty (see Working Committee of the Central Associations of Statutory Health Insurance Funds 2004: 14). Nonetheless, the SpiK saw a further opening of the principle of cash benefits for benefits received in another EU Member State "als Ausnahme ... die die Regel zugunsten von Qualität und Wirtschaftlichkeit im deutschen Gesundheitssystem bestätigt" (Central Associations of Statutory Health Insurance Funds 2005: 3).[19] The SpiK reiterated this position because in 2004 the FDP had wanted to extend choice of cash reimbursement instead of in-kind benefits to all insured and all situations without restrictions (see *Deutscher Bundestag* 2004a: 2). In addition, the CDU/CSU had demanded free choice of reimbursement for certain types of ambulatory benefits (see *Deutscher Bundestag* 2004b: 7).

The Federal Association of Statutory Health Insurance Dentists also welcomed Paragraph 13 of the Draft of the Statutory Health Insurance Modernization Act. It saw the recognition of the principle of cash reimbursement only as a first step towards a feasible EU-wide system of reimbursement:

> Das nunmehr vorgesehene System einer Regelung des Kostenerstattungsver-
> fahrens in den Satzungen der einzelnen Krankenkassen sowie der in diesem
> Zusammenhang unbeschränkt eingeräumten Möglichkeit der satzungsrechtlichen
> Normierung von Erstattungsabschlägen für Verwaltungskosten und fehlende
> Wirtschaftlichkeitsprüfungen, stellt nach wie vor eine wesentliche Erschwerung
> der Inanspruchnahme entsprechender Leistungen im EU-Ausland dar. (2003:
> 19–20)[20]

---

18 See for instance *Techniker Krankenkasse* (2003b); the Association of the *Angestellten-Krankenkassen/Arbeiter-Ersatzkassen* stated that the reorganization of Paragraph 13 met the demands of the SpiK and was to be welcomed in principle (2003); the AOK Federal Association equally welcomed the change (2003: 18); a representative of the Federal Association of Company Health Insurance Funds stated that the regulation was "sachgerecht" [appropriate] (see *Deutscher Bundestag* 2003c: 67).

19 "As an exception that confirms the general rule of quality and economic efficiency in the German health care system" (translation of the author).

20 "The now conceived system of regulating cash reimbursement proceedings in the statutes of the individual insurance funds as well as the unrestricted option of regulating deductions for administrative costs and missing controls of economic efficiency still present considerable obstacles for using services in other EU-countries" (translation of the author).

The Statutory Health Insurance Modernization Act: Full Compliance

The German *Bundestag* passed the Statutory Health Insurance Modernization Act on September 26, 2003, and the *Bundesrat* on October 17, 2003 (see *Bundesgesetzblatt* 2003). The act became effective on January 1, 2004. In its Article 1, the Social Code Book V (SGB V) was modified. With the amendment of Paragraph 13 SGB V, the German Parliament transposed the ECJ rulings *Kohll* and *Decker*, *Geraets-Smits/Peerbooms* and *Müller-Fauré/van Riet* (see *Deutscher Bundestag* 2003d: 80–82).

The new fourth section of Paragraph 13 SGB V relaxed the territorial restriction of the demand for benefits. It determined as a matter of principle that insured persons were entitled to care providers in other Member States of the EU and EEA, and also entitled to choose cash instead of in-kind benefits (see *Bundesgesetzblatt* 2003: 2191).

The new section 5 of Paragraph 13 limited the choice of cash reimbursement to out-patient care and left hospital care abroad still dependent on prior authorization by the competent insurance fund. Following the ECJ jurisprudence, prior authorization was only to be refused if an equal or an equally effective treatment could be obtained in due time from a contractor of the insurance fund (see *Bundesgesetzblatt* 2003: 2191).

In Paragraph 13(4) SGB V several precautions were taken. Before reimbursing, the insurance funds must deduct costs for administrative additional work and expenses and costs for the missing efficiency controls as well as other extra payments, for example charges for medical visits (see *Bundesgesetzblatt* 2003: 2191). Paragraph 13(4) SGB V was again slightly reformulated in 2006 in the framework of the Law for the Change of the Contracted Physicians' Law (see *Bundesgesetzblatt* 2006).

The reimbursement of health care costs was not limited to foreign care. In fact, according to Paragraph 13(2) all insured persons could choose cash benefits instead of in-kind benefits. However, two restrictions were inserted: the insurance funds have to advise the insured before making this choice, and the insured have to stick to reimbursement for at least one year. A restriction of the reimbursement mechanism to the out-patient sector was made possible (see *Bundesgesetzblatt* 2003: 2191). Paragraph 13(2) was again reformulated in 2007 in the framework of the Law for the Strengthening of Competition in the Statutory Health Insurance (see *Bundesgesetzblatt* 2007). Two provisions were changed: the duty of the insurance funds to advise the insured persons about the choice of reimbursement and the restriction to the out-patient sector. Now, in case of reimbursement the insured persons only have to inform their insurance funds before the utilization of the benefit. In turn, the insurance funds have to inform their clients about the possibility that some of their costs might not be covered. In addition, in order to facilitate the choice of reimbursement the German legislator made it possible to restrict this option to several areas: out-patient care, out-patient dental care, in-patient care, or occasioned care (pharmaceuticals, medical devices) (see German *Bundestag* 16/4247: 31).

Prior to the Statutory Health Insurance Modernization Act, the importance of the in-kind benefit principle was already occasionally undermined in German law (see for example Zerna 2003: 253–254). Between 1997 and 1998, all persons with compulsory health insurance could choose cash benefits. This option was restricted in 1999 to the voluntarily insured and their co-insured family members, a rather small circle. Compulsorily insured persons who had opted for cash benefits before January 1, 1999 could also stick with cash reimbursement. Despite these past breaches, the amendment of Paragraph 13 of Book 5 of the Social Code was a substantial strengthening of the cash reimbursement principle in the German health care system.

In addition to the amendment of Paragraph 13, Paragraph 140(e) of Book 5 of the Social Code extended the in-kind benefit principle to foreign cases. Insurance funds may sign contracts with health providers from the EU/EEA in order to provide their insured with health services (see *Bundesgesetzblatt* 2003: 2225). Paragraph 140(e) was slightly reformulated in 2006 (see *Bundesgesetzblatt* 2006). To be able to contract with foreign providers, as is customary in the Netherlands, was an explicit demand of the insurance funds. Paragraph 140(e) now allows them to provide their insured members with health care abroad through contracts with foreign providers. The contracted providers have to supply health care in conformity with the German regulations. The care provided has to be billed directly to the contracting German health insurance fund. This is not restricted to the out-patient sector. The *Siemens Betriebskrankenkasse* (SBK) had demanded it should be allowed to contract with foreign providers and to thus export the German in-kind benefit system. Even before Parliament allowed contracts with foreign providers, German health insurance funds had taken the initiative and started to experiment with such contracts. The Federal Insurance Authority, however, pointed to the missing legal mandate and prohibited these initiatives (see Interview G2).

Even though the insurance funds demanded contracts with foreign providers, it is highly questionable whether they will be used extensively except for border regions (see Schreiber 2004). In 2005, the *AOK Brandenburg*, for instance, made a contract with a Polish dental prostheses provider (see Interview G2). In 2006, the SBK had established about ten contracts (see Interview G5). According to the *Deutsche Krankenversicherung* in Brussels there were approximately 20 contracts in 2006, mainly in the rehabilitation sector (see Interview M1).

When the Statutory Health Insurance Modernization Act became law, three different legal foundations for receiving health care in another EU/EEA Member State existed: first, the European Regulations 1408/71 (Article 22) and 574/72 (Articles 21 to 23); second, reimbursement according to Paragraph 13(4–6) of the German SGB V; and third, contracts of insurance funds with health care providers in EU/EEA countries based on Paragraph 140(e) SGB V.

Shortly before the new law took force, the Central Associations of Statutory Health Insurance Funds and the *Deutsche Verbindungsstelle Krankenversicherung –*

Ausland issued a detailed common recommendation in November 2003 on how to apply it since they wanted to assure a uniform application of the law (see Central Associations of Statutory Health Insurance Funds and *Deutsche Verbindungsstelle Krankenversicherung – Ausland* 2003).

The 2004 ECJ decision in *Leichtle* (see Chapter 4) revealed a further incompatibility of the Social Code Book 9 with the *Kohll/Decker* jurisprudence:[21] Paragraph 18 entitled insured persons to the rehabilitation in-kind benefits only "wenn sie dort bei zumindest gleicher Qualität und Wirksamkeit wirtschaftlicher ausgeführt werden können."[22] Karl-Jürgen Bieback considered this stipulation to be an unjustified discrimination against foreign providers (2005: 266).

Conclusion

How did Germany implement the ECJ jurisprudence under discussion? In the beginning, the German government left legislation unchanged because *Kohll* and *Decker* raised sufficient doubts about their transferability. The Ministry of Health and, more importantly, the government were not prepared to accept ECJ interference in an area which was seen as one of the few remaining "reservations" of purely domestic politics. An additional motive may have been to gain time, to wait and see. However, as soon as the ECJ unmistakably applied the *Kohll/Decker* jurisprudence to in-kind benefit systems in 2003, the German government quickly transposed the jurisprudence into the Social Code. The requirements of the *Kohll/Decker* jurisprudence were unambiguously incorporated into the Statutory Health Insurance Modernization Act. The legal implementation took place in one legislative step. However, several insurance funds had already started to apply the *Kohll/Decker* jurisprudence to the advantage of their patients, even though they lacked a sound domestic legal basis.

Why did the Ministry of Health and the Central Associations of Statutory Health Insurance Funds change their views on this jurisprudence? And why was the implementation in Germany in comparison to other countries so quick? Several factors are at work here. First, the Ministry of Health and the insurance funds feared that the implementation of the ECJ jurisprudence would create considerable political and legal pressure for an opening of its health care system based on in-kind benefits for foreign cases, and that this disruption would affect the entire system. Two factors helped to overcome this fear: First of all, no decisive health care actor argued that the in-kind principle should be completely abolished and that the principle of cash reimbursement should be introduced as a general principle instead. Secondly, the predominant principle of providing in-kind benefits for

---

21   SGB IX concerns rehabilitation and the participation of handicapped persons in the labor market.

22   Only "if the in-kind benefits can be performed there at least with equal quality and effectiveness and with greater economic efficiency" (translation of the author).

foreign cases could be relaxed without major repercussions: voluntarily and compulsorily insured persons got the opportunity to opt for cash reimbursement only under quite restrictive conditions.

A second important factor driving the prompt implementation was the fine-tuning of the ECJ jurisprudence. The Ministry of Health and the insurance funds had feared that not only out-patient but also unlimited in-patient mobility would be triggered by the ECJ decisions. In this case the political and, more importantly, financial costs would have been considerable. Therefore, as a matter of principle, they fiercely rejected the entire jurisprudence on patient mobility. However, the ECJ excluded in-patient cases in general from benefit exports and handled permission very restrictively. Consequently, the skepticism toward the ECJ and its decisions – which was widespread among insurance funds and in the Ministry – decreased substantially. The self-restrained ECJ approach paved the way for the smooth transposition of the jurisprudence.

A third factor: for many years *Kohll* and *Decker*, as well as subsequent decisions and their outcomes, had been studied in numerous working groups in which these fears were assuaged or dissipated, and where hopes for cost-saving effects were even expressed.

Fourth, domestic party political preferences played a role: CDU/CSU consent to the Statutory Health Insurance Modernization Act was required. The first draft of this law was not far-reaching enough for the CDU/CSU, on whose political agenda patient sovereignty and patient choice was a high priority. Therefore, it pressed successfully for a more ambitious implementation. It was the *de facto* grand coalition between the red-green government and the CDU/CSU that extended the conditional choice of cash reimbursement to all insured persons and to health care received abroad.

A fifth factor: the first national court cases arose in 2001 and presented an additional disturbing factor for the administration and government that had to be borne in mind.

Lastly, the fact that some insurance funds had already started to apply at least parts of the jurisprudence and others had not was an additional impetus for the Ministry of Health. It wanted to put an end to the legal uncertainty created by the ECJ and national court decisions, although the Ministry usually refrains from transposing the Court jurisprudence into social law.

Interaction with the European Commission through infringement procedures and negotiations cannot be reported for the German case. Until clarification by further ECJ jurisprudence, the situation for Germany could be considered unclear. After further ECJ decisions put an end to this uncertainty, the German legislator reacted instantly and no intervention by the Commission was possible or necessary.

The implementation of the *Kohll/Decker* jurisprudence indeed eroded the principle of territoriality enshrined in the German Social Code. Insured persons can now consume out-patient care within the EU/EEA wherever they want. Nevertheless, the actual effect may not be very dramatic. The ECJ jurisprudence limited the de-territorialization effect to out-patient care, several restrictions were built into the law, and de-territorialization had, to a certain extent, already existed beforehand in Germany. The fears that the German health care system would experience internal de-structuring through the backdoor of the transposition of this jurisprudence were never realized. The introduction of the principle of cash reimbursement in foreign cases did not lead to further legislative and administrative changes. In fact, this introduction for the compulsorily insured was motivated by CDU/CSU political preferences. The extension to foreign cases harmonized with these domestic preferences and did not require much effort. In addition, no financial destabilization can be perceived. The number of mobile patients did not increase considerably. The insured did not choose cash reimbursement for domestic care *en masse*. For foreign cases the number of patients is, according to all available sources, very low. If there would be a huge increase in patients in the future or if the legislative restrictions were dropped, however, the still predominant in-kind benefit principle could be more seriously endangered.

If we consider the overall German health care reform processes in the last years and the Statutory Health Insurance Modernization Act, the ECJ's jurisprudence and its repercussions had only minor effects.[23] Indeed, the ECJ jurisprudence became part of the very important reform in 2003. However, there were no observable major conflicts about the incorporation of the ECJ jurisprudence in the legislative process nor did the likely repercussions of European law receive much attention by the insurance funds and governmental/administrative actors. On the contrary, the EU was of very little importance while domestically related concerns prevailed.

---

23   For a detailed discussion of the health care reforms since the 1990s, see Busse and Riesberg (2004: 185–205).

Chapter 8

The Case of the United Kingdom (England and Wales)

The United Kingdom's Beveridge model of a National Health Service (NHS) can be characterized as follows: It relies on a directly state-run administration that is financed through general tax revenue which is apportioned among the various Primary Care Trusts (PCTs) according to the needs of the population of a given geographical area.[1] In-patient and out-patient medical services are delivered free of charge to all ordinarily resident UK citizens, regardless of age, income, or state of health. No co-payments are charged. There is no reimbursement of health care costs and, thus, no regulation of the issue. Health care services are primarily provided through public health providers. Nonetheless, the NHS has a long tradition of using private contractors (see Newdick 2005: 231). The National Health Service makes use of its scarce resources by rationing or, more euphemistically, by setting clinical priorities for the type, location, and timing of specific in-patient treatments. This results, naturally, in waiting lists for less urgent treatment. PCTs receive an annual budget from the Secretary of State for Health in order to manage and deliver health care on a local basis. They commission treatments to the NHS trusts that run all UK hospitals on a contractual basis.[2]

The UK is not a single legal entity. There are several legal jurisdictions: England and Wales, Northern Ireland, Scotland and Gibraltar (see Montgomery 2003: 6). In this chapter I mainly deal with the NHS in England and Wales.

Cross-border Provisions: Strict Territorial Restriction

Until important legal amendments caused by the *Kohll/Decker* jurisprudence were made, UK legislation allowed the referral of NHS patients outside the UK for

---

1 The PCTs, statutory health care bodies, are awarded a fixed annual budget from the Secretary of State for Health that covers the expenditure on in-patient and out-patient treatment and administrative costs. There are over 300 PCTs in England that "act as the 'purchasers' or 'commissioners' of medical, dental, pharmaceutical, and optical NHS care for their local communities" (Newdick 2005: 78).

2 For a more detailed review of the organization of the UK NHS, see for instance Newdick (2005).

health care treatment only in very exceptional cases.[3] The NHS Act from 1977 determined in section 5(2)(b) that "[t]he Secretary of State may ... arrange to provide accommodation and treatment outside Great Britain for persons suffering from respiratory tuberculosis" (3). Based on this restriction that targeted only a very small group of people, the Department of Health (DoH) argued that the UK legislator had not intended to empower the NHS to purchase health care services outside the UK. Nevertheless, it was possible to get approval for treatment outside the UK and the EEA from the DoH on an *ex-gratia* basis, if four specific criteria were met: "the condition involved is of a serious nature; suitable treatment is not available within the UK or EEA; the treatment abroad is well-established, not merely experimental; there is a probability of significant benefit to the patient" (DoH 1995).

European Community law (Article 22, Regulation 1408/71) determined that UK patients had under specific circumstances the right to be treated in another Member State. An NHS patient could invoke these rights under Article 22 through the application of an E111 form for an emergency treatment while staying abroad, or an E112 form for a planned specialist treatment not available in the UK. Both forms were freely available in post offices. The E112 system was deliberately controlled by the central government, which advised patients to first seek the favorable opinion of their NHS consultant and PCT. The DoH as the ultimate arbiter had to approve who could be referred abroad (see Interview UK2). In 1998, 812 patients were authorized to receive treatment abroad under the E112 procedure, and 860 in 1999 (see *The Daily Telegraph* 2001). According to the UK government, 1,100 persons were authorized in 2000, and 1,134 the following year (see European Commission 2003c: 28). The figure for referrals under the E112 scheme was quite stable over the years. For the E111 procedure no numbers are available.

Degree of Misfit: High

The UK NHS was incompatible with the *Kohll/Decker* jurisprudence in three ways. First, reimbursing health care costs to its patients was alien to the NHS tradition. It provided in-kind benefits, had no financial reimbursement mechanism and no fund out of which treatment abroad could be paid for. Second, its strict territorial principle prevented the NHS from sending patients abroad. Third, patient referral under the European Coordination Regulation 1408/71 with its E112 scheme was handled restrictively in the UK. The version of Article 22(2)(c) of Regulation 1408/71 valid in 1998 could be seen as violated by the UK practice. The DoH's policy was to refer patients abroad only if the waiting time was being excessive

---

3   More precisely, this restriction existed in the English/Welsh and Scottish legislation. Northern Ireland and Gibraltar, the other two separate jurisdictions, had no such restrictions (see Interview UK2).

according to UK standards. The logic of rationing health care was overriding the health and the probable course of the disease of a patient, consideration of which was demanded by the ECJ decisions. The *Kohll/Decker* jurisprudence did not generate misfit in the politics/polity dimension. The expected financial costs for the UK NHS resulting from the implementation of the *Kohll/Decker* jurisprudence were estimated to be high due to its structural underfunding and the consequential long waiting times for UK patients. The three dimensions of misfit taken together produced a high overall misfit for the UK (see Table 8.1).

Table 8.1 Overall misfit in the UK

Degree of legal misfit	(Expected) Financial costs	Politics/polity misfit	Degree of overall misfit
High	*High*	*None*	*High*
• Very strict principle of territoriality; • Cash reimbursement inexistent; • Restrictive application of the prior authorization scheme of Regulation 1408/71.	• Underfunded; • Long waiting times and lists; • High numbers of patients traveling abroad.		

À-la-Carte Implementation

The UK concentrated a great deal of attention on the *Kohll/Decker* jurisprudence as can be seen from the fact that the UK was the only EU Member State that commented on all rulings of this line (see Table 5.1). According to John Collins from the Treasury Solicitor's Department, "[i]t is the policy of the U.K. to take an active part in proceedings before the Court of Justice" (2002: 359).[4]

---

4 Although the DoH was leading in the elaboration of the statements for the *Kohll/Decker* jurisprudence, the Treasury Solicitor's Department, a separate legal office within the Government Legal Service, represented the UK government in the correspondence with the ECJ. The European division of the Treasury Solicitor's Department, headed by the Cabinet Office Legal Adviser on European Union matters, is divided into the Advisory Section and the Litigation Section. "The Advisory Section's role is to advise the Cabinet Office on Community law questions and co-ordinate the views of departmental lawyers on questions of Community law which raise, in particular, questions of general horizontal interest in which it is important that lawyers in other government departments adopt the same approach. ... the Litigation Section's role is to maintain consistency in the UK's submissions, co-ordinate

In the proceedings of *Kohll*, the UK government stated that Articles 49 and 50 EC Treaty "ne s'appliquent pas à la fourniture de prestations de services de santé publique par un organisme de sécurité sociale qui constitue une entité à but non lucratif, dont les frais sont financés en tout ou en partie à l'aide de fonds publics" (ECJ, Rapport d'audience, *Kohll*: para. 85).[5]According to its opinion, maintaining prior authorization schemes was justified for the financial stability of the domestic social security regimes (para. 87).

Immediate Reaction: No Transferability

The UK government denied that the rulings were transferable to its NHS immediately after *Kohll* and *Decker* were decided (see Palm et al. 2000: 86–87). At the conference "The new Public Health Policy of the European Union" in Potsdam in January 1999, the British representative officially stated that the UK did not fear that the rulings *Kohll* and *Decker* would call its NHS into question, because it simply was not concerned by it (see Gobrecht 1999a: 103). The main argument was that the UK NHS was not comparable to a reimbursement-style system like Luxembourg's. If patients obtained health services privately they had to pay them from their own resources: the NHS did not refund the costs of treatment provided privately within the UK, and services obtained privately outside the UK should be treated similarly (see Interview UK2).

In response to the subsequent rulings, the UK government consistently maintained that the principles elaborated by the ECJ in the *Kohll/Decker* jurisprudence should not be applied to the NHS. The government feared two aspects of the ECJ jurisprudence particularly: First, in more general terms, it was afraid that the ECJ would push the boundaries of applying the EU basic principles to health care systems further and further (see Interview UK2). Second, and more specifically, the main rationing instrument of the UK NHS, the waiting list, was potentially creating incentives for patients to travel abroad for treatment. A massive outflow of patients would have distorted this integral part of the functioning of the NHS.

Patient Choice, Private Sector Involvement and the Reduction of Waiting Lists

After a period of inactivity, the Labour party that took power in 1997 aimed at restructuring the NHS in a more market-oriented manner (see Allsop and Baggott 2004: 34). According to Judith Allsop and Rob Baggott, the reforms undertaken

---

the approach to be adopted in cases where a number of Departments have an interest and identify points of general horizontal interest" (Collins 2002: 359–360).

5   The proceeding is only available in French. Therefore, the citation is in French. They "do not apply to public health services provided by social security institutions who constitute a non-profit entity, whose costs are overall or partly financed out of public funds" (translation of the author).

were characterized by "elements of both modernisation and marketisation" (2004: 29). Three elements of the broader governmental plan – the patient choice agenda, the involvement of the private sector, and the overall agenda to reduce waiting lists and times – fed into the implementation of the *Kohll/Decker* jurisprudence.

In 2000, the political pressure on the government led by Prime Minister Tony Blair to combat the system failures of the NHS rose considerably. Therefore, in July the government presented its future "NHS Plan," "designed around the patient." Patient choice was among the central principles elaborated in this plan, and it was to be strengthened in the NHS (see DoH 2000b: 89).

In its first term in power Labour was opposed to an increased involvement of the private sector in the NHS (see Smith 2005: 274). However, the Blair government signed a much-publicized "concordat" with the Independent Healthcare Association in October 2000 "to set out the parameters for a partnership between the NHS and private and voluntary health care providers" (see DoH 2000a: para. 1.1). It seemed unrealistic to reduce waiting times in the short term without the help from the private sector. Because of pragmatic and fiscal reasons, capacity constraints concerning doctors, nurses, and beds, and spending limits, the Labour government expanded the contribution of private providers to the NHS in order to use their spare capacity (see Newdick 2005: 231–232). The private sector "came to be seen (at least in New Labour circles) as not the nemesis of the NHS but, rather, its saviour" (Smith 2005: 274). The principle aim of this governmental health policy of increasing the NHS capacity through spare capacity of the private sector was to reduce waiting lists and times. Its ambitious objective was that,

> by 2005, no patient is to wait more than 3 months for an initial out-patient appointment and no longer than 6 months for the in-patients treatment they may need. By 2008, the wait for in-patient treatment is set to reduce to 3 months. (DoH 2002b: 4)

Alan Milburn, then Secretary of State for Health, explained the intention of the DoH as follows:[6]

> I think what we need is a bigger relationship not a smaller relationship between the National Health Service and the private sector in general. I think there should be a long term relationship and not a one night stand. I think we want to see improved capacity, more services being made available to more NHS patients and if, as we all accept, there is a problem with capacity as far as health care is concerned, and if we have spare capacity, whether those are resources, infrastructure or expertise, and we can harness that for the benefit of NHS

---

6   Alan Milburn succeeded Frank Dobson as Secretary of State for Health in October 1999. The Secretary of State for Health has overall responsibility for NHS and social care delivery and system reforms, finance and resources as well as communications.

patients, then that is precisely what we should do. (House of Commons Health
Committee 2002: para. 971)

The possibility of contracting with the private sector was a crucial development
in the implementation of the *Kohll/Decker* jurisprudence, as the opening to the
private sector could not be restricted only to the UK but had to be extended to
overseas providers as well. According to an assessment by Diane Dawson in 2002,
"[t]he purely domestic policy decision to open the English provider market to a
richer mix of non public sector for-profit and not-for-profit companies will force
the NHS to pay more attention to EU competition law" (4). Not only competition
law but also the free movement of services had to be taken into account. Unable to
restrict its new openness toward the private sector to the UK only, the New Labour
government nevertheless preferred to attract overseas providers to the UK instead
of encouraging patients' travel abroad for treatment. In a session in the House of
Commons in October 2001, Alan Milburn argued as follows:

> What I would prefer to do and what we are actively doing is, talking to colleagues
> in the States, talking to colleagues in Germany, Italy and Spain, and it is just
> far more sensible in the great scheme of things if there is spare capacity – for
> example, as you well know there is a surplus of doctors in Germany ... if we
> could bring some of those doctors here and get them into the National Health
> Service providing treatment and care for NHS patients. That is a much more
> comfortable and convenient thing for the NHS patients. (House of Commons
> Health Committee 2001: para. 69)

However, the DoH admitted that "where it makes sense in terms of value for
money and convenience for patients overseas treatment does offer a further means
to add to the capacity of the NHS, to reduce waiting times and to extend the choice
available to patients under choice pilots" (DoH 2002c: para. 1.1).

Long waiting times for treatment was a central problem identified within the
NHS. The government itself had to admit that

> [a]t present the average wait to see a consultant for an outpatient appointment is
> seven weeks and the average time that people have been waiting for an operation
> is three months. But some people wait much longer than this – up to 18 months
> for inpatient treatment – and it is this which so concerns the public. (DoH 2000b:
> 103)

In order to reduce these long waiting times the government planned a
"combination of investment and reform" (DoH 2000b: 101). First, it intended to
inject more money into the NHS:

> To fund the increase in health care services, the Government has made an
> unprecedented investment in the NHS, undertaking to increase the money that

is to be spent on health care by 7.4% real terms over each of the next 5 years. (DoH 2002b: 4)

And second, reforms in primary care, intermediate care, and hospital care were envisioned (see DoH 2000b: 101–103).

Vanbraekel and Geraets-Smits/Peerbooms:
Catalyst Rulings for Legislative Change

The three governmental policy agendas of more patient choice, increased involvement of the private sector, and the reduction of waiting times initially did not cause any visible changes in the implementation of the ECJ jurisprudence. However, with *Vanbraekel* and particularly *Geraets-Smits/Peerbooms* in 2001, the first implementation steps were set in motion. These two decisions created major difficulties for the UK, especially the statement that in-kind benefit systems, in the case at hand that of the Netherlands, fell within the scope of the free movement of services, and that if a Member State could not provide a treatment "without undue delay," it had to refer the patient to another Member State (see ECJ, *Geraets-Smits/Peerbooms*: para. 55). Essentially, the UK government argued against *Geraets-Smits/Peerbooms*:

> First … the NHS, in contrast to the ZFW scheme [from the Netherlands, AJO], is not a sickness insurance fund. It is itself a provider of health care and, in the overwhelming majority of cases, delivers that health care itself direct to its patients. Only exceptionally, and for a comparatively small number of patients, does it discharge its responsibilities by purchasing hospital services from other providers, either within the United Kingdom (from the private health sector) or abroad. Second, and a related point, that even though under both the NHS and the ZFW scheme treatment is free at the point of delivery to the patient, the doctors are remunerated differently, the Dutch doctors being reimbursed preset scale fees by the state whilst in the United Kingdom hospital doctors are salaried employees of the state. (Administrative Court 2003, *Watts*: para. 97)

In the wake of *Vanbraekel* and *Geraets-Smits/Peerbooms*, UK (print) media showed considerable interest in the two decisions, whereas the DoH according to *The Guardian* reacted with "classic ostrich behaviour" in the beginning.[7] It claimed that the wider legal implications of the rulings still had to be studied (see *The Guardian* 2001b). Nevertheless, according to official sources, sending patients abroad was not considered to be a valid option for the UK (see *Daily Mail* 2001) and priority was given to investment in the NHS (see *The Daily Telegraph* 2001a). A spokesperson from the DoH was cited in *The Sunday Times* accordingly: "It is

---

7 *The Guardian* is a left-of-center broadsheet attracting more educated readers with higher income.

not the policy of the government to send patients abroad for healthcare ... It is our policy to recruit more doctors and nurses and improve the NHS" (2001d).

In an internal "Background Note – Undue Delay," the DoH set out its understanding of *Geraets-Smits/Peerbooms*. According to its reading the ECJ did not define "undue delay" and left this to national law and practice. In the background note the DoH went on to explain that

> [i]f the wait to see a consultant is in excess of the NHS target maximum outpatient waiting time, or the waiting time for an operation is in excess of the maximum inpatient waiting time for surgery (currently 15 months), this would be prima facie evidence of undue delay. (Cited in Administrative Court 2003, *Watts*: para. 5)

The Sunday Times, the right-of-center sister Sunday paper of the broadsheet newspaper Times, virtually mounted a campaign supported by other newspapers in which it pressed for the utilization of spare capacities in other EU Member States. The campaign started three days after the ECJ decisions and lasted for more than a month.[8] In the first of a line of articles, *The Sunday Times* stated prophetically:

> Losing cash to the health systems of our neighbours is not a clever way of improving our own service though it may be a catalyst that will accelerate reform. The analogy is not perfect, but once sufficient numbers of British motorists started buying cars on the Continent, prices here fell. If the threat of patients going abroad has the same galvanising effect on the NHS, then the European Court will have done us all a favour. (2001b)

The press also reported that a group of British patients, advised by the former social services minister Frank Field, prepared to take the government before the ECJ (see *The Guardian* 2001b).

It was not only the press coverage that increased dramatically: the pressure from the ECJ itself and the European Commission rose at the same time. A spokesperson for the ECJ, Fionnuala Connolly, was cited in *The Sunday Times* with the words that "the British government will have to ensure that it complies [with *Geraets-Smits/Peerbooms*, AJO]" (2001h). The Commission was faced with complaints brought forward by British residents that the government was not complying with the rulings (see *Sunday Times* 2001f, g and *The Daily Telegraph* 2001b). The Commission was cited that if complaints by UK patients were upheld "the British government will have to back down or be in breach of its treaty obligations" (*Sunday Times* 2001f).

In addition, single PCTs started to consider plans to send some of their patients abroad in order to meet governmental waiting list targets and doctors expressed

---

8   The campaign of *The Sunday Times* started on July 15, 2001. The following weeks it published numerous articles concerning the rulings (2001b, c, d, e, f, h, i).

themselves in favor of these initiatives. However, the government was against these activities (see *Sunday Times* 2001e and *The Guardian* 2001a).

As a consequence of this pressure mounted from many sides, Alan Milburn announced in August 2001 an "historic shift" (*The Guardian* 2001c), possibly one of the "biggest shake-ups of the National Health Service since its inception" (*Sunday Times* 2001g), a "seismic change" (*The Express* 2001). Prior to that, Section 5(2)(b) of the NHS Act from 1977, which applied only to England and Wales, precluded the access to NHS health care treatment outside the UK. Treatment outside the UK was allowed under very special circumstances only. Alan Milburn declared that the general possibility of contracting with health care providers from other EU Member States should be given to the NHS. In *The Sunday Times* a spokesperson of Milburn stated that the forthcoming policy change had to be understood as a pragmatic decision going back to the ECJ rulings: "This is a big change in outlook for the Department of Health. It wasn't in the NHS plan and this court ruling has forced us to think about it" (2001g).

The press rejoiced over the major "Labour U-turn" (*Daily Mail* 2001). *The Sunday Times* explicitly welcomed the decision of the UK government to change its policy (2001a). The British Medical Association (BMA) also welcomed the policy change (see *Daily Mail* 2001 and *The Express* 2001).[9] Alan Milburn expressed his intentions as follows:

> The Government's top priority is to ensure patients receive high quality treatment when they need it. That is why we are making record levels of investment in the NHS, using spare private sector capacity where it is appropriate, and encouraging Health Authorities and Primary Care Trusts to use capacity elsewhere in the EU where that is the best option. (DoH 2001)

The media suspected that after having returned from vacation in Florida, Milburn had been pressed by the ongoing events and the Prime Minister. According to this reading he ignored advice from his civil servants and hurried ahead with the announcement (see *Sunday Times* 2001a, g and *The Guardian* 2001c). It took more than a year, though, before Milburn's full-bodied announcement, the removal of the territorial principle enshrined in the NHS Act from 1977, was realized. In the meantime, the government tried to relieve the internal pressure coming from the press, politicians, doctors, health authorities, and patients, and the external pressure from the ECJ and the Commission. It regulated treatment received abroad.

Despite the announcement of legislative changes in 2001, the DoH still denied a direct effect of *Kohll* and *Decker* on the NHS.[10]

---

9   The BMA is a voluntary professional association representing physicians in the UK from all branches.

10   The then Parliamentary Under-Secretary of State from the DoH, Lord Hunt of Kings Heath, brought forward this assessment of *Kohll* and *Decker* in a session of the House of Lords (2001).

Pilot Scheme for Overseas Treatment

The Labour government started to set up a centrally planned pilot scheme for treating patients overseas, funded by the government and run by the local health authorities. This scheme fed into the governmental plan to increase the number of patients treated, and at the same time, to reduce waiting lists and times in respect of particular conditions in particular areas. The three selected sites for the national pilot scheme were located in Southern England: Portsmouth, Isle of Wight and South East Hants Health Authority; East Kent Health Authority; and West Sussex and East Surrey Health Authorities. West Sussex was among those parts of the UK in which patients faced the longest waiting times (see *Sunday Times* 2001e). The official objective of the pilot scheme was to increase patient choice and to assess its impact on the local health economies, especially on the waiting times (see DoH 2002a: 4).

In January 2002, right before the first patients were sent abroad to receive planned treatment within the framework of the pilot scheme, the New Labour government quickly changed – for England only – by means of statutory instrument the regulation "National Health Service (Travelling Expenses and Remission of Charges)." The Statutory Instrument 4043, which came into force January 18, 2002, regulated the reimbursement of costs for traveling abroad for health care treatment and put it on a par with reimbursement of travel expenses in the UK.[11] The Liberal Democrats and the Conservatives, the parliamentary opposition, both challenged the Statutory Instrument 4043. Therefore, it had to be debated in the Fourth Standing Committee on Delegated Legislation on February 5, 2002, more than two weeks after it had come into force. In this Committee debate, John Hutton, then Minister of State for Health, pointed several times to the political constraints emanating from the internal market and claimed that the pilot scheme was necessary to comply fully with the ECJ rulings *Vanbraekel* and *Geraets-Smits/Peerbooms* from July 2001 (see House of Commons 2002a: columns 6, 10, 11, and 13). He declared:

> Those court decisions provide the backbone against which the regulations have been introduced and should be judged. … [T]he Government were under a clear obligation to ensure that the framework of NHS legislation in this country fully reflected the impact of the two decisions. (House of Commons 2002a: column 10)

---

11 Statutory instruments are a form of secondary, delegated or subordinate legislation in the UK in which ministers exercise legislative power delegated by the Parliament. They are the predominant legislative instrument in the UK. Statutory instruments are used because they are faster and simpler to implement than full Acts of Parliament. The legal office of the responsible Government Department normally drafts them. Statutory instruments are also used to incorporate provisions of EU directives into UK law.

Hutton disavowed the criticism coming from the parliamentary opposition, saying, "[i]t is wrong to caricature the arrangements as an underhand way for the Government to reduce average waiting times for patients in the UK; that is simply not true" (House of Commons 2002a: column 13).

At the same time, he imbedded the pilot scheme rhetorically into the broader Labour choice agenda:

> It would have been wrong not to take the opportunity offered by the rulings to widen the opportunities for access to high-quality health care, which will be provided free under the NHS at the point of delivery. (House of Commons 2002a: column 10)

It has been contested whether the introduction of the pilot scheme was the direct result of *Vanbraekel* and *Geraets-Smits/Peerbooms*. According to Diane Dawson, this causality brought forward especially by the press had to be called into question. She argued that the press coverage in July and August had "an important effect on public opinion and consequently on the enthusiasm with which the Government appears to have embraced the need to reverse its long standing policy against contracting with hospitals abroad" (2002: 1). From Dawson's point of view *Vanbraekel* and *Geraets-Smits/Peerbooms* did not imply rights for NHS patients to shorter waiting times because the rulings were dealing with a specific piece of Dutch legislation without clarifying the important questions for the UK. Nevertheless, the DoH allowed the NHS to contract with hospitals on the continent. Dawson explained this shift with the publicity of the possibility, admitted in October of 2000, for the NHS to contract with the UK private sector. She pointed out that the pilot scheme, which was developed through bilateral contracts, was independent from the ECJ decisions. First, patients sent abroad within the framework of the pilot scheme did not apply for authorization, and secondly, the UK did not change its handling of requests for authorization of treatment abroad (Dawson 2002: 3).

Nonetheless, there is overwhelming evidence that the ECJ rulings and the UK pilot scheme were highly connected. The statements of John Hutton during the Committee debate in the House of Commons cited above, the statements by Alan Milburn, and the final evaluation report of the overseas pilot scheme all point in this direction.

The centrally run pilot scheme started in January 2002 and ended in April. Its estimated costs, according to John Hutton amounted to £1.1 million for 190 patients (see House of Commons 2002b). The pilot scheme was favorably evaluated and carried out on a local basis. Single NHS Trusts or PCTs, approved by the DoH, continued to send patients abroad for treatment in order to reduce their waiting times. The DoH tried to control and to manage these decentralized referrals with guidance to the NHS trusts and PCTs. It established an overseas commissioner, Guy's and St Thomas' Trust, that is responsible for contracting with overseas hospitals. It negotiated prices, organized the travels by patients, and monitored quality on behalf of the NHS (see DoH 2004a).

Referral abroad generally followed a certain procedure: First, an Overseas Assessment Clinic in the UK, which was run by an overseas consultant, assessed the selected patient. If the patient was deemed fit and suitable to travel and fit for the operation or treatment, she was sent to the overseas hospital (see DoH 2004a).

In a debate in the House of Commons in 2003, John Hutton reported that UK patients had been referred to three hospitals in France and eight in Germany (2003). The exact number of patients sent abroad for treatment within the local referral procedures, which continued the pilot scheme, is not known, because the commissioning bodies do not have to report to the DoH (see Interview UK2). However, in March of 2004, the DoH stated in a public guidance that since January 2002 almost 600 patients had received treatment in France, Belgium and Germany, the majority being orthopedic and cardiac treatments (see DoH 2004a).

Removal of the Territorial Restriction in the NHS Act from 1977

More than one year after the announcement by Milburn, minister Hutton put into force the Statutory Instrument 2759.[12] This statutory instrument came into force in November 2002 and removed the territorial restriction within the NHS from the English and Welsh legislation. Section 5(2)(b) of the NHS Act from 1977 was repealed and after Section 3(1) the following was inserted:

> The Secretary of State may provide or secure the provision of anything mentioned in subsection (1) above outside England and Wales. (The National Health Service Act 1977 and National Health Service and Community Care Act 1990 (Amendment) Regulations 2002: Section 3(1)(A))

In addition, the NHS and Community Care Act from 1990 was amended. Paragraph 15(A) now determined that "[a]n NHS Trust may arrange for the provision of accommodation and services outside England and Wales" (The National Health Service Act 1977 and National Health Service and Community Care Act 1990 (Amendment) Regulations 2002).

The amendments effected by the Statutory Instrument 2759 created the explicit power for the NHS to purchase health care from outside the UK without having to ask the DoH for approval. Primary health care trusts could now buy services from the private sector abroad with

---

12   The Statutory Instrument 2759 was made by the responsible designated minister, John Hutton, Minister of State for Health, with reference to the European Communities Act 1972 to implement obligations of the UK arising from European requirements. This statutory instrument was not contested in the House of Commons and passed Parliament without discussion.

the caveats that nobody is forced to go to another member country against their wishes, that the issues of value for money and cost criteria that would be considered in UK apply, as well as those of quality care and follow up treatment. (Roberts 2003: 28)

Domestically, the UK government justified the pilot scheme and the continuing practice of sending patients abroad, as well as the legislative changes, with European requirements. However, toward the ECJ, it maintained the alleged non-transferability of the principles progressively elaborated in the *Kohll/Decker* jurisprudence. In fact, sending patients abroad served to channel the pressure from the media campaign and to relieve pressure from the NHS because of continuing high waiting lists and times. The main advantage of the pilot scheme and the continuing practice for the DoH and the NHS was that they were in complete control of sending patients to other Member States, instead of having unplanned patient travel abroad, as was the result of *Watts* (see Interview UK1), which will be discussed below. According to the DoH, the legislative changes were not only provoked by the ECJ decisions but also induced by broader political considerations to reduce waiting times and lists in the NHS. As a high-ranking DoH official put it, *Geraets-Smits/Peerbooms* was "instrumental" in changing national legislation. It helped to create a climate prone to policy change (see Interview UK2). One piece of evidence for this is the fact that the restrictions were lifted for the whole world not only for the EU. Nevertheless, the explanatory note of the Statutory Instrument 2759 emphasized that the amended regulations were meant

to implement European obligations (arising from decisions of the European Court of Justice, in particular case C-157/99 B.S.M. Geraets-Smits v Stichting Ziekenfonds VGZ and H.T.M. Peerbooms v Stichting CZ Groep Zorgverzekeringen) and enable rights to be enjoyed relating to the freedom to provide services. (The National Health Service Act 1977 and National Health Service and Community Care Act 1990 (Amendment) Regulations 2002)

Watts brings about Further "Trouble"

The DoH had unquestionably relieved much of the public pressure with the help of the practice to refer patients abroad. However, by the end of 2002, it became clear that the problem for the government was not solved. According to the press, several persons threatened court action because their case had not been considered under the new schemes (see *Sunday Times* 2002).

The next urgent problem for the DoH arose with *Müller-Fauré/van Riet*, a case that was decided by the ECJ in May of 2003. The DoH especially disliked the distinction made by this ruling between out-patient and in-patient services because according to its view, both required the same amount of planning and financing (see Interview UK2).

The UK Administrative Court of the Queen's Bench Division of the High Court had explicitly awaited *Müller-Fauré/van Riet* to be able to lay down its own decision in *Watts* in October 2003 (para. 36).[13] This UK case had caused considerable (media) attention. In March 2003, Yvonne Watts, a United Kingdom resident, had her hips replaced in France. The competent British Bedford Primary Care Trust refused to reimburse her costs with the argument that she had not accepted the required waiting time.

After *Müller-Fauré/van Riet* was handed down, the responsible judge of the first-instance Administrative Court, Mr. Munby, ruled that the passive free movement of services applied to the NHS also. According to him,

> the fundamental principles articulated by the ECJ ... in *Muller-Fauré* [sic] *and van Riet* ... were intended to be, and are, as applicable in the case of the NHS as in the case of the Dutch ZFW. (*Watts*: para. 108)

In detail, judge Munby found the then-existing waiting time of the NHS for in-patient treatment of 15 months intolerable; according to him it had to be much less than a year, though he did not set a specific time figure (see *The Guardian* 2003). In addition, the judge found fault with the official public guidance by the DoH and said that it should be altered in order to make UK patients aware of their rights under Article 49 EC Treaty (see Administrative Court 2003, *Watts*: paras. 196 and 199). However, the DoH thought that the Administrative Court read too much into the ECJ rulings (see Interview UK1). Mrs. Watts finally lost the case on the facts, because according to Mr. Munby, in her specific case the waiting time had been cut appropriately.

Watts explicitly contradicted John Reid, Alan Milburn' successor as Secretary of State for Health in 2003. He had claimed before that people who were on a waiting list for less than a year could not receive reimbursement. Since this ruling, in principle, patients who suffer "undue delay" waiting for an operation in the NHS could go to another EU Member State to get treatment and will then be reimbursed by the NHS. However, in official statements the DoH claimed that *Watts* was complex and needed to be studied in detail (see *The Independent* 2003). The British Medical Association (BMA) in principle welcomed the ruling:

> However, if NHS resources are used to treat patients abroad it will be even less able to treat patients quickly at home. The BMA believes the way forward is to continue cutting waiting lists by increasing capacity in the UK. We support the government's commitment to sustained investment in the NHS. (2003)

Both parties – Mrs. Watts and the DoH – appealed the national court decision. Therefore, it went on to the Court of Appeal that referred it in July 2004 in seven questions to the ECJ. In the first and most important question, the Court of Appeal

---

13   For a more detailed description of Watts, see Chapter 4.

asked whether, in principle, in the light of the ECJ jurisprudence *Geraets-Smits*, *Müller-Fauré* and *Inizan*, UK nationals were entitled to receive hospital treatment in other EU Member States. The Court of Appeal specifically wanted to know whether the state-funded UK NHS had to be distinguished from the health care system of the Netherlands. The UK government proposed to answer this question with "yes" (see ECJ, Report for the Hearing for *Watts*: paras. 46 and 67). The ECJ stated in its preliminary ruling that the obligation to reimburse the cost of a hospital treatment provided in another Member State also applied to the UK NHS. A prior authorization scheme like the one in the UK had to prove that the waiting time did not exceed a medically acceptable period of time considering the condition of the patient and her clinical needs.

The NHS Confederation was rather critical about the ECJ preliminary ruling in *Watts*.[14] It declared that it was unfair that more affluent patients could afford treatment abroad and claim reimbursement afterwards, which would have negative consequences for other patients with higher clinical needs. Nevertheless, according to its Chief Executive, Gill Morgan, "[a]s the NHS moves towards treating every patient within 18 weeks, problems like this should cease to be an issue" (NHS Confederation 2006). The British Medical Association welcomed *Watts*. Its chairman, Edwin Borman, stated that "[w]hen patients seek treatment overseas, doctors should be free to make a decision based on their clinical need" (British Medical Association 2006).

As one source of UK law is the practice of the courts called "common law," the *Watts* ruling by Mr. Munby in 2003 was the law in England (see Montgomery 2003: 7). Accordingly, the DoH changed its guidance to the public. However, these guidelines were rather unclear about what would happen if patients traveled abroad outside the established structures:

> Following decisions by the European Court of Justice and our domestic courts, a patient can also approach a provider in an EU country directly, i.e. outside the E112 procedure or NHS-commissioned service. As you would have to pay from your own resources for such treatment and then claim reimbursement from the NHS retrospectively for such treatment, you are strongly advised to seek advice from your PCT or board before proceeding. As this is a complex area of developing law you are also strongly advised to take your own legal advice. If you go ahead without both a recommendation from your consultant and the agreement of the PCT you may find that you are subsequently unable to obtain reimbursement. (see DoH 2005)

As can be seen from this doubtful interim guidance to the public, the DoH tried to deter patients from using the possibility of getting treatment abroad, rather than encourage them. Already in *Watts*, Mr. Munby had claimed that the DoH

---

14   The NHS Confederation represents more than 90 percent of all NHS organizations, statutory, non-profit, and commercial.

public guidance was "unhelpful and somewhat opaque" (Administrative Court 2003, *Watts*: para. 196). According to a DoH official, patients who traveled abroad on their own account and claimed reimbursement afterwards were frequently reimbursed. The two reasons given were that the decision by Mr. Munby was the law in the UK and that the DoH wanted to prevent additional national court cases (see Interview UK2). This practice of preventing court cases seems to have started quite early. Already in a general report for the European Commission DG Employment in May 2000 Palm and others had observed that, "[i]n some cases which could potentially have ended up before the ECJ, the regional authorities reimbursed the patients in order to avoid possible precedents" (2000: 87).

In more recent public guidance the DoH admitted that, following ECJ and domestic rulings, under certain circumstances patients could travel abroad for treatment and were then entitled to the reimbursement of some of their costs. According to this guidance, the competent local health commissioners were considering two major factors to decide on a referral abroad:

> Amongst the factors to be considered are whether treatment which is the same or equally effective can be obtained without undue delay under the NHS; and all the circumstances of your individual case including, if appropriate, how much pain you are in, the nature of any disability and whether your condition is affecting your ability to work, as well as your medical history. (DoH 2006)

The DoH continued to warn UK patients that they should bear in mind "that the extension to tax-funded health systems such as the NHS of the ECJ case law on the rights of patients to go abroad and claim reimbursement is under challenge" (2006).

Conclusion

The UK is well known for administrative efficiency and its "impeccable" implementation record of EU legislation (see Kassim 2000: 22). This study tries to figure out whether the same is true for the much-contested *Kohll/Decker* rulings.

The UK government has accomplished important legislative and administrative adaptations as a reaction to the *Kohll/Decker* jurisprudence. First, two major legislative changes were made. In 2001, the government amended the English NHS regulations concerning travel expenses and extended these regulations to cases in which patients went abroad to receive treatment. A year later, the government removed the strict territorial restriction enshrined in the 1977 NHS Act. The competent NHS institutions could from then on – independently from the Secretary of State – seek health care from providers abroad. Secondly, the UK government adopted a "contractual approach" with regard to patient mobility. In order to relieve political and media pressure from the NHS, it introduced a centralized pilot scheme to give patients who were on a waiting list the choice to be treated in health care centers in other EU Member States, though only in centers that had a contract with the NHS. After the phasing-out of this centralized pilot scheme, the local health authorities carried on the referral mechanism. Finally, the DoH altered the relevant guidance to the public in reaction to the ECJ jurisprudence several times.

Regardless of these legislative and administrative changes, the UK government remained strictly opposed to the application of the principles elaborated in the *Kohll/Decker* jurisprudence to the NHS. In the proceedings before the ECJ case *Leichtle*, the government even requested that the Court determine that national health services like the one in the UK were not bound by Article 49 EC Treaty. The UK government stated at the same time that it could be applied to systems like the German or Dutch social security systems (see ECJ, Report of the judge rapporteur, *Leichtle*: para. 47).[15]

The UK government remained reluctant to change its attitude even after the *Watts* decisions by its Administrative Court and by the ECJ. The continuous administrative practice by the DoH has been to informally grant individual reimbursement claims in order to prevent national court cases. Because of the reluctance to take full account of the *Kohll/Decker* jurisprudence, it will be up to the national courts and the ECJ to decide future cases and to apply the *Kohll/Decker* jurisprudence to the UK, case by case. It is very unlikely that without this judicial activity the UK will voluntarily move further toward the implementation of the *Kohll/Decker* jurisprudence.

Three factors can explain the administrative and legislative changes in the UK. First, an aggressive press campaign, which revealed major problems within the NHS, caused considerable public and political pressure on the UK government in the summer of 2001. The government immediately reacted by announcing the insertion of a pilot scheme to treat patients overseas, as well as some major legislative changes. Secondly, this strategic move fitted perfectly into the governmental agenda to increase patient choice, involve the private sector and therewith shorten waiting lists and times. Parts of the *Kohll/Decker* jurisprudence were compatible with the broader governmental agenda. Finally, the *Watts* decision by the Administrative Court thwarted the strategy of the government to pre-empt court cases. It was very likely that additional cases would arise. In order to anticipate this development, the government changed its legislation and administrative practices.

Because the implementation of the *Kohll/Decker* jurisprudence is not yet fully accomplished in the UK, its effects are difficult to assess. De-territorialization has certainly been increased with the removal of the territorial restriction from the NHS Act. At the same time, de-territorialization is rather limited and takes place mainly within contractual parameters. The ECJ jurisprudence has not directly caused internal de-structuring. The patient choice agenda and the involvement of the private sector were part of the governmental program.

---

15 The judge rapporteur writes the report for the oral hearing, which sums up the facts of the case and the legal arguments.

In the past, patients in the UK generally had very circumscribed choice. They had no choice where to get treatment, when to get it, what to get, and from whom to obtain it. The *Kohll/Decker* jurisprudence in general and *Watts* in particular, although they concerned treatment abroad, were considered to be a general danger to this system (see Interview UK2). The DoH feared that the implementation of the jurisprudence would open a gateway and endanger the NHS in its entirety. However, the Labour government's policy since its accession and especially since 2000 was to increase patient choice (see DoH 2003). Since December 2005, patients who have waited for more than six months for elective surgery have the choice of moving to another hospital for faster treatment. In this case,

> [t]he referral will be made by the GP [General practitioner, AJO][16] and may be to another hospital, treatment centre, GP with a specialist interest, private, or overseas hospital. Responsibility for entering into arrangements with alternative providers will fall to PCTs which will appoint 'patient care advisors' to advise and assist patients in making a choice. (Newdick 2005: 61)

Parts of the *Kohll/Decker* jurisprudence were in line with this patient choice agenda. Therefore, the strict rejection of this jurisprudence was difficult to uphold. As an official of the DoH put it "if choice [exists, AJO] within the UK there has to be choice outside" (Interview UK2). Nevertheless, the DoH wanted to proceed at its proper pace and did not want to be pushed by the ECJ (see Interview UK2).

The *Kohll/Decker* jurisprudence certainly has been an important driving force behind the implementation of the patient choice agenda by the Labour government. *Watts*, though, bears the ability to shake up the entire rationing mechanism, which is central to the NHS. If waiting times do not decrease and patients start to travel to other EU Member States *en masse*, the setting of clinical priorities might be disturbed drastically.

From the beginning, the reduction of waiting lists and times was a priority for the Labour government (see Leathard 2000: 226-257). Therefore, it sought to inject more money into the NHS so as to reduce waiting times. Accordingly, waiting times have decreased considerably. For August 2006, the DoH reported the lowest number of people on waiting lists since the beginning of the data collection in 1988. The number of in-patients waiting was 769,000, a reduction of 389,000 since 1997, with an average of eight weeks wait (see DoH 2006b). The *Kohll/Decker* jurisprudence was an additional means to shorten waiting lists. Several hundred, possibly thousands, of NHS patients received treatment abroad, which allowed the NHS to free its own resources. Additionally, some of the ECJ rulings were explicitly geared to systems with long waiting lists. With the continued presence of these lists, further intrusion by the ECJ was inevitable. This fact was

---

16   GPs are the gate-keepers within the NHS. Patients must first consult them and are then referred to specialists. GPs are self-employed and have to conclude a contract with the competent health authority.

a strong incentive for the UK government to invest ever more money into its own NHS to shorten waiting lists, and once achieved to keep them short. Only with such a policy could the assumed flood of patients traveling abroad for treatment be reduced to a trickle. The UK government made it clear that it was not willing to co-finance other countries' health care systems through the reimbursement of treatment abroad. In this respect, the *Kohll/Decker* jurisprudence has had a considerable influence on the NHS.

Available information from the DoH does not suggest a direct financial destabilization of the NHS. The number of those who travel abroad and ask for reimbursement is still negligible and no substantial increase is observable (see Interview UK2). A major reason to believe that this is not going to change for the moment is that there is a knowledge gap in the UK. Patients usually do not know what their entitlements are under EU law, neither Regulation 1408/71 nor their rights elaborated by the ECJ in the *Kohll/Decker* jurisprudence (see Interview UK3).

To sum up, the *Kohll/Decker* jurisprudence has indeed fed into the political agenda of the Labour government. However, only those elements of the jurisprudence which fit these domestic preferences were implemented. The transferability of the *Kohll/Decker* jurisprudence was consistently denied. Overall, with respect to the broader governmental program of reforming the NHS, the implementation of limited elements of the ECJ jurisprudence was and is a rather small and therefore negligible phenomenon.

Chapter 9

Fine-tuning Doctrines by the ECJ:
Judicial Activism and Self-restraint?

Despite the initial obstruction to the principles enshrined in *Kohll* and *Decker*, Germany, France and the UK incorporated them into their social codes in a later stage. Member States did not have to alter core features of their social protection systems; the actual impact of the rulings was therefore rather modest when compared to the one postulated. What role did the ECJ's fine-tuning in the follow-up rulings to *Kohll* and *Decker* play in all this? Did the fine-tuning interact with domestic implementation efforts?

Conventional models of judicial politics have conceived the ECJ either as a strategic rational actor that tries to accommodate Member States' preferences (see, for example, Garrett 1995, Garrett et al. 1998, Alter 2001, Hartley 2007), or as an autonomous judicial actor that exercises considerable discretion *vis-à-vis* Member States (see, for example, Burley and Mattli 1993, Stone Sweet 2004, Cichowski 2007).

I argue that the ECJ in the *Kohll/Decker* jurisprudence oscillated between "judicial activism" and "self-restraint." According to Hjalte Rasmussen, judicial activism "connotes regular judicial policy-making in pursuance of policy-objectives which usurp the rule and policy-making powers of other branches of government" (1998: 26–27). The concept of judicial self-restraint is "commonly used to designate the situation in which judges defer their judgements to some extent ... to the political branches of government" (Rasmussen 1986: 33). I claim that the ECJ is both a strategic and an autonomous actor. It enjoys considerable autonomy from Member State interference and has its own agenda of applying EC law uniformly across Member States. At the same time, its autonomy is constrained by Member State interests. Ultimately, the Court wants to ensure that Member States accept its rulings and incorporate them in their laws and administrative practices.

Three Layers of Judicial Politics

If we want to observe the (partially contradicting) aims of applying EC law uniformly and of guaranteeing compliance at work, we have to take a look at three distinct layers of judicial politics. The first layer consists of a leading case (or cases) in which the ECJ decides a question of principle and lays down the doctrines with which the question at hand has to be answered. The second layer consists of an ensuing process of fine-tuning the principles developed in the leading case in follow-up rulings. Even though, outside the formal structure of interaction between the ECJ, national courts, the European Commission and Member State governments, communication is categorically denied (see Interviews ECJ1, ECJ2), they engage in a subtle "dialogue" via the fine-tuning process.[1] If the ECJ has delivered a key ruling for a specific question in a specific country, further questions about its actual scope remain open. To close this gap, national courts submit additional preliminary questions. This may either concern another Member State, potentially with a different system, or it may regard a different question related to the first ruling. The ECJ in the course of fine-tuning its decisions then applies the principles elaborated earlier to other Member States and other case constellations. At the same time, it further refines the already existing principles and adds new ones. This process of fine-tuning the jurisprudence leads to the third layer of judicial politics: interaction of ECJ rulings and implementation processes at the Member State level. The repeated interaction between national courts (as well as Member State governments in the proceedings) and the ECJ allows the latter to steadily refine its earlier rulings. In doing so, the Court is able to accommodate concerns and criticism by Member State governments. In turn, the fine-tuning may help to overcome Member state non-compliance, it may help governments and national courts to better understand the meaning and impact of the ECJ decisions, and it may allow governments to draw horizontal conclusions for their implementation.[2]

Judicial Activism and Self-restraint in the *Kohll/Decker* Jurisprudence

In the development of the *Kohll/Decker* jurisprudence we can observe this layered interaction between the ECJ and Member States. The former showed both judicial activism and self-restraint. By applying the principles of the free movement of services and goods to health care in *Kohll* and *Decker* and thereby challenging national welfare states the ECJ was activist. The Member States assumed that they would be confronted with enormous political, administrative and financial costs associated with the rulings. They tried to convince the ECJ to limit the implications of the decisions. In the proceedings before the ECJ, the Member States expressed the fear that destabilization effects would follow from a Europe-wide patient mobility. Therefore, when it came to the actual design of the intrusion of the principles of the free movement of services and goods into the domestic sphere

---

1   See Section 4 EC Treaty, as well as the statute and the rules of procedure of the ECJ. For a detailed description of the procedural framework in preliminary rulings, see Granger (2004).

2   With horizontal conclusions I do not only mean that Member States apply the principles elaborated by the ECJ to the same cases in their system but also to other similar cases.

of social security, the ECJ exercised self-restraint by limiting the impact of its decisions largely to the less costly out-patient sector. In *Geraets-Smits/Peerbooms* and *Watts*, the ECJ extended the application of the general principle of the passive free movement of services to systems based on in-kind benefits and to national health systems. Simultaneously, the ECJ conceded in *Geraets-Smits/Peerbooms* that there might be justifiable grounds for Member States to put restrictions on patient mobility for in-patient health care. *Kohll* and *Decker* and patient mobility in out-patient health care were already heavily contested by Member States; the application of the jurisprudence to in-patient care was an even more ominous threat for them. Therefore, they argued that the entire organization of their health care systems would be at stake. The ECJ could have extended its jurisprudence also to the in-patient sector without restrictions. Nevertheless, it refrained from doing so and referred to the stability of the social security systems of the Member States. The ECJ thus partly followed the arguments of the Member States. It applied the general principles from *Kohll* and *Decker* to in-patient health care, but expressed its willingness to accept more justifications for restrictions than it would accept in other areas. Until the 1990s, the strict orthodox reasoning of the ECJ with respect to the effects of the basic freedoms was to ignore justifications based on economic grounds. However, the *Kohll/Decker* jurisprudence signaled a change of this reasoning regarding social security systems (see O'Leary and Fernández-Martín 2004: 165 and 171–172).

Why did the ECJ act like that? First of all, most Member States initially reacted with hostility toward the *Kohll/Decker* jurisprudence. Only with the ECJ's fine-tuning and its application to one group of countries while leaving the rest undecided did the united front of rejection start to crumble. The most visible sign of this development was the French observation in the *Watts* proceedings. In earlier cases the French government had been fiercely opposed to the *Kohll/Decker* jurisprudence; nevertheless, it finally implemented the jurisprudence (see Chapter 6). In *Watts*, the French government surprisingly did not back the position of the UK government and all the other national health systems, but rather, on the contrary, claimed that the *Kohll/Decker* jurisprudence also had to be applied to them. Secondly, the Member States' hostile reactions sensitized the ECJ to their concerns. Member States succeeded in persuading the Court of the peculiar nature of national social security systems and the dangers of an unrestricted application of the basic freedoms. The ECJ recognized the sensitivities in this area, which is one of the last quasi-exclusive domains of the Member States.

To sum up, in the *Kohll/Decker* jurisprudence, the ECJ applied the passive free movement of services and the free movement of goods to the health sector, one of the last spheres of Member States' sovereignty. The original two cases concerned out-patient care of the Luxembourg system based on cash reimbursement. The transferability of the same principle to in-patient health care and to other Member States' systems remained open. All Member States were strictly opposed to these decisions. While the application of the free movement of services to out-patient care could be gradually extended to other Member States' systems, the

ECJ refrained from extending the principle without restrictions to the even more contested in-patient sector. This fine-tuning and the limitation to out-patient care facilitated Member State implementation. Counterfactually speaking, had the ECJ extended the jurisprudence without restrictions to all systems and circumstances, the resistance and containing measures by Member States would have been much more powerful. It took Member States some time to implement the rulings. Nevertheless, a containment of the rulings in the sense of Conant, that is a conscious and systematic bypassing, is virtually absent.

Chapter 10

The European Commission: Enforcement and Alternative Management Strategies

In addition to the fine-tuning of the ECJ, the activities of the European Commission help to understand why EU Member States implemented the ECJ rulings. They initially strongly contested the *Kohll/Decker* jurisprudence; none of them welcomed these decisions. Some countries, for instance France, deliberately decided not to implement them. In the Council of Ministers meeting that took place right after *Kohll* and *Decker*, ministers insisted on blockading them. In particular, the German Minister of Health at the time, Horst Seehofer, argued against *Kohll* and *Decker*. The debates in the Administrative Commission on Social Security for Migrant Workers also revealed fierce resistance against the two ECJ decisions. The European Commission faced a united front of rejection. Could it have overcome this obstruction and, if so, how? First, I discuss the infringement policy of the Commission to make Member States implement *Kohll* and *Decker*. Second, I analyze the alternative strategies that were promoted by the Commission after these decisions, and that went beyond country-specific infringement proceedings.

Enforcement through Infringement Proceedings

As the European Commission was faced with Member States' initial open non-compliance with *Kohll* and *Decker*, which strategies did it employ to encourage compliance? It faced three major problems related to ECJ decisions in general or the *Kohll/Decker* jurisprudence in particular. First, ECJ decisions generally concern very specific, often rather technical single cases, which leaves much room for interpretation on whether they can be applied to other cases and other Member States. Secondly, the lead role in monitoring compliance fell to two competing Directorate Generals, with a third DG involved as well. The DG Employment and Social Affairs was in charge of supervising compliance with Regulation 1408/71. After *Geraets-Smits/Peerbooms*, where the ECJ's reasoning was based exclusively on Article 49 (free movement of services), and where Regulation 1408/71 was not even mentioned, the dossier was transferred to the DG Internal Market, which deals with the free movement of services. Since then both DGs worked on the issue of patient mobility. In addition, the DG Health and Consumer Protection, the DG promoting health in all community policies, was involved as well (see Interview EC1). A third problem related to ECJ decisions was that the Commission had not anticipated the result of the decisions and was as surprised as the Member States were (see Interview EC1).

The reticence of the Commission in applying the free movement of services can best be seen in its observation in *Kohll*, where it stated that "une certaine "territorialisation" des soins médicaux s'avère nécessaire" [a certain 'territorialization' of medical care proves to be necessary, AJO] and that "le risque potentiel de déséquilibre financier des régimes de sécurité sociale justifie l'existence du système d'autorisation préalable qui entraîne une restriction à la liberté absolue de prestation des services" (ECJ, Rapport d'audience, *Kohll*: 24–25).[1]

After *Kohll* and *Decker* were decided in 1998, the Commission did not launch any major offensive against Member States. It started its infringement policy with a proceeding against France concerning *Decker* in 1999. The French government had openly argued soon after *Kohll* and *Decker* against their transferability to France and urged its insurance funds to ignore the cases. In addition, beginning in 1996, the Commission had received an unusual amount of individual complaints especially against the French practice of not reimbursing health care costs incurred abroad or the refusal to authorize health care abroad (see Interview EC1 and Chapter 6). In 2001, after *Geraets-Smits/Peerbooms* further clarified the jurisprudence, the Commission stepped up the pressure on the French government and launched a new action under Article 226 concerning bio-medical analysis laboratories. In December 2001, the Commission brought the case before the ECJ. It declared that France required from foreign bio-medical analysis laboratories that they have their place of business on French territory in order to be able to obtain the authorization for operating. In addition, France precluded any reimbursement of the costs incurred abroad by such laboratories and thus failed to fulfill its obligations under Articles 43 and 49 EC Treaty (see the ECJ case C-496/01). It took the ECJ two and a half years to finally decide the case, which it did in March of 2004. Already in October 2004, the Commission started another infringement proceeding under Article 228 EC Treaty with a Letter of Formal Notice, because the French government had not complied with the ECJ ruling from March. Its Reasoned Opinion followed in April 2006.

Because a formal *erga omnes* effect of ECJ rulings is missing, the UK and to a lesser extent Germany could argue with the Commission that the *Kohll/Decker* jurisprudence could not be applied to their systems. The Commission did not initiate infringement proceedings against these Member States.

In addition to its proceedings against France, the Commission started two infringement proceedings against Finland, one against Belgium and one against Portugal (see Table 10.1).

---

1 "The potential risk of a financial disequilibrium of social security regimes justifies the existence of preliminary authorization systems which leads to a restriction of the absolute freedom to provide services" (translation of the author).

Table 10.1 Infringement proceedings on the *Kohll/Decker* jurisprudence initiated by the European Commission

	Letter of formal notice	Reasoned opinion	Referral to the ECJ
Belgium		July 2002 Reimbursement of Medical Analyses	
Finland		July 2005 Patient mobility	
		July 2005 Medical Rehabilitation	
France		January 2000 Medicinal Products	
	October 1999 Pair of Eyeglasses	October 2000 Pair of Eyeglasses	
		March 2001 Medical Laboratories	October 2001 Medical Laboratories
	October 2004 Medical Laboratories	April 2006 Medical Laboratories	
Portugal	March 2002 Medical Laboratories		

Note: The data for this table have been assembled with help from DG Internal Market and DG Employment and information provided on the EU websites. Usually, the European Commission publishes infringement proceedings beginning with the second stage. Therefore, it cannot be said with certainty how many Letters of Formal Notice have been sent to the Member States with respect to the *Kohll/Decker* jurisprudence.

Finland received two Reasoned Opinions in 2005 on patient mobility and medical rehabilitation. In the first case, the Finnish government informed the Commission that it would change the registration and authorization requirements for foreign health care providers laid down in its Health Insurance Act. The requirements for medical rehabilitation were still under consideration in 2005 (see Jorens and Hajdú 2005: 58–59). Belgium received a Reasoned Opinion in 2002 on the reimbursement of medical analyses, and finally, Portugal received a Letter of Formal Notice in 2002 on medical laboratories. In total, with regard to the *Kohll/ Decker* jurisprudence, the Commission initiated eight infringement proceedings and referred only one case to the ECJ. There is no data available with which we could compare this infringement policy. Nonetheless, it can be established that it has been rather unsystematic.

Gerda Falkner and others distinguished between four different effects of infringement procedures of the Commission on the implementation in Member

States: First, if domestic implementation remains inert, an infringement procedure may kick-start such a process. Second, the Commission can accelerate an implementation process that is already under way in neutralizing national opposition or helping the government to circumvent potential veto players. Third, the Commission can correct domestic implementation. And fourth, infringement procedures may have no direct effect at all (see Falkner et al. 2005: 225–228). With the initial outright rejection of the jurisprudence by the French government, the activities of the Commission since 1999 seem to have kick-started the administrative debate on the applicability of the ECJ jurisprudence and its gradual implementation. Although France could rather easily achieve conformity to the ECJ cases with a simple circular on optical products and very minor financial costs involved, the first infringement proceeding can be seen to have been quite successful and to have accelerated the implementation process in general.

Alternative Management Strategies

The official infringement procedures initiated by the European Commission are only the tip of the iceberg in overall Member State non-compliance. The Commission only initiates such procedures against violations of European law that it can detect, and sometimes even refrains from doing so when it discovers such violations. As we can see from Table 10.1, the Commission did not pursue a systematic infringement policy as regards the *Kohll/Decker* jurisprudence, although the majority of Member States were clearly in violation with that jurisprudence. Apart from France, it initiated proceedings only against Finland, Belgium, and Portugal. This conservative behavior seems to be consistent with the typical Commission approach. Regarding innovative ECJ interpretation, Conant held that the Commission "rarely acts on the basis of a few rulings, but usually waits to see that a legal principle develops consistently through a series of cases" (2003: 75).

Evidently, the Commission did not systematically force Member States to comply with the *Kohll/Decker* jurisprudence through infringement proceedings. But does such a fragmentary enforcement policy mean that the Commission was sitting back with hands folded? The answer is "no" as will be seen in the following section. The Commission did not want to push the non-compliant countries to implement the ECJ decisions through infringement proceedings; rather, it opted for alternative management strategies.

High Level Process of Reflection and the Ensuing High Level Group

The inevitable political debate amongst Member States about the *Kohll/Decker* jurisprudence started under the Spanish EU presidency at a ministerial conference in Malaga, Spain, February 2002. A meeting of national experts with the Commission followed this conference (see Sauer and Fahy 2004: 505). In June 2002, initiated by the DG Health and Consumer Protection, a Health Council started a "High Level Process of Reflection on Patient Mobility and Healthcare Developments in the European Union," where health ministers of Member States, representatives from the European Parliament, and representatives of patients, professionals, providers and purchasers of health care discussed health care matters including how to reconcile national health policies with European obligations (see European Commission 2003e). Officially, the Commission declared that the High Level Reflection Process intended

> to provide an informal and flexible forum bringing together relevant stakeholders for joint reflection on issues affecting health and health services in the internal market, and to make recommendations to guide future work at Community and Member State level, without duplicating or substituting for discussions within the formal institutional structures of the EU. (European Commission 2002: 15)

The underlying goal was to assemble EU health ministers around one table and let them discuss patient mobility and other health issues. The major impetus for the reflection process came from the *Kohll/Decker* jurisprudence; consequently, one of the four working groups dealt with patient mobility and these ECJ decisions. The health ministers were surprised that Health Commissioner David Byrne personally invited them to participate in the reflection process. This invitation implied a far-reaching watershed. The ministers were not used to discussing health issues other than *public* ones at the European level and thought that all other health issues were an exclusively domestic issue.

The objectives of the reflection process were perceived differently: one side understood the process as an effort to stop the ECJ jurisprudence (see Interview EC1); the other side regarded it as an initiative to discuss the impact of the European level on national health systems (see Interview EC2). One important objective was the perceived necessity to reduce the legal uncertainty created by the ECJ rulings.

The general results of the reflection process were documented in 2003. The recommendations on the ECJ jurisprudence were very general and noncommittal in nature. One rather cryptic recommendation was

> to invite the Commission in consultation with the Member States to explore how legal certainty could be improved following the Court of Justice jurisprudence concerning the right of patients to benefit from medical treatment in another Member State and to bring forward any appropriate proposals. (European Commission 2003d: 11)

The real success seems to have been the mere fact that health ministers were even discussing patient mobility supranationally.

In order to implement the recommendations and the proposals set out in a Communication from the Commission in 2004, a High Level Working Group on Health Services and Medical Care was established and launched in July 2004. Since then, this standing committee has been a permanent feature and has reported annually to the Council of Employment, Social Policy, Health and Consumer Affairs. In contrast to the committee constructed for the reflection process, this committee comprises only representatives from the Commission and the Member States. Among its seven main competencies figures "cross-border healthcare purchasing and provision," in which patient mobility is prominent. Also in 2004, the European Parliament (EP) pressed the Commission to develop "as quickly as possible, a coherent policy on patient mobility using the open method of coordination" (2005b).

Consultation Process on the Implementation of ECJ Jurisprudence

When *Kohll* and *Decker* were decided by the ECJ in 1998, general knowledge about the extent and conditions of patient mobility was very limited even at the Member State level. The European Commission with its limited resources was unable to comprehensively grasp this phenomenon. Therefore, in July 2002, the DG Internal Market launched a "Consultation Process" on the implementation of this ECJ jurisprudence in Member States. The official reason for this "constructive dialogue with member states and other stakeholders" was to come up with "a concerted and coherent approach" (European Commission 2002: 15). However, the Secretariat General of the Commission spoke of a "pre-litigation stage of the investigation process" (European Commission 2005b). The Consultation Process was initiated for four reasons: First, the DG Internal Market received an increasing number of complaints from individuals about the non-implementation of the ECJ's jurisprudence. Second, the DG wanted to make Member States aware of their duties vis-à-vis the jurisprudence. Third, because there was no monitoring mechanism, the DG did not know whether Member States were making progress in complying with the rulings or not. Before initiating infringement proceedings, it needed better knowledge about what was happening on the Member State level. Fourth, the *Kohll/Decker* jurisprudence was on the European agenda. The EP had asked the Commission several questions about the ECJ cases, and in two Councils – Health and Employment and Social Affairs – a debate on patient mobility had started (European Commission 2003c: 20).

To start the Consultation Process, the DG Internal Market sent out a questionnaire and a letter to all Member States asking them to detail the national measures taken to implement the *Kohll/Decker* jurisprudence. Unfortunately, the Commission did not disclose the answers to this questionnaire to me.[2] The aggregate responses of

---

2   The Secretariat General justified its refusal to the author as follows: "As already explained by the said Directorate-General [Internal Market, AJO], the aforementioned documents were received as a reply to a questionnaire launched by the Commission services

the Member States, though, were condensed in a public Commission report that was meant to increase the pressure on the Member States although a direct naming and shaming was avoided (2003c). According to the report, few Member States had taken steps to change national legislation or practice and implementation varied considerably, leaving patients to face different obstacles concerning their reimbursement rights depending on the Member State to which they belonged. As a reaction to these results which were unsatisfying for the Commission, it perceived two options: it could either pursue individual complaints on a case-by-case basis and then initiate infringement proceedings against countries that did not comply with the ECJ jurisprudence, or it could codify the concerned ECJ jurisprudence in a piece of secondary legislation. The Commission deemed the first path inefficient and chose the second one. A proposal for a directive on services was already being drafted. The Commission wanted to include the ECJ jurisprudence on medical services into this directive and felt this was the best way to make Member States respect the *Kohll/Decker* jurisprudence (see Interview EC1).

Including the Jurisprudence in the Proposal for a Directive on Services

In January 2004, Internal Market Commissioner Frits Bolkestein, who had participated in the reflection process, came up with a proposal for a directive, later labeled the "Bolkestein Directive," that aimed at facilitating the internal market in services. In pushing forward his broader agenda – namely the realization of the internal market – Bolkestein wanted to remove obstacles against the internal market of services across several sectors including health. In its *Kohll/Decker* jurisprudence, the ECJ had found that health services were services according to the EC Treaty (see *Kohll*: para. 29, *Müller-Fauré/van Riet*: para. 103). Therefore, the Commission thought it was on safe ground when it included health services in the services directive. In Article 23 of the proposal it inserted a passage on "assumption of health care costs" that entailed four points and in which the Commission attempted to clarify the conditions for patient mobility.

---

on July 12, 2002 in a pre-litigation stage of the investigation process in order to verify the Member States' compliance in the domain of public health care services. Consequently, the objective was to ensure that Member States would take the necessary measures to comply with Community law as interpreted by the Court of Justice. Considering the fact that the Commission is in the process of the investigation, the Commission services were of the view that all Member States should be involved in a constructive dialogue to make full use of the pre-litigation stage and to encourage the Member States to conform voluntarily with their treaty obligations. Since the date of launching this questionnaire, a number of infringement procedures according to Article 226 EC Treaty have been initiated (against France, Sweden and Finland) and it cannot be excluded that more are to come. The investigations are therefore fully ongoing. Disclosure of the requested documents at this stage would therefore undermine the protection of the purpose of investigations of the Commission" (European Commission 2005b).

First of all, it suggested that out-patient health care received abroad does not require prior authorization. Second, the Member States were to authorize in-patient treatment abroad under certain conditions. Third, the reimbursement rates were specified. And fourth, domestic authorization procedures should conform to the overall authorization provisions of the Services Directive (see European Commission 2004b: 60–61). In Articles 4 to 10 of the directive, in addition, the Commission tried to define in-patient health care.

In Commission language, Article 23 "codifies and complements the well-established case law" of the ECJ (2004a: 2). According to the Commission, the objectives of Article 23 are

> *strengthening the rights of patients* with respect to the freedom to receive, under certain conditions, health care in another Member State; *increasing legal certainty and transparency* for patients and for Member States and their social security systems by clarifying a certain number of issues which to date are not sufficiently clear in the jurisprudence of the Court; and *giving the opportunity to the European legislator* to deal with practical issues left open by the jurisprudence. (2004a: 2, emphases in the original)

The majority of German insurance funds were against including health in the Services Directive. In 2004, the German Working Committee of the Central Associations of Statutory Health Insurance Funds criticized the fact that social security systems, non-economic services, and the ECJ jurisprudence were included in the Services Directive. According to them, the proposals made were incompatible with the characteristics of domestic social security systems. In addition, the organization of these belongs to the inviolable competence of EU Member States (see Working Committee of the Central Associations of Statutory Health Insurance Funds 2004: 19). The Supervisory Board of the AOK feared the broader implications combined with further ECJ jurisprudence, that is deregulation and privatization of domestic statutory health care systems and therefore strictly refused the interference by the Commission (see AOK Federal Association 2005).

Most of the Member States – even those who had already complied with the ECJ jurisprudence – strictly opposed the inclusion of the "particularly sensitive" health sphere into the Services Directive, they pleaded for excluding health. The "Gebhardt-Report," which summarized the amendments by the EP to the proposed Services Directive, suggested the deletion of Article 23 and of Articles 4 to 10 (see European Parliament 2005a: 55–56, 84–85). The proposed cancellation of Article 23 was justified as follows:

> As regards the assumption of health care costs, provisions aiming at transposing into law the case-law on patient mobility established by the European Court of Justice should not be covered by this Directive, which, when amended, will not deal with health services. The fact that certain Member States do not comply with

the case-law on patient mobility, as was indicated by the Commission, should be addressed in the framework of Regulation (EEC)1408/71 and/or within a separate and more appropriate secondary legislation based on the outcome of the high level reflection process on patient mobility and health care developments in the European Union. (European Parliament 2005a: 85)

Because of the continuing pressure by European interest organizations, the European Parliament, and several Member States, the health sphere and thus Article 23 were finally removed from the directive.[3] The EP voted for a condensed version of the directive in February 2006. In July of the same year, the Council adopted a common position, from which only Belgium and Lithuania abstained. After a three-year political struggle, the Bolkestein Directive finally passed the second and last reading of the EP on November 16, 2006, without including health.

The Commission ultimately failed to include the ECJ health services jurisprudence into the Services Directive. However, this is not the end of the story. In his statement on the Services Directive at the EP Plenary Session, made a few days before its vote in the EP, Charlie McCreevy, then Commissioner for Internal Market and Services, announced that the Commission would make a separate legislative proposal on health services to address the ECJ jurisprudence:

[I]f health services are excluded from the scope of the Directive this does not take away from the necessity to address the increasing jurisprudence of the Court of Justice in regard to patient mobility. A separate proposal from the Commission addressing this issue will therefore be necessary. (European Parliament 2006: 3)

Indeed, in September 2006 the Commission, now led by the new Commissioner of the DG Health and Consumer Protection Markos Kyprianou, launched a four-month public consultation on EU action on health services. This consultation aimed at gathering input from the Member States, the EP, and other stakeholders such as patients, health professionals, purchasers and providers of care, and was intended to end the legal uncertainty created by the ECJ jurisprudence and to improve the coordination between the health systems of Member States.

Draft Directive on the Application of Patients' Rights

The European Commission failed to include patient mobility rights in the Services Directive. In their refusals, the EP and the Council had invited the Commission instead to come up with a more specific instrument for the area of patient mobility. Therefore, the patient mobility agenda was referred to DG Health and Consumers, which then developed and propelled a separate directive only for this issue. First

---

3   The then European Commissioner for Internal Market and Services, Charlie McCreevy, announced the exclusion of health services from the Services Directive in a statement to the EP (2005a).

of all, the Commission started a public consultation in September 2006 in order to identify the major problems of cross-border care and to assess the opinions of various stakeholders about the issue.[4] This effort led in July 2008 to the adoption of a draft directive on the application of patients' rights in cross-border health care as part of the Renewed Social Agenda for the twenty-first century (see European Commission 2008).

Revising Coordination Regulations 1408/71 and 574/72

In addition to the Commission activities described above – the Consultation Process, the High Level Reflection Process and the High Level Group, the proposal for the Services Directive, and the proposal for a patients' rights directive – the European Coordination Regulations 1408/71 and 574/72 were amended routinely. Many of these reforms were caused by ECJ decisions. Some of these reforms took place in reaction to the *Kohll/Decker* jurisprudence.

Article 34 of Regulation 574/72 dealt with patients who needed health care in another Member State during a temporary stay and who had to pay cash in advance because the doctor refused to accept their E111 form. Here, the responsible insurance fund had to refund the costs up to 500 ECU (see Administrative Commission on Social Security for Migrant Workers 1996). In June 1999, the Administrative Commission on Social Security for Migrant Workers increased the sum reimbursable to €1,000, with the actual level to be set by each Member State (see Administrative Commission on Social Security for Migrant Workers 2000). Germany implemented this new level of reimbursement already in October 2001 and France in January 2002. The revision of Article 34 of Regulation 574/72 was caused by physicians in several countries refusing the E111 form and the wish to bypass the bureaucratic costs resulting from the cumbersome, normal bi-lateral billing mechanism provided for in the coordination regulation. However, there is also some evidence supported by the French Circular DSS/DACI/2002/31 that the new push for unbureaucratic reimbursement was meant to reflect the new ECJ jurisprudence and to prevent the growth of *Kohll*- and *Decker*-like cases.

In 2004, the new Regulation 883/2004 should have replaced Regulation 1408/71.[5] The recent ECJ jurisprudence on questions of coordination was the major impetus for this reform. The *Kohll/Decker* jurisprudence was part of this coordination package. Article 20(2) of Regulation 883/04 – in line with the *Kohll/Decker* jurisprudence – requires prior authorization for health care received abroad if the insured person cannot receive the treatment in her country "within a time-limit which is medically justifiable, taking into account his/her state of health and the probable course of his/her illness." Other important components of the

---

4   The responses to the consultation were summarized in a report (see European Commission 2006).

5   Regulation 883/2004 has entered into force in May 2004, but it is not yet applicable, because the procedural regulation and several annexes are still under discussion.

jurisprudence could not be incorporated into the new regulation because several Member States, especially the UK and Ireland, were strictly opposed to this.[6] Thus as soon as Regulation 883/04 will become applicable, it will coexist with *Kohll*- and *Decker*-like cases, which are based on the free movement of services.

Conclusion

The description of enforcement and management activities of the European Commission in the development of the *Kohll*/*Decker* jurisprudence has yielded three insights. First, Commission activities shape and interact with domestic implementation efforts. It kick-started the implementation process in France. Despite this success, it set aside a coherent infringement policy for efficiency reasons and, instead, opted for broader alternative management strategies to make Member States comply with the *Kohll*/*Decker* jurisprudence. The Commission tried to revive the topic through the High Level Reflection Process and the High Level Group, it attempted to codify the jurisprudence in the Services Directive and in a separate patients' rights directive, and it amended the relevant Coordination Regulations. A second conclusion thus is that the central instrument of the Commission to make Member States comply with European law, namely the infringement proceeding, is not always that central. Managerial activities are sometimes more prominent. In the follow-up to the *Kohll*/*Decker* jurisprudence, the Commission preferred management to enforcement. It deliberately abstained from pressing Member States too much with infringement proceedings but rather opted for a more encompassing approach. Thirdly, ECJ rulings may not only influence implementation at the domestic level but may also trigger important processes at the European level. Before *Kohll* and *Decker*, Member States pointed to the EC Treaty and the subsidiarity principle, arguing that health care and social security systems were an exclusively domestic issue. In their view the influence and competency of the European Union was restricted to public and occupational health.[7] Health ministers were not used to meeting each other in an EU context and to discussing health issues beyond public health; with *Kohll* and *Decker* this situation changed radically. Suddenly it became clear that, even though there was no direct European competency, Member States had to respect the indirect impact of internal market regulations when organizing their social security systems.

---

6   Bernhard Spiegel reported this about the negotiations in the Administrative Commission on Social Security of Migrant Workers at the Seminar "Training and Reporting on European Social Security" in Berlin on July 1, 2005.

7   Article 152(5) EC Treaty determines that "community action in the field of public health shall fully respect the responsibilities of the Member States for the organisation and delivery of health services and medical care."

Chapter 11

Making Sense of Implementation

This chapter is divided into four parts: First, I explain the main reasons for the initial non-implementation of the *Kohll/Decker* jurisprudence in Germany, France, and the UK. Second, I describe and explain the divergent pathways of implementation in the three Member States under study. Third, I analyze the most pertinent forces driving the implementation process. Fourth, I discuss the de-territorialization, internal de-structuring, and financial destabilization effects of this jurisprudence.

Explaining Non-implementation

In order to understand Member State implementation performance, it is necessary and instructive to first look at the reasons for their non-implementation. Governments/administrations, insurance funds and other health care actors stated four main reasons: the differences among social security systems; fears of financial consequences; fears of policy changes, which were contradicting entrenched social security principles; and fears of disturbing health care steering mechanisms.

Differences among Social Security Systems

Some EU Member States have centralized mechanisms, which are used to monopolize the interpretation of ECJ rulings and to decide on the further implications of those rulings.[1] However, in many EU countries, administrations do not necessarily draw conclusions from an individual ECJ decision for areas which are not directly linked to the case at hand. Since there is no legal *erga omnes* effect, the material doctrines that the ECJ develops in an individual case are usually not applied to other circumstances. The frequent reaction of national administrations is that a given ECJ case is unique and that their system, being so different, has no lesson to be learned from it.

In line with this behavior, the main argument against the non-implementation of the *Kohll/Decker* jurisprudence was the supposed non-transferability of its doctrines. Germany and the UK argued that the decisions referred to social

---

1 The Netherlands and the UK have such mechanisms. In the Dutch administration each ECJ decision is analyzed according to a fixed procedure by a group of civil servants that looks at the possible effects for national policy and legislation. Then a "*fiche*" is drawn and distributed among high civil servants and, if necessary, transmitted to the cabinet. This formal system amounts to an acceptance of the *erga omnes* effect of ECJ decisions.

security systems based on cash benefits, such as Luxembourg's, and not to systems based on in-kind benefits, like in Germany, or national health systems, like in the UK. The differences among the distinctive types of health care systems were considered sufficient to make the assumption that *Kohll* and *Decker* could not be transferred. Thus, Germany refused the implementation of these rulings. The German arguments against transferability weakened, though, after *Müller-Fauré/ van Riet* and *Geraets-Smits/Peerbooms*. These were cases from the Netherlands, which operates an in-kind benefit system. However, the Central Associations of Statutory Health Insurance Funds and the German administration emphasized more subtle system differences between Germany and the Netherlands. Throughout this whole period, the UK insisted that the jurisprudence could not be transferred to the NHS.

Fears of Financial Destabilization

In the discussion on the effects of the *Kohll/Decker* jurisprudence, fears surfaced in Germany, France, and the UK that its implementation would financially destabilize social security systems. First, patient mobility would create additional expenditures for the insurance funds. The funds would have to pay the amounts fixed domestically and would, in addition, have to finance foreign out-patient cases, which would mean an added financial burden. Second, even if significant in-patient treatments could be out-sourced to other EU countries, the domestic maintenance costs for hospitals and their equipment would remain the same, but foreign treatment costs would also need to be covered.

Territorial Restriction/In-kind Benefits

A third concern especially brought forward in Germany and the UK was that the implementation of the *Kohll/Decker* jurisprudence would break up the territorial enclosure of health care. The social security systems of all three Member States were stamped by the principle of territoriality, which was called into question by the ECJ decisions. In addition, Germany and the UK provided health care predominantly through in-kind benefits. The *Kohll/Decker* jurisprudence made an adjustment of this principle necessary.

Disturbed Health Care Steering Mechanisms

In all three Member States objections were raised that domestic health care steering mechanisms would be disturbed if *Kohll* and *Decker* were implemented. France limited its health care expenditures since the mid-1990s with the help of sanctioning mechanisms, which were aimed primarily at French physicians. The extension of this mechanism to the medical personnel of other EU countries seemed to be impossible. In the UK, the government sets clinical priorities. It feared that the implementation of the *Kohll/Decker* jurisprudence would either force it to increase the general budget or create injustices among patients, as some could get quicker treatment abroad although their clinical priority was considered to be lower. In Germany, the government feared that its health care steering instruments such as budget and quality regulations would be rendered ineffective.

Diverse Pathways of Implementation

The results of the three case studies in this book confirm previous findings that European requirements – here ECJ rulings – impact differently on domestic structures (see Héritier et al. 2001). Analyzing Germany, France and the UK, two main differences appear. First, the pathways through which the *Kohll/Decker* jurisprudence was implemented differed. While in Germany all happened in one big step, in France it was a slow and gradual process. Because the UK government constantly refused to apply the jurisprudence, its implementation was more unsettled and à la carte (see Table 11.1).

Table 11.1 Different implementation processes in Germany, France, and the UK

Germany	A quick, one-step implementation process (1998–2003)
	1. Refusal to implement *Kohll/Decker*: no transferability because of differences in the health care system (1998);
	2. Application of reimbursement practices to voluntarily insured by individual insurance funds (from 2002 onwards);
	3. Change of the administrative reimbursement practices by individual insurance funds (from 2003 onwards);
	4. Statutory Health Insurance Modernization Act (in force since January 2004).
France	**A slow, gradual implementation process (1998–2005)**
	1. Refusal to implement *Kohll/Decker*: common national and European strategy (ministerial letter from June 1998);
	2. Restrictive implementation of Decker, causing very few costs (circular in March 2001);
	3. Transitory extension of the implementation of the *Kohll/Decker* jurisprudence (circular in June 2003);
	4. Essentially full legal transposition into the CSS (decree in April 2005 and circular in May 2005);
	5. Full legal transposition into the CSP (decree in March 2006).

Table 11.1 continued

UK	An à-la-carte and unfinished implementation process (1998–2006)
	1. Refusal to implement *Kohll/Decker*: no transferability (expressed in 1998 and maintained until Watts);
	2. Reform of travel expenses regulations (statutory instrument, January 2002);
	3. Introduction of centralized pilot scheme to send patients abroad (January 2002);
	4. After its phase-out continuation by local health authorities (from 2002 onwards);
	5. Removal of the strict territorial restriction from the NHS Act 1977 (statutory instrument, November 2002);
	6. First Watts decision by the Administrative Court (October 2003);
	7. Change of the guidelines for patients (from 2003 onwards);
	8. Second Watts decision by the ECJ: change of the guidelines for patients (May 2006).

The second difference lies in the various instruments through which the jurisprudence was implemented. In 2003, the German government incorporated the *Kohll/Decker* jurisprudence into the Statutory Health Insurance Modernization Act, which had to pass the *Bundesrat*, the chamber of the *Länder*. In 1998, the French government determined its approach in a simple ministerial letter and continuously adapted its position in the following years in ministerial circulars. This process was concluded through two ministerial decrees and a procedural circular in 2005/06. The UK government, in legal and administrative terms, adjusted its NHS in minor ways, predominantly through governmental statutory instruments.

Driving Forces for the Implementation of the *Kohll/Decker* Jurisprudence: Competing and Complementary Explanations

A combination of factors led to the different patterns of implementation of ECJ jurisprudence in the three EU countries. This study confirms the results of studies by Falkner et al. about the implementation of six EU directives (2005: 26, 277, Chapter 14), and by Héritier et al. (2001: Chapter 8), which dealt with the differential impact of European legislation on domestic rail transport and road haulage policy.

The French government was mainly pushed along by the European Commission through several infringement proceedings, and by the decisions of its own national courts. In the case of Germany, the intensive preoccupation with the ECJ jurisprudence in numerous semi-official working groups slowly led to a gradual shift of the governmental position toward compliance with the jurisprudence. Once the main actors were convinced of the necessity to implement and national courts applied pressure, implementation moved forward. In the UK, or more precisely in England and Wales, the Administrative Court of the Queen's Bench Division of the High Court with its *Watts* decision was the main driving factor behind à-la-carte implementation of the *Kohll/Decker* jurisprudence.

Falkner and others identified three different "worlds of compliance": a world of law observance, a world of domestic politics, and a world of neglect. Each cluster of countries develops a distinct procedural pattern of implementing EU-induced reform requirements (see Falkner et al. 2005: Chapter 15). Countries of the world of law observance comply with EU-induced adaptation requirements because compliance per se is highly valued and overrides domestic concerns. The countries of the world of domestic politics are marked by cost-benefit reflections in each single case of adaptation to EU requirements, and domestic preferences and ideologies usually prevail in case of conflicts of interest. Finally, in the world of neglect the first typical reaction is inactivity because compliance is not seen as an obligation and only attained when powerful action from outside intervenes (see Falkner et al. 2005: 321–324). In this typology, Germany and the UK clearly belong to the world of domestic politics, whereas France is the "prime example of neglect" (see Falkner et al. 2005: 333–338).

Do the findings of this study for France, Germany and the UK support the thesis of the three worlds of compliance? From the available evidence, I cannot conclude that France was inactive and that "national arrogance" toward ECJ decisions prevailed. The French administration was aware of the ECJ rulings from very early on. It immediately refused to implement them but installed working groups to discuss the problems resulting from the jurisprudence. Finally, the Commission had to enforce compliance through infringement procedures. The French government only made a minor concession at first, and then implemented the jurisprudence incrementally.

In Germany, party political preferences played a role. The red-green coalition needed the consent of the CDU/CSU in the *Bundesrat* for implementing the *Kohll/Decker* jurisprudence in the Statutory Health Insurance Modernization Act in 2003, but only for the voluntarily insured. The extension of the implementation to all insured persons fit with the general political goals of the CDU/CSU, which favored patient sovereignty. Therefore, it demanded this additional reform in the negotiations with the government and succeeded in expanding the implementation.

In the UK, only those elements of the *Kohll/Decker* jurisprudence were implemented that fit with the general governmental policy of increased patient choice.

Goodness-of-Fit

Goodness-of-fit has been the most prominent, but also most criticized, approach to explain compliance with EU requirements (see Mastenbroek 2005 and Treib

2008). In this study, goodness-of-fit has served as a first analytical step, but it has not yielded conclusive insights.

In all three Member States patient mobility was not reflected sufficiently in the domestic legal provisions, while EU regulations applied to all of them equally. The *Kohll/Decker* jurisprudence required that the principle of territoriality, on which the legislation of the three Member States was built, be partially abandoned. All of them applied the prior authorization scheme, provided for in Regulation 1408/71, restrictively. France had a comparatively good substantive fit as it allowed for cash reimbursement. In Germany, this option was only provided to the voluntarily insured; the delivery of in-kind benefits prevailed. In the UK, cash reimbursement was virtually nonexistent. The potential financial costs for the three Member States varied: the underfunded UK-NHS with its long waiting lists and times had to expect the highest costs; the costs would most likely be minor in Germany and France. The fit/misfit of the three EU countries with the requirements of the *Kohll/Decker* jurisprudence is summarized in Table 11.2. If we add the legal policy misfit to the expected financial costs, the overall adaptational pressure was medium in France and high in Germany and the UK.

Table 11.2 Overall misfit

EU Member State	Degree of legal misfit	Politics/ polity misfit	(Expected) Financial costs	Degree of overall misfit
France	*Medium*	*None*	*Low*	*Medium*
	• Strict principle of territoriality; • Restrictive application of the prior authorization scheme of Regulation 1408/71.		• No waiting lists; • Low numbers of patients traveling abroad.	
Germany	*High*	*None*	*Low*	*High*
	• Strict principle of territoriality; • Restrictive application of the prior authorization scheme of Regulation 1408/71; • Cash reimbursement only for voluntarily insured.		• No waiting lists; • Low numbers of patients traveling abroad.	
UK	*High*	*None*	*High*	*High*
	• Very strict principle of territoriality; • Restrictive application of the prior authorization scheme of Regulation 1408/71; • No cash reimbursement.		• Underfunded; • Long waiting times and lists; • High numbers of patients traveling abroad.	

Note: A high degree of misfit in one of the three dimensions is rated as high overall misfit.

The case studies have shown that goodness-of-fit can only partly explain the pace, timing, and extent of implementing the *Kohll/Decker* jurisprudence. We would have expected France to be the first to implement the ECJ jurisprudence. Indeed, among the three EU countries studied, France took the first implementation steps. Germany followed shortly thereafter and was even quicker in complying fully with the jurisprudence. The UK was the most reluctant to implement the jurisprudence. All three countries had to weaken to some extent the territorial principle, a cornerstone of their health care legislation.

In the static institutional fit/misfit of the three Member States the ECJ jurisprudence is not very influential; therefore, we have to conceive fit/misfit more dynamically. In both the UK and Germany the *Kohll/Decker* jurisprudence fit with domestic demands for patient sovereignty and patient choice. Demands by patients to receive treatment in another EU country and to be reimbursed could not be totally dismissed if, at the same time, the government pushed an agenda of patient choice, as in the UK. Similarly, the German government could not (re)introduce the freedom of choice between cash benefits and in-kind benefits without allowing for an extension to foreign cases. If it would have done so, the arguments that such a change would be a breach of principle could not be maintained.

The goodness-of-fit argument has been a very prominent determinant for explaining implementation of EU rules since the late 1990s. However, my results also support those who criticize it: goodness-of-fit cannot satisfactorily explain the implementation of the *Kohll/Decker* jurisprudence in Germany, France and the UK. But the goodness-of-fit concept and its operationalization provide a useful analytical tool to check alternative explanations like those presented in the following analysis.

Legal and Political Mobilization through Organized Interest Groups

According to Lisa Conant, the variety of domestic and European policy responses to innovative legal interpretation of the ECJ can be best explained by different patterns of legal and political mobilization to support or oppose the implementation of legal doctrines. These variable patterns are "a function of variations in the aggregation of interests and institutional support" (2003: 33). The legal and political mobilization of pressure, which has to overcome obstructive Member State policy responses, "derives from the activism of organized societal actors and the responsiveness of public institutions that support legal claims." These activities consist of, amongst others, "strategic litigation campaigns of copycat cases, the mass filing of parallel claims before bureaucracies, the systematic prosecution of parallel cases by enforcement agencies, and the lobbying of officials and elected representatives" (Conant 2003: 3).

In contrast to the telecommunications and electricity sectors, in social benefits – especially for migrants – Conant identified three prevailing strategies of national governments to deal with ECJ decisions: first, "contained compliance," that is applying legal innovation in single cases only instead of acknowledging wide-ranging implications; second, "preemptive design of social measures," that is the construction of European and domestic law to avoid interference by ECJ rulings; and third, "legislative overrule," "when member states directly overturn the ECJ via treaty revision or statutory reform" (Conant 2003: 32–33 and 192).

Conant observed that, like in the United States, in the EU "business interests are much better organized than less privileged groups, including labor, consumer, and environmental groups" (2003: 28). Patients in the EU do not have powerful interest organizations that speak on their behalf. However, there are single interest organizations at the European level. There is, for instance the European Public Health Alliance (EPHA), a loose alliance of non-governmental and other non-for-profit organizations that promote and protect the health interests of European citizens and monitor European health policies.[2] The *Centre Européen des Consommateurs/ Europäische Verbraucherzentrale* in the German city of Kehl, which is separated by the Rhine from Strasbourg, is an example of a bi-national French-German association that provides consumers with legal advice and information.[3] Other actors in the health care sector clearly have more influential interest groups. It would be beyond the scope of this study to detail these various interest groups and their strategic position in the EU institutional configuration. The insurance funds of EU Member States for instance are organized in the European Social Insurance Platform (ESIP), or the more encompassing *Association Internationale de la Mutualité* (AIM).[4] The organizational capacity of patients and their advocates, and consequently their prospects for successful legal and political mobilization to achieve the implementation of the ECJ jurisprudence on patient mobility, are relatively insufficient.

I could not analyze systematically which groups, if any, were backing the individual national court and ECJ cases that were part of the *Kohll/Decker*

---

2   EPHA represents over 90 non-governmental and other non-for-profit organizations that work on public health issues in Europe (http://www.epha.org).

3   The *Centre Européen des Consommateurs/Europäische Verbraucherzentrale* resulted from the merging of a German and a French consumer protection association in 1993 with the launch of the Single European Market. The Center has four broad missions that are tackled on the European and the national level: informing and advising consumers, reaching out court settlements on cross-border consumer disputes, promoting mediation and conciliation, and raising the awareness and understanding on consumer issues.

4   ESIP was created in 1996. It represents a transnational alliance of over 30 European social security organizations. Its official goals are reinforcing solidarity-based social insurance systems and maintaining the quality of European social protection. ESIP tries to facilitate the dialogue and the exchange of information between the different domestic social security institutions. Common positions are developed from this exchange and they influence the decision-making process in the EU. AIM was set up in 1950. It represents European, Southern American, Central and Eastern Asian, Middle Eastern, and African mutualist organizations. AIM serves as a platform to exchange information and know-how among its members and to represent and defend its common principles in European and international institutions.

jurisprudence and the ensuing administrative and legislative changes. However, there is convincing evidence that legal and political mobilization efforts were rather unsystematic and non-strategic. As concerns the *Kohll/Decker* ECJ jurisprudence, two aspects are striking. First, many EU Member States were involved with one or two cases: Belgium (1), France (1), Germany (1), Greece (1), Luxembourg (2), the Netherlands (2), Spain (2), and the UK (1). It follows that there was, secondly, no country from which ECJ cases originated *en masse*. Looking at the national court cases that were in the pipeline, we observe for our three Member States that in the UK there was only one case, in Germany a few cases, and in France a larger number of cases. Looking at the ECJ and national court cases together, systematic legal mobilization did not take place. Concerning political mobilization, the following effects could be discerned: in the UK, the changes in legislation and administrative practice harkened back to, amongst other things, a major media campaign fueled by diverse interest groups. In Germany, two insurance funds (TK and SBK) initiated one national court case each. The CDU/CSU wanted to please the medical interest groups, therefore it pushed for the extension of the originally rather small changes to the German Statutory Health Insurance Modernization Act in 2003.

If we follow Conant's argument – that in the absence of powerful interest representation a follow-through of ECJ jurisprudence, i.e. national adjustment of law and policy, is unlikely – the *Kohll/Decker* jurisprudence should have been predominantly contained and circumscribed by the Member States. However, the jurisprudence triggered considerable legislative and administrative implementation efforts. An explanation for this that relies merely on legal and political mobilization does not give us sufficient leverage to explain the implementation. Therefore, we have to look into other pertinent explanations, which will be done in the following subsections.

The National Judiciary: Sword of ECJ Rulings

The behavior of national courts as a bridge between the EU and the Member States has been described as a central variable in explaining the implementation of ECJ rulings (see Golub 1996, Alter 1998, Weiler 1999). The three case studies on France, the UK and Germany show that national courts influenced the implementation of the *Kohll/Decker* jurisprudence, though to a differing degree. I now discuss this influence and to what extent it was relevant.

In France, courts at all levels, including the *Cour de Cassation*, accepted and applied the doctrines elaborated by the ECJ in the *Kohll/Decker* jurisprudence. As early as 2000, the *Tribunal des Affaires de Sécurité Sociale du Bas Rhin* applied *Kohll* and *Decker*. The *Cour d'Appel de Colmar* affirmed these rulings in 2002/03. In addition, the *Cour de Cassation* set important precedents for the French government and administration in decisions such as *Magnan* in 2002 and *Gérona* in 2004. The government faced further court cases. In order to end the legal uncertainty caused by the judicial activism of the national courts and the reluctance of other courts to follow this activism, and to remedy the resulting non-uniform application of the law, it implemented the jurisprudence fully and changed the relevant legal provisions in the *Code de la Sécurité Sociale* and the *Code de la Santé Publique* in 2005/06. *Inizan*, referred to the ECJ by the *Tribunal des Affaires de Sécurité Sociale de Nanterre* in 2000, did not decisively influence the legislative and administrative implementation in France, as it did not declare void French provisions concerning in-patient treatment.

The unofficial policy of the UK government entailed preventing domestic court cases on patient mobility. It deliberately preempted upcoming cases by using its wide discretionary power to reimburse patients who had received health care abroad. Nevertheless, this preventive strategy toward national court cases did not work out entirely. It only needed one court case to bring this strategy down. The Administrative Court of first instance in *Watts* explicitly used the *Kohll/Decker* jurisprudence, notably *Geraets-Smits/Peerbooms* and *Müller-Fauré/van Riet*, without referring the case to the ECJ, and challenged the legislative provisions in the UK. The government appealed against this first-instance decision and "achieved" a referral to the ECJ by the Court of Appeal in the hope that the *Kohll/Decker* jurisprudence would be declared inapplicable to the UK NHS. However, the government ultimately lost the judicial battle and then faced a situation in which it could not perpetuate its overall obstructive attitude. Even before the ECJ decision in *Watts*, the UK government had been forced by the Administrative Court ruling to move toward implementing the jurisprudence. In *Watts* the ECJ left it to the UK national courts to decide case by case whether "undue delay" was given. The ECJ provided the national courts only with several criteria to determine what is "due":

> an objective medical assessment of the patient's medical condition, the history
> and probable course of his illness, the degree of pain he is in and/or the nature
> of his disability at the time when the request for authorisation was made or
> renewed. (ECJ, *Watts*: para. 119)

With this case-by-case approach, the UK courts have considerable discretion and power in the future. However, legal certainty for the individuals will suffer.

In Germany, the *Siemens Betriebskrankenkasse* (SBK) and the *Techniker Krankenkasse* (TK) both initiated legal proceedings to prevent the government and the Federal Insurance Authority from blocking the implementation of the jurisprudence. The SBK explicitly wanted to bring its case concerning a refused statute change to the ECJ. However, the Social Court Munich denied this request in 2003: a similar German case, namely *Bautz*, was already pending before the Court and, therefore, it suspended the SBK case in order to await the results of the ECJ ruling. The two German cases, *Weller* and *Bautz*, were referred to the ECJ in March and October 2002. The first was referred by the first-instance Social Court Augsburg and the second by the highest social court in Germany, the *Bundessozialgericht*. Both cases were withdrawn in May and April 2004 with the reasoning that the ECJ had given sufficient indications on how to interpret Article 49 EC Treaty and Regulation 1408/71. None of these national court cases was decided before the *Kohll/Decker* jurisprudence was transposed. However, there is sufficient evidence that these domestic cases did aid in convincing the government to include the *Kohll/Decker* jurisprudence in the Statutory Health Insurance Modernization Act in 2003. *Leichtle*, referred to the ECJ by the first-instance *Verwaltungsgericht Sigmaringen* in 2001, did not decisively affect the implementation of the *Kohll/Decker* jurisprudence.

Karen Alter has ascribed a special role to the lower courts that might become empowered through ECJ rulings (1998a). In France, the *Cour de Cassation* – the highest French civil and criminal court – in particular accepted and applied the *Kohll/Decker* jurisprudence and pushed the government to move toward its legal implementation. In the UK, the first legal initiative came from a lower national court that applied the ECJ doctrines, arguing that the Court had already given sufficient indication to assume that the patient mobility principles are also to be applied to the UK NHS. This advance was partly undone by the Court of Appeal. It referred *Watts* with many detailed preliminary questions to the ECJ to clarify whether the doctrines elaborated in the *Kohll/Decker* jurisprudence were to be applied to the UK. In Germany, a low and a high court each referred one case to the ECJ. Both were withdrawn as soon as the national courts found that the ECJ had clarified the unresolved questions. Of the ECJ patient mobility cases in other EU Member States, some were referred by low, some by high courts.[5] There is no clear pattern in the *Kohll/Decker* jurisprudence as regards the supposed lower-higher inter-court competition, although lower courts have been quite active in this jurisprudence.

All three investigated EU Member States started to change their domestic laws and practices before they faced an ECJ ruling on their country; moreover, the lower courts and the *Cour de Cassation* in France, and the UK Administrative Court, autonomously applied the doctrines elaborated by the ECJ. The national courts obviously thought that they had enough indications at hand to interpret European law on patient mobility without an express ECJ decision on their Member State. This evidence fits with Conant's claim that national courts most often apply European law without formally interacting with the ECJ (2003: 81).

5　The Luxembourg *Cour de Cassation* (*Kohll*) is a high court whereas the *Conseil Arbitral des Assurances Sociales* (*Decker*) is a social court of first instance. The Belgian Higher Labor Court, the *Cour du Travail de Mons* (*Vanbraekel*), is a court of second instance. The Dutch *Arrondissements-Rechtbank te Roermond* (*Geraets-Smits/Peerbooms*) is a court of first instance whereas the *Centrale Raad van Beroep* (*Müller-Fauré/van Riet*) is a social jurisdiction high court. The Spanish *Juzgado de lo Social no 20 de Madrid* (*Keller*) is a social court of first instance, whereas the *Tribunal Superior de Justicia de Cantabria* (*Acereda Herrera*) is the Cantabrian High Court. Finally, the Greek *Diikitiko Protodikio Athinon* (*Stamatelaki*) is an administrative court of first instance.

In conclusion, the national judiciary was the sword of the ECJ in implementing the *Kohll/Decker* jurisprudence. This clearly indicates that national courts are a key variable for understanding and explaining national implementation: they are able to kick-start and accelerate implementation. As soon as national courts accept and apply the doctrines elaborated by the ECJ, governments face accomplished facts. Such national rulings in combination with contradicting legislative provisions and other more reluctant courts created judicial uncertainty in the Member States. The domestic legislator was, therefore, forced to implement the ECJ rulings and to change the law on the books in order to decrease the judicial uncertainty. These results seem to substantiate my initial working hypothesis in Chapter 2 that national court activities kick-start and accelerate legislative and administrative implementation.

The possibility to turn to (social) courts varies among the three researched Member States. Nonetheless, for accelerating compliance it did not make a difference whether in the UK a single court or in France several courts of different instances ruled in accordance with the ECJ jurisprudence. The result, namely accelerated compliance with ECJ rulings through national court rulings, was quite similar.

As a consequence, the behavior of national courts has to be at the very centre of investigation when looking at compliance with EC law, and particularly ECJ rulings. If governments and administrations hamper implementation, and domestic political considerations are incompatible with the ECJ jurisprudence, and if ECJ requirements are incompatible with existing domestic structures and policies, national courts can resolve non-compliance through forcing the legislator to end legal uncertainty with a multiplication of national court cases that contradict domestic legislation.

The European Commission: (Unsuccessful) Management Strategies

The activities of the European Commission have been described as a negligible factor for explaining implementation (see Falkner et al. 2005). The infringement policy of the Commission concerning the *Kohll/Decker* jurisprudence was not very ambitious. France, in a ministerial letter to its insurance funds and undeniably concerned by the jurisprudence, made the mistake of speaking expressly against the application of the jurisprudence. France was the only EU country where the Commission pursued an active and successful infringement policy. France is a typical laggard in complying with European law. It seems that the Commission treated it more strictly than other Member States.

Overall, the Member State rejection of the jurisprudence was overwhelming. To avoid protracted individual infringement proceedings against all non-compliant Member States, the Commission pursued a more managerial way. It came up with several initiatives: The Commission started a Consultation Process and a High Level Reflection Process, followed by a High Level Group, in order to make Member States aware of their obligations to the jurisprudence and to sensitize them to the requirements of adapting to it. In order to ensure Member State compliance with the *Kohll/Decker* jurisprudence, the DG Internal Market tried to incorporate the ECJ doctrines into secondary European law, the Services Directive and a patients' rights directive.

Although the Commission ultimately was not very successful in making Member States comply with the *Kohll/Decker* jurisprudence, its management initiatives made the Member States aware of the interdependence of their social security systems. Already the simple fact that health ministers met and discussed patient mobility regularly can, therefore, be seen as a political success.[6]

Domestic Politics as Driving Force

Falkner and others (2005) found that domestic political preferences are important for explaining Member State compliance. Complying with a European requirement thus is not a matter of principle but depends on national political priorities. Germany and the UK are classified by Falkner and her colleagues as EU Member States that clearly belong to the "world of domestic politics." In both countries, party political considerations are said to play a major role in implementing EU social policy directives (see Falkner et al. 2005: 333–334). France, in contrast, was perceived as "the prime example of neglect motivated by a kind of national 'arrogance'" characterized by inertia in implementation (see Falkner et al. 2005: 338). Do my findings support or contradict these viewpoints?

In the UK, three major interrelated political health agendas – increasing patient choice, expanding private sector involvement in the NHS, and the overall aim of reducing waiting lists and times – interacted with the implementation efforts. The UK attributed major legislative and administrative changes and some new pilot schemes to the ECJ jurisprudence. This was a deliberate strategy to blame the EU. The "à la carte implementation" stemmed from the insight that it would be impossible to completely reject the jurisprudence. However, the justifications used

---

6 At the Health Council Meeting in June 2006 during the Austrian Presidency common values and principles that underpin EU health systems were discussed as a response to the ECJ jurisprudence and Commission activities. EU Health Ministers were still rather skeptical about EU interventions in the health area. In the Council Conclusions EU Health Ministers stated: "We strongly believe that developments in this area [health care, AJO] should result from political consensus, and not solely from case law," and "it is for individual member states to determine their own approach with specific interventions tailored to the health system concerned" (2006). At an "Informal Council Meeting" in April 2007, EU Health Ministers met in the German town of Aachen to discuss patient mobility. The Notes of the Trio Presidency still considered health a predominantly national competence but stated that health care policies – as an initial example patient mobility – should be taken forward at the EU level. The Presidency postulated that "[t]he case-law of the Court of Justice of the European Communities and the principles and conditions with regard to the reimbursement of health care abroad have to be codified and clarified in some respects" (German EU Presidency 2007a).

domestically cannot be found in the statements aimed at the ECJ and its fellow EU Member States. The UK government argued constantly that, in principle, the *Kohll/Decker* jurisprudence was non-transferable to its NHS.

In Germany, the CDU/CSU and the FDP pursued an agenda of increasing patient sovereignty in the statutory health care system. The governing red-green coalition needed the approval of the CDU/CSU to the Statutory Health Insurance Modernization Act in the *Bundesrat*. Therefore, it went further in implementing the ECJ jurisprudence than its own initial proposal would suggest. The *de facto* grand coalition between the government and the CDU/CSU extended the range of cash benefits to all insured persons and to health care received abroad.

In France, the political agenda of the government opposed patient mobility as promoted by the ECJ jurisprudence. However, the French health care system lacked capacities especially in border regions. For the French government it seemed reasonable to increase cross-border cooperation to cope with these existing shortages. Accordingly, it made treaties with the neighboring countries and tried to restrict patient mobility to close cross-border cooperation. However, the principles espoused by the ECJ went far beyond this cross-border cooperation, which is why the French government constantly opposed them.

To sum up, in the UK the domestic political priorities of the government and the opposition were heavily reflected in how the *Kohll/Decker* jurisprudence was implemented. In Germany and France this was less the case.

Fine-tuning the Jurisprudence: The ECJ's Judicial Activism and Self-restraint

In the *Kohll/Decker* jurisprudence both judicial activism and self-restraint can be detected. The ECJ was an activist court in that it applied, against the unified interests of EU Member States, the basic freedoms of services and goods to health care and thereby challenged national welfare states. However, when it came to the actual design of this intrusion into the domestic sphere of social protection, the Court exercised considerable self-restraint by limiting the impact of its decisions largely to the less costly ambulatory sector and by accepting – contrary to other policy areas – justifications of an economic nature for the restriction of free movement.[7]

Why did the ECJ restrain itself? First, from the beginning most Member States reacted very negatively toward the *Kohll/Decker* jurisprudence and refused

---

7   Before the 1990s, the ECJ rejected in numerous cases that aims of an economic nature were able to justify restrictions of free movement (see for example Case C-352/85 para. 30; Case C-353/89 or Case C-398/95 para. 23). In its reasoning in *Kohll* and *Decker* the ECJ signalled a change in this orthodox position. The ECJ held in *Kohll* that the maintenance of a balanced medical and hospital service could fall within the grounds of public health under Article 46 EC (para. 50). The acceptance of justifications by the ECJ can be seen in the follow-up jurisprudence in which the Court was interested to obtain evidence from Member States with regard to the impact of its former rulings.

to implement it. With the ECJ's fine-tuning and its application to one group of Member States while maintaining legal uncertainty for the others, the united rejection started to crumble. This development can be seen in the French position in the *Watts* proceeding. In earlier cases the French government had been fiercely opposed to the *Kohll/Decker* jurisprudence. Nevertheless, it finally implemented the jurisprudence. In *Watts*, the French government did not back the position of the UK and all the other national health systems but claimed that the *Kohll/Decker* jurisprudence also had to be applied to the national health systems. A second reason for the ECJ's self-restraint was that the Member State reactions sensitized the Court to their concerns. It is plausible to assume that in the ECJ proceedings, Member State governments succeeded in persuading the Court of the peculiar nature of national social protection systems and the dangers of an unrestricted application of the basic freedoms, for example by providing empirical "evidence."[8] The ECJ thus seems to have recognized the sensitivities in this area, which is one of the last exclusive domains of the Member States. In return, Member States implemented the narrowed requirements of the jurisprudence.

In Germany, France and the United Kingdom (UK) the fine-tuning of the jurisprudence by the ECJ – and along with that ECJ self-restraint – influenced implementation processes and outcomes, though to differing degrees.

In Germany, widespread skepticism toward ECJ rulings in general and the *Kohll/Decker* jurisprudence in particular hampered implementation. *Kohll* and *Decker* were seen as an example of "activist" ECJ policy-making. Horst Seehofer, German Federal Minister of Health, commented on *Kohll* and *Decker* in a press release on the very day they were issued. He considered them to be highly problematic (see Federal Ministry of Health 1998a). In the Administrative Commission on Social Security for Migrant Workers, Seehofer was less diplomatic and, according to participants, called for the immediate revision of the rulings. The German Ministry of Health, most of the statutory health insurance funds and also medical associations perceived the rulings as an intrusion into a sphere that was held to be under exclusive control of the Member States: the organization of the fundamental principles of the social protection system. They feared that not only out-patient but also unlimited and unconditioned mobility in the in-patient sector would be triggered by the ECJ decisions. In this case the political and, more importantly, financial costs would have been considerable. Therefore, as a matter of principle, they initially rejected the entire jurisprudence on patient mobility. In the proceedings before the Court in the follow-up cases, the German government reiterated its position that health care services were not of an economic nature.[9]

---

8 According to the Opinion of Advocate General Ruiz-Jarabo Colomer, the Dutch government informed the Court in the oral hearing in *Müller-Fauré/van Riet* that about 14.000 insured persons had made use of treatment abroad although prior authorization was still required (see footnote 30 of his Opinion).

9 After the ECJ delivered *Müller-Fauré/van Riet* in 2003, Germany stopped commenting on the follow-up cases (see Table 5.1).

If the Court was to decide differently, the German government found prior authorization procedures justified in the in-patient sector.

In the follow-up rulings, notably *Geraets-Smits/Peerbooms* (2001) and *Müller-Fauré/van Riet* (2003), the ECJ confined the scope of the jurisprudence *de facto* to the out-patient sector, that is the Court extended the scope in principle to hospital cases, however, only under restrictive conditions. This narrowing down of the original broad *Kohll/Decker* doctrines convinced the German Ministry of Health and the other health care actors that the ECJ, first, acknowledged the complexities and specificities of domestic health care systems and, second, took into account Member States' concerns about the *Kohll/Decker* jurisprudence. Consequently, the skepticism toward the ECJ in general, and the *Kohll/Decker* jurisprudence in particular, decreased substantially. The self-restrained ECJ approach thus helped to overcome the most abrasive lines of resistance and paved the way for implementing the *Kohll/Decker* jurisprudence.

Despite the initial resistance, in 2003, the German government incorporated the requirements of the jurisprudence into its fifth book of the social code (*Sozialgesetzbuch*, SGB) with the help of the Statutory Health Insurance Modernization Act.

The UK government, similar to Germany and France, rejected the *Kohll* and *Decker* rulings and their transferability to the National Health Service (NHS). The refinement of the jurisprudence by the ECJ influenced both the implementation process and outcome in the UK. *Vanbraekel* and particularly *Geraets-Smits/ Peerbooms* clarified in 2001 that, first, in-kind benefit systems fell within the scope of the free movement of services, and that, second, if a Member State could not provide a treatment "without undue delay," it had to refer the patient to another Member State. Because of the NHS logic of rationing health care, waiting times for an operation were extremely long for UK patients. The question of what "undue delay" meant in practice was therefore of great importance to the UK government. The rulings *Vanbraekel* and *Geraets-Smits/Peerbooms* forced the UK to set in motion the first implementation steps in 2001/02. The ECJ follow-up ruling *Müller-Fauré/van Riet* in 2003 had additional direct consequences for the UK case *Watts*. The first-instance Administrative Court of the Queen's Bench Division of the High Court ruled in *Watts* that *Müller-Fauré/van Riet* was applicable to the NHS. Although the government appealed the national court decision, it set further steps toward compliance.

In France, the constant refinement of the jurisprudence was not decisive for the pace of the implementation, but all the more for the outcome. The French case *Inizan* (2003), which was part of the fine-tuning process, was an additional element to take into account for the French government but not of great importance. Since the ECJ narrowed down the original doctrines, the changes in the French social code remained minor.

To sum up, the ECJ's fine-tuning influenced the implementation process in Germany, to a lesser degree in the UK. More importantly, the implementation outcome was affected by the fine-tuning of the *Kohll* and *Decker* rulings. All three countries allowed patient mobility to a certain degree, but only under restrictive conditions. Since the ECJ narrowed down the doctrinal content of the original rulings and limited the scope *de facto* to out-patient care, the actual effect diminished accordingly. Ultimately, the tremendous impact which was postulated by legal and political science scholarship, that is the massive change of the institutional configuration of domestic health care systems, did not come true.

Interplay of Different Implementation Explanations

The results of the preceding sections are summarized and represented in Table 11.3. We have seen that several factors explain the implementation of the *Kohll/ Decker* jurisprudence: national court rulings, domestic political preferences, the management and enforcement activities of the European Commission, and the fine-tuning of the ECJ jurisprudence.

Table 11.3 Cross-national variation of implementation: The empirical evidence

Competing explanations for cross-national variation of implementation processes	Process/Mechanism	Explanatory power for Germany, France, and the United Kingdom
Goodness-of-Fit Model Match or Mismatch Model	Congruence or incongruence of European arrangements and existing legal and administrative domestic policies and structures.	Germany: High misfit, but comparatively quick one-step implementation; France: Medium misfit, slow gradual implementation; UK: High misfit, selective unfinished implementation.
Legal and political mobilization	Different patterns of interest aggregation and institutional support.	Germany: Moderate legal and political mobilization; France: No legal and political mobilization; UK: No legal mobilization, moderate political mobilization.
National judicial system	National courts adjudicate cases in accordance with ECJ jurisprudence and force the legislator or the administration to end judicial uncertainty.	Germany, France, and the UK: National courts played a crucial role.
Fine-tuning of the jurisprudence by the ECJ in further decisions	In the process of differentiating its jurisprudence the ECJ exercises self-restraint and thus facilitates compliance by EU Member States.	France and Germany: The de-facto exclusion of in-patient care from the free movement of patients was crucial for the implementation.

Table 11.3 continued

Competing explanations for cross-national variation of implementation processes	Process/Mechanism	Explanatory power for Germany, France, and the United Kingdom
Influence of the European Commission	Overall interaction between the European Commission and the EU Member States (formal and informal).	France: Major role.
Domestic politics	Domestic political preferences prevail over European requirements and each case of implementing an ECJ ruling tends to happen based on a fresh cost-benefit estimate.	Germany: Increased patient responsibility fitted with the jurisprudence; UK: Patient choice agenda, involvement of the private sector, and reduction of waiting lists fitted partly with the jurisprudence.

The case studies have shown that several factors together led to the implementation of the jurisprudence on patient mobility in the three Member States (see Table 11.4).

Table 11.4 Weighted influence of the major explanations for implementation

	Germany	France	UK
Domestic politics	+	+	+++
National courts	+	+++	+++
Activities of the European Commission		+++	
Fine-tuning of the jurisprudence by the ECJ	+++	++	+

Note: + = moderate influence; ++ = strong influence; +++ = very strong influence.

In Germany, the ECJ's refinement of its jurisprudence, and to a lesser extent the activities of national courts and domestic political preferences of the CDU/CSU, eased implementation. In France, it was a combination of national court rulings, Commission infringement procedures, the ECJ's fine-tuning, and to a lesser degree domestic political priorities. In the UK, domestic political preferences together with the *Watts* ruling by the Administrative Court forced the government into its first implementation steps. The fine-tuning of the jurisprudence by the ECJ contributed to the implementation only indirectly.

In addition, the four factors have a distinctive function in the implementation process, which is different in every case study (see Table 11.5). They either kick-started, accelerated, or helped to finalize the implementation of the *Kohll/Decker* jurisprudence.

Table 11.5 Function of alternative explanations in implementation

		Domestic politics	National courts	Activities of the European Commission	Fine-tuning of the jurisprudence by the ECJ
Germany	Kick-start				+++
	Acceleration		+		+
	Finalization	+			
France	Kick-start			+++	
	Acceleration		+++	++	
	Finalization	+	+++	++	+
United Kingdom	Kick-start	+++	+++		+
	Acceleration				
	Finalization				

Note: + = moderate influence; ++ = strong influence; +++ = very strong influence.

De-territorialization, Internal De-structuring and Financial Destabilization: Much Ado about Nothing?

In the following part, I analyze the changes of legislation and administrative practices in Germany, France, and the UK (summarized in Table 11.6) that were directly caused by the *Kohll/Decker* jurisprudence. I can then answer the question of whether and to what extent the ECJ jurisprudence led to de-territorialization, internal de-structuring and financial destabilization effects. De-territorialization is about the weakening or abolishing of the territorial principle embedded in national health systems, de-structuring about the concomitant effects on the internal functioning of those systems, and destabilization about the financial effects. All three elements together make an assessment of the overall impact of the *Kohll/ Decker* jurisprudence possible.

Table 11.6 Legislative and administrative changes caused by the
***Kohll/Decker* jurisprudence**

	Legislative changes	Administrative changes
Germany		
2001		Reimbursement for voluntarily insured by some insurance funds.
No exact date		Reimbursement of ambulatory care for all insured by some insurance funds.
2003	SGB V, Paragraph 13(2) changed, Paragraph 13(4–6) inserted: cash benefits are optional; reimbursement of ambulatory treatment received abroad; for hospital treatment, prior authorization is still necessary; SGB V, Paragraph 18 changed: differentiation between EU and non-EU cases; SGB V, Paragraph 140(e) inserted: contracts between German insurance funds and foreign providers.	
France		
2001		Circular DSS/DACI/2001/120: reimbursement of optical products purchased abroad and prescribed in France, very low French tariff.
2003		Circular DSS/DACI/2003/286: reimbursement of registered medications and medical equipment purchased abroad; reimbursement of ambulatory treatment received abroad, very low French tariff.
2004		Circular DSS/DACI/2004/134: case by case reimbursement of non-registered medical products.
2004	CSS, L. 332–3 changed: differentiation between EU and non-EU cases.	
2004	CSP, L. 6211–2–1 inserted: reimbursement of medical analysis in EU/EEA laboratories is possible, administrative authorization is necessary.	
2005	CSS, R. 332–2 changed and R. 332–3 to 6 inserted: reimbursement of ambulatory treatment received abroad.	
2006	CSP, R. 6211–46 to 56 inserted: authorization of EU/EEA analysis laboratories.	

Table 11.6 continued

	Legislative changes	Administrative changes
France		
2006	CSP, L. 6211–2–1 changed: reimbursement of medical analysis in EU/EEA laboratories without administrative authorization.	
UK		
No exact date		Discretionary reimbursement in individual cases.
2001 to date		Centralized pilot scheme for patient referral; individual local authorities continue to refer patients abroad.
2002	NHS Act 1977, Statutory Instrument 4043: change of travel expenses refund; NHS Act 1977, Statutory Instrument 2759: removal of territorial restriction for Secretary of State; NHS and Community Care Act 1990, Statutory Instrument 2759: removal of territorial restriction for NHS Trusts.	
2003 to date		New guidance to the public and local health care commissioners.

De-territorialization:
The Principle of Territoriality Remains Intact but is Further Weakened

A "trend" toward an opening of territorially closed health care systems has been described by a number of authors (see Ferrera 2005, Leibfried 2005). The principles elaborated by the ECJ in its jurisprudence served as evidence for this argument. However, these authors did not look at actual legislative changes. Therefore, the question remains whether and how these principles have been translated into domestic legislation and into the practice of Member States. Has the implementation of the *Kohll/Decker* jurisprudence further weakened or destroyed the territorial demarcation lines of domestic health care systems?

I have shown in the empirical chapters that prior to the *Kohll/Decker* jurisprudence all three countries studied had more or less strict territorial principles inscribed into their domestic legislation. The European Coordination Regulations for the Social Security of Migrant Workers – progressively extended to all citizens – as well as other provisions indeed made exceptions from the principle of territoriality. However, the principle itself remained untouched by these exceptions. The German *Sozialgesetzbuch V (SGB V)*, the French *Code de la Sécurité Sociale* (CSS) and the *Code de la Santé Publique* (CSP), and the *1977*

UK National Health Service Act suspended health care benefit claims for the time that an insured person stayed abroad.

In the course of implementing the *Kohll/Decker* jurisprudence, the three Member States changed the existing regulations at the core of their health care systems: the German SGB V, the French CSS/CSP, and the UK NHS Act. However, the degree of change varied among the three countries.

In Germany, Paragraph 16(1)(1) still suspends the rights to receive health care for persons who reside abroad. In 2003, an exception from this general rule was created with the new Paragraph 13(4) SGB V. It allowed insured persons to receive out-patient treatment in another EU/EEA Member State and to be reimbursed by their insurance fund. However, in-patient treatment still depends on prior authorization from the insurance fund. The basic principle of suspending health care remained intact, but it was further softened, although still confined to out-patient care. Independent from this legislative change, from 2001 onwards several insurance funds started to reimburse, first, voluntarily insured patients, and then all insured patients without express legislative backing. An additional legislative change caused by the *Kohll/Decker* jurisprudence was the insertion of Paragraph 140(e), which allowed insurance funds to make contracts with foreign health care providers under the same conditions as with domestic providers. Presently, very few contracts have been made because the administrative effort is considered too high as compared with any possible gains.

In its Articles L. 332–3 and R. 332–2 the French CSS determined that health care benefits were restricted to the French territory. With the restatement of these articles and the insertion of new regulations in 2004/05, Article R. 332–3 to 6, France for the first time distinguished between EU and extra-EU cases. The fundamental principle of suspending health care provision as long as a person resides abroad – spelled out in Article L. 332–3 – remained unchanged. However, similar to Germany, it was eroded further by the making of more exceptions. Out-patient treatment can be obtained in any EU/EEA Member State and reimbursement has to be provided. In addition, in Articles L. 6211–2–1 and R. 6211–46 to 56 of the CSP, the French government determined that EU/EEA laboratories could offer their services to French patients under the same conditions as French providers.

Except for the deviations contained in the European coordination regulations, the UK had an even stricter territorial confinement in the NHS Act of 1977. Section 5(2)(b) only allowed sending patients abroad with respiratory tuberculosis and in limited goodwill cases. With the removal of this principle from the NHS Act 1977 and the NHS Community Care Act 1990 in 2002, a change that was nearly imperceptible to the public, the Secretary of State and NHS trusts could now make use of health care services from abroad, be they from the EU or beyond. Before that, the UK government had already amended the regulations on travel expenses in 2002 to facilitate a pilot scheme that was destined to test referrals of patients to overseas hospitals. The removal of the territorial restriction had little practical relevance for patient mobility; referral abroad still happened at the discretion of the NHS institutions in which patients had virtually no say where and when to get treatment.

To sum up these legislative changes, the strict territorial principles of all three health care systems have been further eroded in the implementation of the *Kohll/Decker* jurisprudence. In the UK, the territorial confinement has been removed entirely. The opening has, though, taken place within rather confined limits. In France and Germany, only out-patient health care was affected. In the UK, sending patients abroad still happens at the discretion of the local health authorities and the Department of Health.

How can we classify these institutional changes? They unquestionably weakened the core of the principle of territoriality, which was a central feature of almost all domestic health care systems. However, these were "second order changes." Although the "instruments of policy as well as their setting" (Hall 1993: 278) have been partially altered in response to the ECJ rulings, the overarching goal of the three governments was nevertheless the perpetuation of the territorial principle. The German and French governments clearly limited the extent of legislative changes and tried to leave the principle of territoriality intact. The UK government removed the territorial restriction as a basic principle; however, financial investment in its own NHS combined with an emphasis on the treatment of patients inside the UK remained the central goal.

Germany, France, and the UK represent three different types of health care systems. France and Germany admitted that they were concerned by the *Kohll/Decker* jurisprudence as the year 2001 unfolded. The UK government officially did not accept that the jurisprudence was transferable to its system. Even after *Watts*, it adopted a rather obstructive position. Nevertheless, I have shown that the principle of territoriality has been weakened in all three Member States, regardless of the system and whether or not they officially admitted to being concerned by the jurisprudence. The principles elaborated by the ECJ in the *Kohll/Decker* jurisprudence had horizontal effects.

Internal De-structuring: Moderate to Nonexistent

EU Member States have indeed changed their legislation with regard to the principle of territoriality in order to comply with the *Kohll/Decker* jurisprudence; however, were these changes limited to patient mobility or did they spill over into the regulation of domestic health care systems in general as has been postulated? (see Ferrera 2005, Martinsen 2005b).

In Germany, a central principle of the social security system was breached in the implementation of the *Kohll/Decker* jurisprudence: delivering in-kind health care benefits. This breach of the system was not limited to cross-border cases; all patients now had the opportunity to opt for cash benefits. However, several restrictive conditions characterized the new regulation of Paragraph 13(2) SGB V: the insured may not restrict reimbursement to out-patient care only; the reimbursement is limited to the amount that an insurance fund would have had to pay for the equivalent in-kind benefit; insurance funds will deduct their administrative costs; obligatory co-payments have to be deducted as well; and patients have to commit themselves for at least one year to cash benefits. These restrictions might explain why, according to several insurance funds, very few insured persons took up the reimbursement option. This prompted the CDU/CSU to demand optional reimbursement for individual service types such as dental treatment (see *Deutscher Bundestag* 2004b: 7). The breach was not only negligible in practical terms but also dogmatically. First of all, the breach was legislated the first time in 1997 before *Kohll* and *Decker*. It was abolished in 1999 and then reintroduced in 2003. Second, voluntarily insured persons continued to opt out of in-kind benefits after 1999. And third, the principle of in-kind benefit delivery was and is accepted by all main actors as the superior mode of organizing health care. As the *Kohll/Decker* jurisprudence was implemented, some marginal actors, especially FDP politicians, pleaded to extend the cash benefits principle to the entire system. However, major political actors never considered such an extension a viable political option. An additional potential dynamic of de-structuring could have been triggered by the annulment of the quantity and quality control mechanisms which are essential features of the German health care system. However, no such repercussions could be ascertained.

In France, none of the basic internal features had to be changed in the implementation of the *Kohll/Decker* jurisprudence. The problem that contractual relationships between insurance funds and physicians through which health care expenditures were controlled could not be extended to foreign physicians, was circumvented by applying a very low tariff to such care providers. Laboratories from other EU/EEA Member States, according to Article L. 6211–2–1 and the corresponding Procedure Regulations R. 6211–46 to 56 in the newly created Section 5 of the CSP, have to submit a declaration which certifies that they are in conformity with the regulations of their Member State and that their personnel possesses the necessary diplomas. In order to receive an administrative authorization, foreign laboratories must conform to the French requirements. With these arrangements the French government exported its requirements and limited the internal impact of the jurisprudence.

Theoretically, the UK had the most reason to fear the *Kohll/Decker* jurisprudence. These decisions potentially endangered its main rationing device, the waiting list. However, the rulings have not triggered any direct internal de-structuring. Still, to preempt a massive outflow of patients, the UK now had a strong incentive to invest more money into its NHS.

Many EU Member States feared that provisions which were deemed necessary to make health care systems compatible with European law would have additional negative effects on these systems. However, in the three countries studied, major internal de-structuring processes could not be detected. The regulations which aimed at complying with European requirements generally did not spill over into other areas. And if they did, as was the case with the breach of the principle of in-kind benefits in Germany, the consequences were quite moderate.

Financial Destabilization: In the Short Run Nonexistent

Did the *Kohll/Decker* jurisprudence destabilize domestic health care systems financially? *Kohll* and *Decker* and the later rulings opened a new dimension in European health care policy-making. Its (financial) implications, according to Brouwer and others, were "quite compelling and far-reaching in the long-run" (2003: 290). However, for the Netherlands they claimed that due to the inertia in patient mobility, "cross-border care will probably remain an insignificant phenomenon in terms of quantities of patients travelling abroad" (Brouwer et al. 2003: 289). Brouwer and others based this claim on the results of three experiments in the Netherlands which showed that "even under circumstances in which cross-border care was facilitated and sometimes stimulated, only few patients considered it a real option" (2003: 293). But what about other EU Member States? What conclusions can we draw for the short, middle and long run?

In several studies and surveys, large numbers of people in Germany, France, and the UK have expressed their willingness to travel abroad for medical treatment.[10] However, for the time being, the number of patients who make use of mobility rights is negligible.[11] Hans Vollaard observed that "[l]'ampleur réelle des soins transfrontaliers contraste violemment avec cette predisposition à se rendre à l'étranger pour des soins" (2005: 237).[12]

The actual number of people who consume health care abroad is quite limited in all countries except Luxembourg. Numbers from the Administrative Commission on Social Security for Migrant Workers suggest that EU Member States spend very little on health care costs received abroad.

Table 11.7 shows that the average costs per inhabitant are very low in Germany, France, and the UK, and that they are far from increasing constantly and considerably. However, these numbers cover only people who are mobile within the established European coordination regulations. Reliable data on people who travel abroad deliberately to receive health care outside this structure and who take advantage of the *Kohll/Decker* jurisprudence is not available. None of the Member States collects such data centrally. This is also due to administrative problems,

---

10   The UK research company, MORI Social Research Institute, found in a survey that 42 percent of all patients would be willing to travel outside the UK for treatment (2002); a Stockholm Network/Populus poll and analysis revealed that a majority of 73 percent of British people said that they would travel abroad for treatment, 37 percent in France, and 50 percent in Germany (Disney et al. 2004: 34, 74, 93). A Flash Eurobarometer on "Cross-border health services in the EU" commissioned by DG SANCO confirmed these results (see European Commission 2007).

11   Martinsen – based on incomplete data – presented low numbers of people who request and obtain prior authorization for treatment abroad (2005b: 1047).

12   "The real scope of cross-border health care is in sharp contrast to the predisposition to travel abroad for health care" (translation of the author).

but it seems that Member States tacitly accept these data problems and leave the phenomenon of patient mobility undisclosed.

Table 11.7 Average costs for health care received abroad per inhabitant for selected countries

	1989	1993	1997	1998	2004
	Euro	Euro	Euro	Euro	Euro
Austria	–	–	0.48	1.87	8.90
Germany	1.77	1.83	2.08	2.21	1.87
France	0.79	1.87	1.21	1.05	5.79
United Kingdom	0.33	1.61	1.92	0.36	0.76
Luxembourg	58.01	149.55	135.29	116.00	130.33

Note: These data have been kindly provided by the *Association Internationale de la Mutualité* which assembled them from the reports of the Administrative Commission on Social Security for Migrant Workers. However, according to Bernhard Spiegel from the Austrian Federal Ministry of Social Security, Generations and Consumer Protection, who is the Austrian representative in the Administrative Commission, the reliability of these data is highly questionable.

Country-specific data is rare; few insurance funds in Germany were able to provide precise numbers. In 1999, the German *Techniker Krankenkasse* spent about 25.6 million Euro for treatments abroad. That is less than 0.4 percent of its overall expenditures (2001: 12). Unfortunately, the *Kohll* and *Decker*-like cases cannot be extracted from these figures. The *Siemens Betriebskrankenkasse* (SBK), between August 1, 2001 and January 1, 2004, reimbursed its voluntarily insured for in-patient health care costs incurred abroad and its compulsorily insured for out-patient health care costs without prior authorization. Nevertheless, the SBK found in an internal study that the expenses for treatments abroad were – with an average of 0.35 percent in a four years period – negligible (2006: 4). The number of patients reimbursed by the UK NHS for treatments abroad outside the coordination regulations is some several hundreds. For France no reliable data is available. Reinhard Busse and Annette Riesberg noted in a report for the World Health Organization:

> Changes in the utilisation of cross-border ambulatory care services are expected to be hardly noticeable to the country's economy as a whole, and the few increases will remain restricted to border regions. However, dental care, elective treatments and certain high-cost drug treatments in EU countries with lower prices may exert some influence on health expenditure. (2004: 212)

The presently minor impact of the *Kohll/Decker* jurisprudence in financial and quantitative terms, though, has to be regarded skeptically for three reasons: First, few years have passed since *Kohll* and *Decker*. Second, some countries still have to implement the rulings. Third, patients lack information about their rights. In the middle and long run, heavily increased patient mobility is unlikely but possible.

Chapter 12
Conclusion: Five Lessons

This study yields five main findings: First, Member States indeed implement ECJ rulings. Second, no single overriding cause can explain these efforts; combinations of factors drive implementation. Third, de-territorialization, internal de-structuring and financial destabilization effects have been limited so far. Fourth, the temporal periodization of early judicial activism versus later self-restraint of the ECJ does not mirror the complexity of ECJ jurisprudence. Fifth, the conventional models of judicial politics have to be revised; the fine-tuning of the content and scope of a ruling through the ECJ shapes the implementation outcome in Member States.

Different Pathways but Similar Outcomes

After *Kohll* and *Decker* in 1998, the German social security legislation remained the same for several years. The major political and administrative actors were not prepared to accept ECJ interference in the area of health care, perceived to be one of the few remaining bastions of domestic politics. The administrative practices of insurance funds changed slowly beginning in 2001. As soon as the ECJ unambiguously answered, in 2003, the open question of whether the *Kohll/ Decker* jurisprudence also applied to systems based on in-kind benefits, the German government rapidly implemented it. The material doctrines of the *Kohll/ Decker* jurisprudence were incorporated exhaustively into the Statutory Health Insurance Modernization Act in 2003.

The French case was quite different. *Kohll* and *Decker* were applicable already in 1998. Nevertheless, the French government adopted an obstructive strategy, which explains why nine years passed before France fully conformed to the jurisprudence. The hierarchical structure existing between government and insurance bodies, excluding the Parliament, allowed for a rather slow and gradual implementation, which accorded with governmental and administrative preferences. Through circulars that invalidated or complemented preceding circulars, the French government adapted the social security system step by step. With two decrees in 2005/06 and an explanatory circular, the French provisions finally complied with the ECJ requirements.

The UK government made important but overall quite moderate legislative and administrative changes in response to the *Kohll/Decker* jurisprudence. First, two legislative changes were implemented. In 2001, the UK government amended the English NHS regulations on travel expenses and extended them to patients going abroad to receive treatment. In addition, in 2002 the government removed the strict territorial restriction from the 1977 NHS Act. NHS institutions could now seek health care from providers abroad and could do so independently of the Secretary of State. Secondly, the UK government adopted a "contractual approach" to patient mobility in 2001/2002. It introduced a pilot scheme to relieve imminent pressure from the NHS and to give patients on a waiting list the choice to be treated in health care centers in other EU Member States, though only if these foreign centers were under contract with the NHS. After this centralized pilot scheme was phased out, the local health authorities continued the referral mechanism. A third change was in the DoH's several alterations to the relevant guidance to the public. These legislative and administrative changes notwithstanding, the UK government was constantly strictly opposed to the transferability of the doctrines elaborated in the *Kohll/Decker* jurisprudence to the NHS.

These results reveal that the pathways of EU Member States in the implementation of the *Kohll/Decker* jurisprudence were different: Whereas in Germany the necessary legislative changes were made in one big step in a major statutory health insurance modernization act, in France the implementation took place more gradually and was carried out step by step, predominantly through circulars and decrees. In the UK, implementation remains an unfinished business; changes there were achieved through statutory instruments and public guidance. In France, central government and the administration monopolize the implementation of ECJ jurisprudence. Interference by Parliament is negligible and the insurance funds are under the government's direct "tutelle." A step-by-step approach of adaptation to the particular situation therefore became possible. Similarly, the UK government is free to deal with ECJ jurisprudence as it deems necessary. It was more difficult to bring about legislative change in federal Germany. The ground for that was prepared after 1998 in numerous working groups in which the negative and positive effects of implementation were weighed. In 2003, the Statutory Health Insurance Modernization Act provided the occasion to incorporate the *Kohll/Decker* jurisprudence.

The outcomes of these different implementation trajectories were similar. So far, at the end of implementation in each of our three EU Member States, we see a further weakening of the strict territorial principle enshrined in the social security systems.

Important with regard to the implementation of the *Kohll/Decker* jurisprudence is the observation that the level of indirect compliance is high. In all three EU Member States (partial) implementation took place without these members being a direct party to the ECJ cases in question, or they became a party only at a moment when implementation was already quite advanced. The reasons for indirect compliance were diverse. However, this fact and the large number of EU Member States that joined the ECJ proceedings indicate that even though a binding *erga omnes* effect is absent, Member States in practice not only follow the doctrines of ECJ rulings closely, but they also independently draw conclusions for themselves which facilitate compliance.

Combinations of Compliance Factors Instead of Single Causes

In Germany, the Ministry of Health and the Central Associations of Statutory Health Insurance Funds underwent a "paradigm shift" that allowed for the quick implementation by the German legislator in 2003 for six main reasons. First, the predominant fear of great change could not be sustained. The German government did not have to extend the cash-benefit principle to the entire system. The political and legal pressure did not go that far. Second, further ECJ jurisprudence removed the additional fear that not only out-patient but also in-patient cross-border benefits would be allowed. As soon as in-patient benefits were excluded from mobility and only restrictively permitted, the widespread skepticism toward the ECJ diminished, paving the way for the implementation of its jurisprudence. Third, the fears described were removed by and by in numerous working groups and even prospects of potential financial cost saving effects rose on the horizon. Fourth, domestic party political preferences of "increased patient sovereignty" played a role. Fifth, the first national court cases arose in 2001 and forced the legislator to take the first compliance steps. And finally, some insurance funds had already started to apply the jurisprudence and pressed the government to end judicial uncertainty.

In France, the main driving force behind implementation was the combined pressure exerted by the European Commission through its infringement proceedings and by national courts through their rulings. The Commission took initiatives from early on. Although the first infringement proceeding resulted only in a minor concession, the French position began to crumble further and further in following proceedings. The French national courts, especially the *Cour de Cassation*, contributed considerably to the changing position of the French government. In a series of decisions, they put considerable pressure on the government to end judicial uncertainty.

In the UK, administrative and legislative changes can be explained by considering three factors: an aggressive press campaign that stirred public pressure; the partial compatibility of some parts of the jurisprudence with the broader governmental agenda; and the ruling of an administrative court that was inspired by the ECJ's fine-tuning of its jurisprudence. In the summer of 2001, the UK government was under great pressure from a press campaign that exposed problems in the NHS. The government immediately reacted by announcing a pilot scheme to treat patients overseas and major legislative changes. This strategic move suited the governmental agenda aiming at increased patient choice, involving the private sector and decreasing waiting lists and times for patients. From the end of 2003 onwards, *Watts*, a national court case, began to plague the UK government and further weakened its obstructive attitude.

This study supports those scholars who claim that compliance is a complex and multifaceted endeavor. In fact, it is a combination of several factors rather than simply a single cause which makes for the implementation of ECJ rulings. No single factor can explain why Member States implement ECJ decisions. An interaction of two or more factors is necessary to kick-start implementation, to push it further and to bring it to a successful end. The role of national courts, the fine-tuning of doctrines by the ECJ, infringement proceedings of the European Commission, and domestic political preferences are those factors which were shown to have the most leverage in the *Kohll/Decker* jurisprudence. Two factors out of these four were decisive in the three case studies, though to a different degree: national court rulings and the fine-tuning of the doctrines by the ECJ. First, if governments and administrations hamper implementation, if domestic party political preferences are incompatible with the jurisprudence, and if the ECJ requirements are incompatible with existing domestic structures and policies, national courts can resolve non-compliance. In France, the UK, and to a minor degree in Germany, national courts forced the legislator – through a series of cases decided in line with the ECJ jurisprudence – to implement the jurisprudence and end judicial uncertainty. Therefore, the behavior of national courts needs to be at the very center of attention when we study compliance with ECJ jurisprudence. Secondly, the fine-tuning of the doctrines by the ECJ is of great importance. In the course of the *Kohll/Decker* jurisprudence the ECJ pressed ahead and retreated, both virtually at the same time. Through the intrusion into Member States' affairs with *Kohll* and *Decker* the Court provoked their reluctance. In subsequent cases, the ECJ extended the doctrines elaborated to other areas, but showed itself simultaneously responsive to the massive objections by Member States and limited the reach of its doctrines. Through self-restraint, it absorbed the main Member State objections and paved the way for their acceptance of its doctrines and their implementation.

Limited De-territorialization, Internal De-structuring,
and Financial Destabilization

With the implementation of the *Kohll/Decker* jurisprudence, the principle of territoriality enshrined in the German social security system was further eroded. Insured persons can now consume health care wherever they want in the EU/EEA area and be reimbursed. However, this erosion of territoriality was limited for three reasons: First, the ECJ limited de-territorialization to out-patient care. Second, several restrictions were built into the Statutory Health Insurance Modernization Act. Third, de-territorialization had already existed to some extent in Germany. Major internal de-structuring effects – as often posited – did not take place. Cash reimbursement, allowed in foreign cases, did not spread. In fact, the introduction of the principle of cash benefits for the compulsorily insured was domestically motivated. The extension to foreign cases conformed to this claim and did not take much effort. Financial destabilization could not be observed. The numbers of cross-border activities have not increased considerably. They are still negligible in Germany.

In France, the strict territorial principle well-anchored in the *Code de la Sécurité Sociale* and the *Code de la Santé Publique* also was eroded further. Important new clauses were inserted that differentiated for the first time between EU/EEA and non-EU/EEA cases. However, following ECJ jurisprudence, unconditional reimbursement of costs incurred abroad was confined to out-patient health care. De-territorialization takes place within strictly confined limits. The jurisprudence did not result in a much feared internal de-structuring of the French social security system and financial destabilization was limited.

In the UK, de-territorialization was certainly increased as the territorial restriction embodied in the NHS Act from 1977 was removed. However, de-territorialization is limited and patient mobility occurs mainly contractually. Internal de-structuring effects do not seem to have been caused directly by the ECJ. The patient choice agenda and involving the private sector were part of the government program. No direct financial destabilization effects could be detected. However, the UK government invested more and more resources into the NHS and will have to do even more so in the future. Such additional funding is part of the Labour agenda, but it is also necessary to contain the repercussions of the *Kohll/Decker* jurisprudence: the government can only control the impact of the jurisprudence, if it reduces waiting times and thus curbs the necessity for patients to travel abroad for treatment.

In order to comply with the *Kohll/Decker* jurisprudence, the territorial principle was weakened in all three Member States. However, this study shows that this partial erosion had no further repercussions. The skeptical reasoning of Ulrich Becker expressed already in 1998 seems to have its merits:

> [Es bleibt] der Trost, daß der Aufschrei über die Entscheidungen größer ist als es die praktischen Folgen sein dürften. Zwar wird befürchtet, der nun einsetzenden Erosion der Sozialstaatlichkeit könne künftig nicht mehr Einhalt geboten werden. Jedoch sind die Entscheidungen kaum der Stein, der eine Lawine ins Rollen bringt, unter der die Sozialversicherungssysteme zu ersticken drohen. Abgesehen von den zur Verfügung stehenden Rechtfertigungsgründen wird die Inanspruchnahme ausländischer Leistungserbringer aus verschiedenen Gründen auf absehbare Zeit die Ausnahme bleiben und deshalb vom zu erwartenden Ausmaß her gesehen die Gesetzliche Krankenversicherung nicht aus dem Gleichgewicht bringen. (364)[1]

Also, the weakening of the principle of territoriality was not (as was often postulated) accompanied by internal de- or re-structuring and financial destabilization.

---

1 "It is consoling that the outcry against the decisions is bigger than their practical consequences. It is feared that the now starting erosion of the welfare state cannot be stopped in the future. However, the decisions are barely causing the avalance under which the social security systems are threatened to suffocate. In addition to the grounds for justification which are at hand, the use of foreign service providers will remain the exception in the foreseeable future for a number of reasons. Therefore, the scope of this phenomenon will not imbalance the statutory health insurance" (translation of the author).

When we consider the overall health care reforms in the last years in Germany, France and the UK, the ECJ's jurisprudence and its repercussions are only of minor importance. We can neither observe heavily disputed domestic conflicts in the legislative process about the incorporation of the ECJ jurisprudence nor do the repercussions of European law receive much attention by the insurance funds, governmental and administrative actors. On the contrary, Europe continues to be of low importance for social security systems while domestically related concerns prevail and the national perspective remains introverted. Domestic reforms were dominated by internal debates, they followed their own constraints and rhythms, and they were only marginally concerned with ECJ rulings.

The ECJ's Integration Function Revisited

Do we need to reconsider the role of the ECJ based on these results? I plead for a look beyond the simple periodization of early judicial activism versus later self-restraint. The implementation of the *Kohll/Decker* jurisprudence has shown that the ECJ always alternates between these two poles simply to ensure compliance with its rulings.

This book demonstrates that the ECJ – through its piecemeal rulings – can indeed instigate processes that have important repercussions on the national and the European level; indeed, triggering such processes makes the ECJ the real integration engine. First, domestic implementation interacts with and is shaped by the ECJ decision process. In the course of the *Kohll/Decker* jurisprudence, the ECJ developed its doctrines in a subtle "dialogue" with Member States. It oscillated between judicial activism and self-restraint to make them accept and implement the rulings. Second, ECJ rulings may also trigger important processes at the European level. Before *Kohll* and *Decker*, Member States pointed to the EC Treaty and the principle of subsidiarity when saying that health care and social security were an exclusively domestic task. According to their view, the EU's influence and competency was restricted to public and occupational health. Health ministers were not used to meeting each other in an EU context and discussing health issues apart from public health. *Kohll* and *Decker* indirectly changed this status quo. These decisions made it clear: even if there is no direct European competency, Member States have to respect the impacts of internal market regulations when they (re-)organize their social security systems.

A More Encompassing Model of Judicial Politics

Finally, against the background of the empirical observations presented above, the existing models of judicial politics have to be revised. To a certain extent they did take into consideration interactions between the ECJ, national courts, and private litigants, as well as the impact of these relationships on doctrinal outcomes. However, they did not assess legislative and administrative outcomes and the interaction between the follow-up rulings and these outcomes. This book incorporates the interaction between the ECJ's fine-tuning and implementation at the Member State level.

I argue that the gradual fine-tuning of the content and scope of a ruling through the ECJ shapes the implementation behavior of and implementation outcome in Member States. The Court first establishes a new doctrine for a specific country case. Then, in order to guarantee its uniform application across the EU in the follow-up rulings, it tailors the doctrine and its consequences to the systems of other EU Member States. This on-going development, that is the fine-tuning of the jurisprudence by the ECJ, is an important intervening variable that contributes, first, to the willingness of Member States to implement Court rulings and, second, to the pace of implementation.[2] The fine-tuning may kick-start, accelerate, or help finalize an implementation process, and this happens for three reasons: First, the refinement of the jurisprudence by the ECJ provides Member States with more information on what is required to comply with a ruling. The legal uncertainty caused by a first ECJ ruling, which postulates new legal principles, decreases step by step with each subsequent ruling. However, follow-up rulings may also raise new questions. Second, with increased information on the scope and content of new ECJ doctrines, the potential and actual financial, administrative and political costs of the implementation of the Court rulings become more predictable for Member States. Third, in the process of fine-tuning its jurisprudence, the ECJ is responsive to criticism and practical problems that emerge in the follow-up cases. To guarantee Member State compliance, the ECJ is ready to exercise considerable self-restraint with regard to the concrete design of its doctrines.

Legal and, even more so, political science scholars expected a considerable impact of the *Kohll* and *Decker* rulings on domestic social protection systems. Scholars based this assessment on the far-reaching doctrines of the rulings. However, the scholarly and political criticism and concerns were absorbed by the ECJ in its follow-up cases which fine-tuned the *Kohll* and *Decker* principles. Consequently, the actual impact was minor compared to what was postulated.

Pierson distinguished between several types of slow-moving processes, one of them being a "cumulative" type, where a "change in a variable is continuous but extremely gradual" (2004: 82). The ECJ's fine-tuning in the cases of *Kohll* and *Decker* could be understood as such a process, in which the variable, the doctrines of the jurisprudence, changed gradually. Scholarly research has to take into account the fine-tuning of the jurisprudence by the ECJ. The impact of rulings with new doctrinal principles has to be seen against the background of this process.

By not paying attention to the slow unfolding of the ECJ's fine-tuning, scholars may overestimate the doctrinal content in rulings while missing the narrowing of this content. The *Kohll/Decker* jurisprudence, which forms the essence of this book, is a good example for the potential effects of such an omitted variable bias

---

2   Other relevant variables to explain Member State compliance were: domestic political preferences, national court rulings, as well as management and enforcement activities of the European Commission.

on research.[3] However, this is certainly not the only example. Recent social policy cases, such as *Laval* and *Viking* on collective trade union action and *Rüffert* on the posting of workers, run the same risk of being systematically overestimated with regard to their impact on Member States.[4]

---

3   According to Henry Brady and David Collier, an omitted variable bias exists "when a theoretically relevant explanatory variable is missing." As a consequence "the causal estimate for any given variable that is included may be too large, in which case the causal effect attributed to the included variable is at least partially spurious" (2004: 296).

4   For the *Laval* and *Viking* rulings see for example Falkner and Obermaier (2008); Case C-346/06, *Dirk Rüffert vs. Land Niedersachsen* [2008], not yet reported.

Bibliography

Abrahamson, P. and Roseberry, L. 2003. *European Observatory on Social Security for Migrant Workers: National Report: Denmark.* Munich: Max-Planck-Institut für ausländisches und internationales Sozialrecht.

Ales, E. 2003. *European Observatory on Social Security for Migrant Workers: National Report: Italy.* Munich: Max-Planck-Institut für ausländisches und internationales Sozialrecht.

Allsop, J. and Baggott, R. 2004. The NHS in England: From Modernisation to Marketisation?, in *Social Policy Review 16: Analysis and Debate in Social Policy, 2004,* edited by N. Ellison, L. Bauld and M. Powell. Bristol: Policy Press, 29–44.

Alter, K.J. 1996. The European Court's Political Power. *West European Politics,* 19(3), 458–487.

Alter, K.J. 1998. Explaining National Court Acceptance of European Court Jurisprudence: A Critical Evaluation of Theories of Legal Integration, in *The European Court and National Courts – Doctrine and Jurisprudence. Legal Change in Its Social Context,* edited by A.-M. Slaughter, A. Stone Sweet and J.H.H. Weiler. Oxford-Portland: Hart Publishing, 227–252.

Alter, K.J. 2001. *Establishing the Supremacy of European Law. The Making of an International Rule of Law in Europe.* Oxford: Oxford University Press.

Alter, K.J. and Meunier-Aitsahalia, S. 1994. Judicial Politics in the European Community. European Integration and the Pathbreaking *Cassis de Dijon* Decision. *Comparative Political Studies,* 26(4), 535–561.

Alter, K.J. and Vargas, J. 2000. Explaining Variation in the Use of European Litigation Strategies. European Community Law and British Gender Equality Policy. *Comparative Political Studies,* 33(4), 452–482.

Altmaier, P. 1995. Europäisches koordinierendes Sozialrecht – Ende des Territorialitätsprinzips?, in *Die Rechtsprechung des Europäischen Gerichtshofs zum Arbeits- und Sozialrecht im Streit,* edited by E. Eichenhofer and M. Zuleeg. Köln: Bundesanzeiger, 71–91.

Arnull, A. 2008. The Americanization of EU Law Scholarship, in *Continuity and Change in EU Law: Essays in Honour of Sir Francis Jacobs,* edited by A. Arnull, P. Eeckhout and T. Tridimas. Oxford: Oxford University Press, 415–31.

Audretsch, H.A.H. 1986. *Supervision in European Community Law. Observance by the Member States of their Treaty Obligations. A Treatise on International and Supra-National Supervision.* Amsterdam-New York-Oxford-Tokyo: Elsevier Science Publishers B.V.

Bailey, I. 2002. National Adaptation to European Integration: Institutional Vetoes and Goodness-of-fit. *Journal of European Public Policy*, 9(5), 791–811.

Bapuly, B. and Kohlegger, G. 2003. *Die Implementierung des Gemeinschaftsrechts in Österreich – die Gerichtsbarkeit*. Wien: Manz.

Beach, D. 2005. Why Governments Comply: An Integrative Compliance Model that Bridges the Gap between Instrumental and Normative Models of Compliance. *Journal of European Public Policy*, 12(1), 113–142.

Becker, U. 1998. Brillen aus Luxemburg und Zahnbehandlung in Brüssel – Die Gesetzliche Krankenversicherung im europäischen Binnenmarkt, zu EuGH v. 28.4.1998, Rs. C-120/95 (Decker), und EuGH v. 28.4.1998, Rs. C-158/96 (Kohll). *Neue Zeitschrift für Sozialrecht*, (8), 359–364.

Becker, U. 2003. Gesetzliche Krankenversicherung im Europäischen Binnenmarkt. *Neue Juristische Wochenschrift*, (32), 2272–2277.

Belcher, P.J. 1999. *The Role of the European Union in Healthcare*. Zoetermeer: Council for Health and Social Service.

Bieback, K.-J. 2001. Etablierung eines Gemeinsamen Marktes für Krankenbehandlung durch den EuGH. Das Urteil des EuGH "Smits/ Peerbooms," v. 12.7.2001. *Neue Zeitschrift für Sozialrecht*, 10(11), 561–569.

Bieback, K.-J. 2005. Abschnitt 2: Arbeitnehmer und Selbständige sowie deren Familienangehörige, in *Europäisches Sozialrecht*, edited by M. Fuchs. Baden-Baden: Nomos, 229–267.

Bleckmann, A. 1983. Die Rolle der richterlichen Rechtsschöpfung im Europäischen Gemeinschaftsrecht, in *Rechtsvergleichung, Europarecht und Staatenintegration. Gedächtnisschrift für Léontin-Jean Constantinesco*, edited by G. Lüke, G. Ress and M.R. Will. Köln-Berlin-Bonn-München: Carl Heymanns Verlag, 61–81.

Bloemheuvel, A.G. 2003. Die Folgen der Urteile Kohll und Decker für das System der Krankenfürsorge in den Niederlanden, in *Grenzüberschreitende Inanspruchnahme von Gesundheitsleistungen im Gemeinsamen Markt. Belgisch-deutsch-niederländische Tagung in Antwerpen*, edited by Y. Jorens and B. Schulte. Baden-Baden: Nomos, 69–92.

Bokeloh, A. 2001. Die Verwaltungskommission für die soziale Sicherheit der Wanderarbeitnehmer. *Deutsche Rentenversicherung*, (8–9), 500–513.

Borchardt, K.-D. 1995. Der Gerichtshof der EG als Ersatzgesetzgeber?, in *Die Rechtsprechung des Europäischen Gerichtshofs zum Arbeits- und Sozialrecht im Streit*, edited by E. Eichenhofer and M. Zuleeg. Köln: Bundesanzeiger, 53–68.

Börzel, T.A. 2000. Improving Compliance through Domestic Mobilisation? New Instruments and the Effectiveness of Implementation in Spain, in *Implementing EU Environmental Policy. New Directions and Old Problems*, edited by C. Knill and A. Lenschow. Manchester-New York: Manchester University Press, 222–250.

Börzel, T.A., Hofmann, T. and Sprungk, C. 2003. *Why Do States not Obey the Law? Lessons from the European Union*, EUSA Conference, March 27–30, Nashville.

Börzel, T.A. and Risse, T. 2002. Die Wirkung internationaler Institutionen. Von der Normanerkennung zur Normeinhaltung, in *Regieren in internationalen Institutionen*, edited by M. Jachtenfuchs and M. Knodt. Opladen: Leske and Budrich, 141–181.

Brady, H.E. and Collier, D. (eds) 2004. *Rethinking Social Inquiry. Diverse Tools, Shared Standards*. Lanham-Boulder-New York-Toronto-Oxford: Rowman and Littlefield.

Brouwer, W., van Exel, J., Hermans, B. and Stoop, A. 2003. Should I Stay or Should I Go? Waiting Lists and Cross-border Care in the Netherlands. *Health Policy*, 63, 289–298.

Burley, A.-M. and Mattli, W. 1993. Europe before the Court: A Political Theory of Legal Integration. *International Organization*, 47(1), 41–76.

Busse, R. and Riesberg, A. 2004. *Health Care Systems in Transition: Germany*. Copenhagen: European Observatory on Health Systems and Policies.

Cappelletti, M., Seccombe, M. and Weiler, J. 1986. Introduction, in *A Political, Legal and Economic Overview*, edited by M. Cappelletti, M. Seccombe and J. Weiler. Florence: European University Institute, 3–68.

Ciavarini Azzi, G. 2000. The Slow March of European Legislation: The Implementation of Directives, in *European Integration After Amsterdam. Institutional Dynamics and Prospects for Democracy*, edited by K. Neunreither and A. Wiener. Oxford: Oxford University Press, 52–67.

Cichowski, R.A. 2007. *The European Court and Civil Society. Litigation, Mobilization and Governance*. Cambridge: Cambridge University Press.

Clever, P. 1994. *Rechtsprechung des EuGH im Sozialbereich auf dem Prüfstand.* Saarbrücken: Europa-Institut der Universität des Saarlandes.

Collins, J. 2002. Representation of a Member State before the Court of Justice of the European Communities: Practice in the United Kingdom. *European Law Review*, 27(3), 359–364.

Conant, L. 2003. *Justice Contained. Law and Politics in the European Union.* Ithaca-London: Cornell University Press.

Cornelissen, R. 1996. The Principle of Territoriality and the Community Regulations on Social Security (Regulations 1408/71 and 574/72). *Common Market Law Review*, 33, 439–471.

Cousins, M. 2003. *European Observatory on Social Security for Migrant Workers: National Report: Ireland*. Munich: Max-Planck-Institut für ausländisches und internationales Sozialrecht.

Daintith, T. (ed.) 1995. *Implementing EC Law in the United Kingdom: Structures for Indirect Rule*. Chichester-New York-Brisbane-Toronto-Singapore: John Wiley and Sons.

Dashwood, A. and White, R. 1989. Enforcement Actions under Articles 169 and 170 EEC. *European Law Review*, 14, 388–413.

Davies, G. 2004a. The Division of Powers between the European Court of Justice and National Courts. *Constitutionalism Web-Papers*, 3, 1–28.

Davies, G. 2004b. Health and Efficiency: Community Law and National Health Systems in the Light of Müller-Fauré. *The Modern Law Review*, 67(1), 94–107.

Dawson, D. 2002. Who is Directing the Traffic to Europe – the European Court of Justice or the Department of Health? *Health Policy Matters*, (7), 1–4.

De Búrca, G. and Weiler, J.H.H. (eds) 2001. *The European Court of Justice*. Oxford: Oxford University Press.

Disney, H., Horn, K., Hrobon, P., Hjertqvist, J., Kilmarnock, A., Mihm, A., Mingardi, A., Philippe, C., Smith, D., van den Broek, E. and Verhoeks, G. (eds) 2004. *Impatient for Change: European Attitudes to Healthcare Reform*. The Stockholm Network.

Döhler, M. and Hassenteufel, P. 1995. Akteurkonstellationen in der Krankenversicherungspolitik: Ein deutsch-französischer Vergleich. *Zeitschrift für Sozialreform*, 41(11/12), 804–822.

Duina, F. 1997. Explaining Legal Implementation in the European Union. *International Journal of the Sociology of Law*, 25(2), 155–179.

Eckstein, H. 1975. Case Study and Theory in Political Science, in *Strategies of Inquiry*, edited by F.I. Greenstein and N.W. Polsby. Reading/Massachusetts-Menlo Park/California-London-Amsterdam-DonMills/Ontario-Sydney: Addison-Wesley Publishing Company.

Ehlermann, C.-D. 1987. Ein Plädoyer für die dezentrale Kontrolle der Anwendung des Gemeinschaftsrechts durch die Mitgliedstaaten, in *Du droit international au droit de l'intégration. Liber Amicorum Pierre Pescatore*, edited by F. Capotorti, C.-D. Ehlermann, J. Frowein, F.G. Jacobs, R. Joliet, T. Koopmans and R. Kovar. Baden-Baden: Nomos, 205–226.

Eichenhofer, E. 1999. Das Europäische koordinierende Krankenversicherungsrecht nach den EuGH-Urteilen Kohll und Decker. *Vierteljahresschrift für Sozialrecht*, 2, 101–122.

Everling, U. 1983. Die Mitgliedstaaten der Europäischen Gemeinschaft vor ihrem Gerichtshof. *Europarecht*, 18(2), 101–127.

Everling, U. 2000. Richterliche Rechtsfortbildung in der Europäischen Gemeinschaft. *Juristenzeitung*, 55(5), 217–227.

Falkner, G. and Obermaier, A. 2008. Aktuelle Reformvorschläge zur EU-Sozialpolitik: Von der Kontroverse zum scheinbaren Konsens. *SWS-Rundschau*, (2), 201–220.

Falkner, G., Treib, O., Hartlapp, M. and Leiber, S. 2005. *Complying with Europe. EU Harmonisation and Soft Law in the Member States*. Cambridge: Cambridge University Press.

Ferrera, M. 2003. European Integration and National Social Citizenship: Changing Boundaries, New Structuring? *Working Paper CIIP*, 3, 1–45.

Ferrera, M. 2005. *The Boundaries of Welfare. European Integration and the New Spatial Politics of Social Protection*. Oxford: Oxford University Press.

Fillon, J.-C. 2001. Les soins de santé face à la libre prestation de services. *Liaisons sociales Europe*, (39), 5–8.

Fillon, J.-C. 2002. Prise en charge de frais d'urgence par une CPAM. *Liaisons sociales Europe* (65), 2–3.

Fuchs, M. 2002. Free Movement of Services and Social Security – Quo Vadis? *European Law Journal*, 8(4), 536–555.

Fuchs, M. (ed.) 2005. *Europäisches Sozialrecht*. Baden-Baden: Nomos.

Garrett, G. 1995. The Politics of Legal Integration in the European Union. *International Organization*, 49(1), 171–181.

Garrett, G., Kelemen, D.R. and Schulz, H. 1998. The European Court of Justice, National Governments, and Legal Integration in the European Union. *International Organization*, 52(1), 149–176.

George, A.L. and Bennett, A. 2005. *Case Studies and Theory Development in the Social Sciences*. Cambridge/Massachusetts-London: MIT Press.

Gerring, J. 2001. *Social Science Methodology. A Criterial Framework*. Cambridge: Cambridge University Press.

Gibson, J.L. and Caldeira, G.A. 1998. Changes in the Legitimacy of the European Court of Justice: A Post-Maastricht Analysis. *British Journal of Political Science*, 28(1), 63–91.

Giesen, R. 2003. *European Observatory on Social Security for Migrant Workers: National Report: Germany*. Munich: Max-Planck-Institut für ausländisches und internationales Sozialrecht.

Gobrecht, J. 1999a. *The Implications of the Kohll/Decker Judgements on the Health Systems of the Member States*, Conference paper, The New Public Health Policy of the European Union – Past Experience, Present Needs, Future Perspectives, January 27–29, Potsdam.

Gobrecht, J. 1999b. National Reactions to Kohll and Decker. *Eurohealth*, 5(1), 16–17.

Golub, J. 1996. The Politics of Judicial Discretion: Rethinking the Interaction between National Courts and the European Court of Justice. *West European Politics*, 19(2), 360–385.

Granger, M.-P.F. 2004. When Governments go to Luxembourg ...: The Influence of Governments on the Court of Justice. *European Law Review*, 29, 3–31.

Green Cowles, M. and Risse, T. 2001. Transforming Europe: Conclusions, in *Transforming Europe. Europeanization and Domestic Change*, edited by M. Green Cowles, J. Caporaso and T. Risse. Ithaca-London: Cornell University Press, 217–237.

Greß, S., Axer, P., Wasem, J. and Rupprecht, C. 2003. *Europäisierung des Gesundheitswesens. Perspektiven für Deutschland*. Gütersloh: Verlag Bertelsmann Stiftung.

Guibentif, P. 2003. *European Observatory on Social Security for Migrant Workers: National Report: Portugal*. Munich: Max-Planck-Institut für ausländisches und internationales Sozialrecht.

Hall, P.A. 1993. Policy Paradigms, Social Learning, and the State: The Case of Economic Policymaking in Britain. *Comparative Politics*, 25(3), 275–96.

Hartley, T.C. 2007. *The Foundations of European Community Law. An Introduction to the Constitutional and Administrative Law of the European Community.* Oxford: Oxford University Press.

Hatzopoulos, V. 2000. Recent Developments of the Case Law of the ECJ in the Field of Services. *Common Market Law Review*, 37(1), 43–82.

Hatzopoulos, V. 2002. Killing National Health and Insurance Systems but Healing Patients? The European Market for Health Care Services after the Judgments of the ECJ in Vanbraekel and Peerbooms. *Common Market Law Review*, 39, 683–729.

Hatzopoulos, V. 2005. Health Law and Policy: The Impact of the EU, in *EU Law and the Welfare State. In Search of Solidarity*, edited by G. De Búrca. Oxford: Oxford University Press, 111–168.

Haverland, M. 2000. National Adaptation to European Integration: The Importance of Institutional Veto Points. *Journal of Public Policy*, 20(1), 83–103.

Héritier, A. 2001. Differential Europe: The European Union Impact on National Policymaking, in *Differential Europe: The European Union Impact on National Policymaking*, edited by A. Héritier, D. Kerwer, C. Knill, D. Lehmkuhl, M. Teutsch and A.-C. Douillet. Lanham-Boulder-New York-Oxford: Rowman and Littlefield Publishers, 1–21.

Héritier, A., Kerwer, D., Knill, C., Lehmkuhl, D., Teutsch, M. and Douillet, A.-C. (eds) 2001. *Differential Europe: The European Union Impact on National Policymaking.* Lanham-Boulder-New York-Oxford: Rowman and Littlefield Publishers.

Héritier, A. and Knill, C. 2001. Differential Responses to European Policies: A Comparison, in *Differential Europe: The European Union Impact on National Policymaking*, edited by A. Héritier, D. Kerwer, C. Knill, D. Lehmkuhl, M. Teutsch and A.-C. Douillet. Lanham-Boulder-New York-Oxford: Rowman and Littlefield Publishers, 257–294.

Hervey, T.K. and McHale, J.V. 2004. *Health Law and the European Union.* Cambridge: Cambridge University Press.

Jacobs, F.G. 1994. The Effect of Preliminary Rulings in the National Legal Order, in *Article 177 References to the European Court – Policy and Practice*, edited by M. Andenas. London-Dublin-Edinburgh: Butterworths.

Jönsson, C. and Tallberg, J. 1998. Compliance and Post-Agreement Bargaining. *European Journal of International Relations*, 4(4), 371–408.

Jordan, A. 1997. "Overcoming the Divide" between Comparative Politics and International Relations Approaches to the EC: What Role for "Post-Decisional Politics"? *West European Politics*, 20(4), 43–70.

Jorens, Y. 2002. The Right to Health Care across Borders, in *The Impact of EU Law on Health Care Systems*, edited by M. McKee, E. Mossialos and R. Baeten. Bruxelles-Bern-Berlin-Frankfurt/M.-New York-Oxford-Wien: P.I.E.-Peter Lang, 83–122.

Jorens, Y. 2004. Impact de la jurisprudence la plus récente de la Cour européenne de justice sur l'influence des règles relatives au marché intérieur sur les systèmes nationaux de santé, plus spécialement les arrêts prononcés après décembre 2001: Les cas Müller-Fauré Van Riet, Inizan et Leichtle. *Revue belge de sécurité sociale*, 46(2), 379–404.

Jorens, Y., Coucheir, M. and Van Overmeiren, F. 2005. Access to Health Care in an Internal Market: Impact for Statutory and Complementary Systems. *Bulletin luxembourgeois des questions sociales*, 18, 1–136.

Jorens, Y. and Hajdú, J. 2005. *Training and Reporting on European Social Security. European Report 2005*. Ghent: Ghent University, Department of Social Law.

Jorens, Y. and Hajdú, J. 2006. *Training and Reporting on European Social Security. European Report 2006*. Ghent: Ghent University, Department of Social Law.

Jorens, Y. and Hajdú, J. 2008. *Training and Reporting on European Social Security. European Report 2008*. Ghent: Ghent University, Department of Social Law.

Jorens, Y. and Schulte, B. (eds) 2003. *Grenzüberschreitende Inanspruchnahme von Gesundheitsleistungen im Gemeinsamen Markt. Belgisch-deutsch-niederländische Tagung in Antwerpen*. Baden-Baden: Nomos.

Kaczorowska, A. 2006. A Review of the Creation by the European Court of Justice of the Right to Effective and Speedy Medical Treatment and its Outcomes. *European Law Journal*, 12(3), 345–370.

Kassim, H. 2000. The United Kingdom, *The National Co-ordination of EU Policy. The Domestic Level*, edited by H. Kassim, G.B. Peters and V. Wright. Oxford: Oxford University Press, 22–53.

Kerschen, N. 2003. *European Observatory on Social Security for Migrant Workers: National Report: Luxembourg*. Munich: Max-Planck-Institut für ausländisches und internationales Sozialrecht.

Kessler, F. 2001. Le principe de libre prestation franchit la porte des hôpitaux. *Liaisons sociales Europe*, (37), 2–4.

Kessler, F. 2002. Frais de soins d'urgence: priorité des règles sur la libre prestation de services (Cass. soc., 28 mars 2002, Magnan c./CPAM Hauts de Seine). *Droit Social*, (6), 649–651.

Kessler, F. 2003. *European Observatory on Social Security for Migrant Workers: National Report: France*. Munich: Max-Planck-Institut für ausländisches und internationales Sozialrecht.

Kilroy, B.A. 1999. *Integration through the Law: ECJ and Governments in the EU*. Unpublished Facsimile, Los Angeles: University of California.

Kingreen, T. 2003. *Das Sozialstaatsprinzip im europäischen Verfassungsverbund. Gemeinschaftsrechtliche Einflüsse auf das deutsche Recht der gesetzlichen Krankenversicherung*. Tübingen: Mohr Siebeck.

Kingreen, T. 2005. Beihilfefähigkeit einer Heilkur im Ausland. *Juristenzeitung*, 60(1), 28–33.

Knieps, F. 1998a. Von Bismarck bis Beveridge. *Gesundheit und Gesellschaft*, (10), 40–46.

Knieps, F. 1998b. Von stationär bis visionär. *Gesundheit und Gesellschaft*, (11), 34–37.

Knill, C. and Lenschow, A. 2000. Do New Brooms Really Sweep Cleaner? Implementation of New Instruments in EU Environmental Policy, in *Implementing EU Environmental Policy. New Directions and Old Problems*, edited by C. Knill and A. Lenschow. Manchester-New York: Manchester University Press, 251–86.

Kremalis, K. 2003. *European Observatory on Social Security for Migrant Workers: National Report: Greece*. Munich: Max-Planck-Institut für ausländisches und internationales Sozialrecht.

Künkele, C. 2000. *Kostenerstattung für medizinische Leistungen im EG-Ausland? Zu den Auswirkungen der EuGH-Entscheidungen Kohll und Decker auf das deutsche Krankenversicherungssystem*. Sankt Augustin: Asgard-Verlag Hippe.

Lascombe, M. 1999. *Droit Constitutionnel de la Ve République*. Paris-Montréal: L'Harmattan.

Leathard, A. 2000. *Health Care Provision. Past, Present and into the 21st Century*. Cheltenham: Stanley Thornes Publishers.

Leibfried, S. 2005. Social Policy: Left to the Judges and the Markets?, in *Policy-Making in the European Union*, edited by H. Wallace, W. Wallace and M.A. Pollack. Oxford: Oxford University Press, 243–278.

Leibfried, S. and Pierson, P. 1995. Semisovereign Welfare States: Social Policy in a Multitiered Europe, in *European Social Policy. Between Fragmentation and Integration*, edited by S. Leibfried and P. Pierson. Washington DC: The Brookings Institution, 43–77.

Leibfried, S. and Pierson, P. 2000. Social Policy. Left to Courts and Markets? in *Policy-Making in the European Union*, edited by H. Wallace and W. Wallace. Oxford: Oxford University Press, 267–292.

Lenaerts, K. 1992. Some Thoughts About the Interaction between Judges and Politicians in the European Community. *Yearbook of European Law*, 12, 1–34.

Lepperhoff, J. 2004. *Wohlfahrtskulturen in Frankreich und Deutschland: gesundheitspolitische Reformdebatten im Ländervergleich*. Wiesbaden: Verlag für Sozialwissenschaften.

Lhernould, J.-P. 2003. Les principaux arrêts de l'année 2002 en sécurité sociale. *Liaisons sociales Europe*, (76), 2–3.

Linos, K. 2007. How Can International Organizations Shape National Welfare States? Evidence from Compliance with European Union Directives. *Comparative Political Studies*, 40(5), 547–570.

Maduro, M.P. 2004. Harmony and Dissonance in Free Movement, in *Services and Free Movement in EU Law*, edited by M. Andenas and W.-H. Roth. Oxford-New York: Oxford University Press, 41–68.

Maher, I. 1996. Limitations on Community Regulation in the UK: Legal Culture and Multi-level Governance. *Journal of European Public Policy*, 3(4), 577–593.

Marhold, F. 1998. Grundsatzfragen der Umsetzung europäischen Sozialrechts in Österreich, in *Soziale Sicherheit in Österreich und Europa. Durchführung der*

Verordnung (EWG) 1408/71 in Österreich, edited by W.J. Pfeil. Wien: Verlag des Österreichischen Gewerkschaftsbundes, 25–42.

Martinsen, D.S. 2005a. Social Security Regulation in the EU: The De-Territorialization of Welfare?, in *EU Law and the Welfare State. In Search of Solidarity*, edited by G. De Búrca. Oxford: Oxford University Press, 89–110.

Martinsen, D.S. 2005b. Towards an Internal Health Market with the European Court. *West European Politics*, 28(5), 1035–1056.

Mastenbroek, E. 2005. EU Compliance: Still a "Black Hole"? *Journal of European Public Policy*, 12(6), 1103–1120.

Mastenbroek, E. and Kaeding, M. 2005. Europeanization Beyond the Goodness of Fit: Bringing Domestic Politics Back in, Conference paper, Leiden University Working Paper, Leiden.

Mattli, W. and Slaughter, A.-M. 1998. Revisiting the European Court of Justice. *International Organization*, 52(1), 177–209.

McCown, M. 2003. The European Parliament before the Bench: ECJ Precedent and EP Litigation Strategies. *Journal of European Public Policy*, 10(6), 974–995.

Mendrinou, M. 1996. Non-compliance and the European Commission's Role in Integration. *Journal of European Public Policy*, 3(1), 1–22.

Menon, A. 2000. France, in *The National Co-ordination of EU Policy*, edited by H. Kassim, G.B. Peters and V. Wright. Oxford: Oxford University Press, 79–98.

Mestmäcker, E.-J. 1994. On the Legitimacy of European Law. *Rabels Zeitschrift für ausländisches und internationales Privatrecht*, 58(4), 615–635.

Montgomery, J. 2003. *Health Care Law*. Oxford: Oxford University Press.

Newdick, C. 2005. *Who Should We Treat? Rights, Rationing, and Resources in the NHS*. Oxford: Oxford University Press.

Nickless, J. 2002. The Internal Market and the Social Nature of Health Care, in *The Impact of EU Law on Health Care Systems*, edited by M. McKee, E. Mossialos and R. Baeten. Bruxelles-Bern-Berlin-Frankfurt/M.-New York-Oxford-Wien: P.I.E.-Peter Lang, 57–82.

Nihoul, P. and Simon, A.-C. 2005. *L'Europe et les soins de santé*. Bruxelles: De Boeck & Larcier.

Numhauser, A. 2003. *European Observatory on Social Security for Migrant Workers: National Report: Sweden*. Munich: Max-Planck-Institut für ausländisches und internationales Sozialrecht.

Nyikos, S.A. 2003. The Preliminary Reference Process. National Court Implementation, Changing Opportunity Structures and Litigant Desistment. *European Union Politics*, 4(4), 397–419.

Obermaier, A.J. 2009. Cross-border Purchases of Health Services. A Case Study on Austria and Hungary. *World Bank Policy Research Working Paper*, 4825, 1–29.

O'Leary, S. and Fernández-Martín, J.M. 2004. Judicially-created Exceptions to the Free Provision of Services, in *Services and Free Movement in EU Law*, edited by M. Andenas and W.-H. Roth. Oxford-New York: Oxford University Press, 163–195.

Palm, W., Nickless, J., Lewalle, H. and Coheur, A. 2000. *Implications of Recent Jurisprudence on the Co-ordination of Health Care Protection Systems*. Brussels: Association Internationale de la Mutualité.

Pierson, P. 2004. *Politics in Time: History, Institutions, and Social Analysis*. Princeton: Princeton University Press.

Rasmussen, H. 1986. *On Law and Policy in the European Court of Justice. A Comparative Study in Judicial Policymaking*. Dordrecht-Boston-Lancaster: Martinus Nijhoff Publishers.

Rasmussen, H. 1998. *The European Court of Justice*. Copenhagen: GadJura.

Raustiala, K. and Slaughter, A.-M. 2002. International Law, International Relations and Compliance, in *Handbook of International Relations*, edited by W. Carlsnaes, T. Risse and B.A. Simmons. London-Thousand Oaks-New Delhi: Sage Publications, 538–558.

Rehder, B. 2007. What is Political about Jurisprudence? Courts, Politics and Political Science in Europe and the United States. *MPIfG Discussion Paper*, 07(5).

Reich, N. 1994. The "November Revolution" of the European Court of Justice: *Keck*, *Meng* and *Audi* revisited. *Common Market Law Review*, 31(3), 459–492.

Risse, T., Green Cowles, M. and Caporaso, J. 2001. Europeanization and Domestic Change: Introduction, in *Transforming Europe. Europeanization and Domestic Change*, edited by M. Green Cowles, J. Caporaso and T. Risse. Ithaca: Cornell University Press.

Roberts, S. 2003. *European Observatory on Social Security for Migrant Workers: National Report: United Kingdom*. Munich: Max-Planck-Institut für ausländisches und internationales Sozialrecht.

Roger, F. 1993. Europe et Fonds National de Solidarité. *Retraite et Société*, 4, 43–73.

Rosenberg, G.N. 1991. *The Hollow Hope. Can Courts Bring About Social Change?* Chicago-London: The University of Chicago.

Ruellan, R. 1998. Le Règlement 1408/71. *Retraite et Société*, 22, 6–9.

Sakslin, M. 2003. *European Observatory on Social Security for Migrant Workers: National Report: Finland*. Munich: Max-Planck-Institut für ausländisches und internationales Sozialrecht.

Sánchez-Rodas Navarro, C. 2003. *European Observatory on Social Security for Migrant Workers: National Report: Spain*. Munich: Max-Planck-Institut für ausländisches und internationales Sozialrecht.

Sandier, S., Paris, V. and Polton, D. 2004. *Health Care Systems in Transition: France*. Copenhagen: European Observatory on Health Systems and Policies.

Sauer, F. and Fahy, N. 2004. Malades à la recherche de soins en Europe. *Revue du Droit de l'Union Européenne*, (3), 499–508.

Scheingold, S.A. 1971. *The Law in Political Integration: The Evolution and Integrative Implications of Regional Legal Processes in the European Community*, Cambridge/Massachusetts: Harvard University Center for International Affairs.

Schepel, H. 2000. Reconstructing Constitutionalisation: Law and Politics in the European Court of Justice. *Oxford Journal of Legal Studies*, 20(3), 457–468.

Schmidt, S.K. 2004. *Rechtsunsicherheit statt Regulierungswettbewerb: Die nationalen Folgen des europäischen Binnenmarkts für Dienstleistungen.* Professorial Dissertation, Hagen: FernUniversität Hagen.

Schreiber, A. 2004. Grenzüberschreitende Inanspruchnahme von Krankenhausleistungen aus der Sicht des BMGS. *Zeitschift für europäisches Sozial- und Arbeitsrecht*, (10), 413–416.

Schulte, B. 2003. "Decker/Kohll" und die Folgen. Fragen und Hypothesen, in *Grenzüberschreitende Inanspruchnahme von Gesundheitsleistungen im Gemeinsamen Markt. Belgisch-deutsch-niederländische Tagung in Antwerpen*, edited by Y. Jorens and B. Schulte. Baden-Baden: Nomos, 169–180.

Schulte, B. and Barwig, K. (eds) 1999. *Freizügigkeit und Soziale Sicherheit. Die Durchführung der Verordnung (EWG) Nr. 1408/71 über die soziale Sicherheit der Wanderarbeitnehmer in Deutschland.* Baden-Baden: Nomos.

Schweitzer, M. and Hummer, W. 1996. *Europarecht. Das Recht der Europäischen Union – das Recht der Europäischen Gemeinschaften (EGKS, EG, EAG) – mit Schwerpunkt EG.* Neuwied-Kriftel-Berlin: Luchterhand.

Shapiro, M. and Stone Sweet, A. 2002. *On Law, Politics and Judicialization.* Oxford: Oxford University Press.

Siegel, S.N. 2007. *Law and Order in the European Union: The Comparative Politics of Compliance.* Doctoral Dissertation, Ithaca-New York: Cornell University.

Sieveking, K. 1997. Der Europäische Gerichtshof als Motor der sozialen Integration der Gemeinschaft. *Zeitschrift für Sozialreform*, 43(3), 187–208.

Sieveking, K. 2007. ECJ Rulings on Health Care Services and their Effects on the Freedom of Cross-border Patient Mobility in the EU. *European Journal of Migration and Law*, 9, 25–51.

Slaughter, A.-M., Stone Sweet, A. and Weiler, J.H.H. (eds) 1998. *The European Court and National Courts – Doctrine and Jurisprudence. Legal Change in Its Social Context.* Oxford: Hart Publishing.

Smith, R. 2005. The Private Sector in the English NHS: From Pariah to Saviour in Under a Decade. *The Canadian Medical Association Journal*, 173(3), 273–274.

Snyder, F. 1993. The Effectiveness of European Community Law: Institutions, Processes, Tools and Techniques. *The Modern Law Review*, 56(1), 19–54.

Somsen, H. 2000. The Private Enforcement of Member State Compliance with EC Environmental Law: An Unfulfilled Promise? in *Yearbook of European Environmental Law*, edited by H. Somsen. Oxford: Oxford University Press, 311–360.

Spiegel, B. 2006. *Die neue europäische Sozialrechtskoordinierung. Überlegungen zur Verordnung (EG) Nr. 883/2004.* Salzburg: Training and Reporting in European Social Security.

St Clair Bradley, K. 2002. The European Court of Justice, in *The Institutions of the European Union*, edited by J. Peterson and M. Shackleton. Oxford: Oxford University Press, 118–138.

Steinmeyer, H.-D. 1995. Die Berücksichtigung der wirtschaftlichen, finanziellen und sozialpolitischen Folgen in der Rechtsprechung des Gerichtshofs der EG, in *Die Rechtsprechung des Europäischen Gerichtshofs zum Arbeits- und Sozialrecht im Streit*, edited by E. Eichenhofer and M. Zuleeg. Köln: Bundesanzeiger, 93–102.

Stone Sweet, A. 2000. *Governing with Judges. Constitutional Politics in Europe.* Oxford: Oxford University Press.

Stone Sweet, A. 2004. *The Judicial Construction of Europe.* Oxford: Oxford University Press.

Stone Sweet, A. and Brunell, T.L. 1998. The European Court and the National Courts: A Statistical Analysis of Preliminary References, 1961–95. *Journal of European Public Policy*, 5(1), 66–97.

Tallberg, J. 1999. *Making States Comply. The European Commission, the European Court of Justice & the Enforcement of the Internal Market.* Lund: Studentlitteratur.

Tallberg, J. 2002. Paths to Compliance: Enforcement, Management, and the European Union. *International Organization*, 56(3), 609–643.

Tallberg, J. 2003. *European Governance and Supranational Institutions. Making States Comply.* London-New York: Routledge.

Treib, O. 2004. *Die Bedeutung der nationalen Parteipolitik für die Umsetzung europäischer Sozialrichtlinien.* Frankfurt-New York: Campus Verlag.

Treib, O. 2008. Implementing and Complying with EU Governance Outputs. *Living Reviews in European Governance*, 3(5). Available at: http://www.livingreviews.org/lreg-2008-5 [accessed 15 June 2009].

van der Mei, A.P. 1999. The Kohll and Decker Rulings: Revolution or Evolution? *Eurohealth*, 5(1), 14–16.

van der Mei, A.P. 2004. Cross-border Access to Medical Care: Non-hospital Care and Waiting Lists. *Legal Issues of Economic Integration*, 31(1), 57–67.

Van Hoogenbemt, H. 2001. *European Observatory on Social Security for Migrant Workers: National Report: Belgium.* Munich: Max-Planck-Institut für ausländisches und internationales Sozialrecht.

Vollaard, H. 2005. Limites et Fondements de la Mobilité des Patients dans l'Union Européenne. *Revue belge de sécurité sociale*, 47(2), 225–53.

von Wulffen, M. 1997. *Erstattungsansprüche im Recht der gesetzlichen Krankenversicherung.* München: C.H. Beck.

Weiler, J.H.H. 1982. Community, Member States and European Integration. Is the Law Relevant? *Journal of Common Market Studies*, 21(1/2), 39–56.

Weiler, J.H.H. 1991. The Transformation of Europe. *The Yale Law Journal*, 100, 2402–2483.

Weiler, J.H.H. 1994a. Journey to an Unknown Destination: A Retrospective and Prospective of the European Court of Justice in the Arena of Political Integration, in *Economic and Political Integration in Europe: Internal Dynamics and Global Context*, edited by S. Bulmer and A. Scott. Oxford/UK-Cambridge/Massachusetts: Blackwell Publishers, 131–160.

Weiler, J.H.H. 1994b. A Quiet Revolution. The European Court of Justice and its Interlocutors. *Comparative Political Studies*, 26(4), 510–534.

Weiler, J.H.H. 1999. *The Constitution of Europe. "Do the New Clothes have an Emperor?" and Other Essays on European Integration.* Cambridge: Cambridge University Press.

Wincott, D. 2003. Containing (Social) Justice? Rights, EU Law and the Recasting of Europe's "Social Bargains." *European Law Review*, 28(5), 735–749.

Zerna, C. 2003. *Der Export von Gesundheitsleistungen in der Europäischen Gemeinschaft nach den Entscheidungen des EuGH vom 28. April 1998 in den Rechtssachen "Decker" und "Kohll".* Frankfurt/M.-Bern-Bruxelles-New York-Oxford-Wien: P.I.E.-Peter Lang.

Zipperer, M. 1999. Die Rechtsprechung des Europäischen Gerichtshofes zur Leistungspflicht der Krankenversicherung aus der Sicht der deutschen Bundesregierung, in *Perspektiven der PKV in Europa*, edited by Verband der privaten Krankenversicherung. Köln, 19–32.

Documents

European Commission

European Commission. 2000. *Letter of reasoned opinion of the European Commission.* COM(2000) 2928 final, 16 October.

European Commission. 2001. *Eighteenth Annual Report on Monitoring the Application of Community Law (2000).* COM(2001) 309 final, 16 July.

European Commission. 2002. *Free movement of workers – achieving the full benefits and potential.* Communication from the Commission. COM(2002) 694 final, 11 December.

European Commission. 2003a. *Better Monitoring of the Application of Community Law.* Communication from the Commission. COM(2002) 725 final/4, 16 May.

European Commission. 2003b. *Communication from the Commission concerning the introduction of a European Health Insurance Card.* COM(2003) 73 final, 17 February.

European Commission. 2003c. *Report on the Application of Internal Market Rules to Health Services. Implementation by the Member States of the Court's Jurisprudence.* Commission Staff Working Paper. SEC(2003) 900, 28 July.

European Commission. 2003d. *High Level Process of Reflection on Patient Mobility and Healthcare Developments in the European Union.* HLPR/2003/16, 9 December.

European Commission. 2003e. *Meeting of the high level process of reflection on patient mobility and healthcare developments in the EU on 3 February 2003.* Minutes of the meeting. HLPR/2003/2 REV1, 4 April.

European Commission. 2004a. *Explanatory Note from the Commission Services on the provisions of the proposed Directive on services in the Internal Market relating to the assumption of healthcare costs incurred in another Member State with a particular emphasis on the relationship with Regulation No 1408/71.* 2004/0001 (COD), 16 July.

European Commission. 2004b. *Proposal for a Directive of the European Parliament and of the Council on services in the internal market.* COM(2004) 2final/3, 5 March.

European Commission. 2005a. *Financial Penalties for Member States who fail to comply with Judgments of the European Court of Justice: European Commission clarifies rules.* MEMO/05/482, 14 December.

European Commission. 2005b. *Confirmatory applications for access to documents according to Regulation 1049/2001.* Secretary General. Letter to the author. SG.B.2/SB/md D (2005) 7053, 13 July.

European Commission. 2006. *Summary report of the responses to the consultation regarding "Community action on health services."* DG Health and Consumer Protection. SEC(2006) 1195/4, 26 September.

European Commission. 2007. *Cross-border health services in the EU.* Analytical Report. Flash Eurobarometer 210.

European Commission. 2008. *Proposal for a directive of the European Parliament and of the Council on the application of patients' rights in cross-border healthcare.* COM(2008) 414 final, 2 July.

European Parliament

European Parliament. 2005a. *Report on the proposal for a directive of the European Parliament and of the Council on services in the internal market.* Final A6-0409/2005, 15 December.

European Parliament. 2005b. *Report on patient mobility and healthcare developments in the European Union.* 2004/2148(INI), 29 April.

European Parliament. 2006. *Commissioner McCreevy's Statement on the Services Directive at the European Parliament Plenary session.* SPEECH/06/84, 14 February.

ECJ Jurisprudence

Bericht des Berichterstatters in Case C-8/02, *Leichtle.*

Case 45/75, *Rewe-Zentrale des Lebensmittel-Großhandels GmbH vs. Hauptzollamt Landau/Pfalz* [1976] ECR I–181.

Case 294/83, *Parti écologiste 'les Verts' vs. European Parliament* [1986] ECR I–1339.

Case C-158/96, *Raymond Kohll vs. Union des caisses de maladie* [1998] ECR I–1931.

Case C-120/95, *Nicolas Decker vs. Caisse de maladie des employés privés* [1998] ECR I–1831.

Case C-228/98, *Kharalambos Dounias vs. Ipourgos Ikonomikon* [2000] ECR I–577.

Case C-368/98, *Abdon Vanbraekel and Others vs. Alliance nationale des mutualités chrétiennes* [2001] ECR I–5363.

Case C-157/99, *B.S.M. Geraets-Smits vs. Stichting Ziekenfonds VGZ and H.T.M. Peerbooms vs. Stichting CZ Groep Zorgverzekeringen* [2001] ECR I–5473.

Case C-385/99, *V.G. Müller-Fauré vs. Onderlinge Waarborgmaatschappij OZ Zorgverzekeringen UA and E.E.M. van Riet vs. Onderlinge Waarborgmaatschappij ZAO Zorgverzekeringen* [2003] ECR I–4509.

Case C-56/01, *Patricia Inizan vs. Caisse primaire d'assurance maladie des Hauts-de-Seine* [2003] *ECR I–12403.*

Case C-496/01, *Commission of the European Communities vs. French Republic* [2004] ECR I–2351.

Case C-8/02, *Ludwig Leichtle vs. Bundesanstalt für Arbeit* [2004] ECR I–2641.

Case C-372/04, *The Queen on the application of Yvonne Watts vs. Bedford Primary Care Trust, Secretary of State for Health* [2006] ECR I–4325.

Case C-145/03, *Heirs of Annette Keller vs. Instituto Nacional de la Seguridad Social, Instituto Nacional de Gestión Sanitaria* [2005] ECR I–2529.

Case C-466/04, *Manuel Acereda Herrera vs. Servicio Cántabro de Salud* [2006] ECR I–5341.

Case C-444/05, *Aikaterini Stamatelaki vs. NPDD Organismos Asfaliseos Eleftheron Epangelmation* [2007] ECR I–3185.

Opinion of the Advocate General, Dámaso Ruiz-Jarabo Colomer, *Müller-Fauré/ van Riet.*

Rapport d'audience in Case C-120/95, *Decker.*

Rapport d'audience in Case C-158/96, *Kohll.*

Rapport d'audience in Case C-56/01, *Inizan.*

Report for the Hearing in Case C-372/04, *Watts.*

France

Assemblée Nationale. 1999. 1st session, 19 January.

Circular DSS/DACI/2001/120 relative au remboursement des frais d'optique engagés dans un autre Etat membre de l'Union européenne et de l'Espace économique européen, sans autorisation préalable de la caisse d'assurance maladie d'affiliation, 1 March.

Circular DSS/DACI/2003/286 relative à l'application de la réglementation pour assurer l'accès aux soins des assurés d'un régime français de sécurité sociale au sein de l'Union européenne et de l'Espace économique européen, 16 June.

Circular DSS/DACI/2004/134 relative à la prise en charge des frais engagés pour l'achat de produits de santé dans un autre Etat membre de l'Union européenne ou partie à l'accord sur l'Espace économique européen, complémentaire à la circulaire DSS/DACI/2003/286 du juin 2003 relative à l'application de la réglementation pour assurer l'accès aux soins des assurés d'un régime français de sécurité sociale au sein de l'UE-EEE, 23 March.

Circular DSS/DACI/2005/235 relative aux modalités de mise en œuvre du décret no 2005–386 du 19 avril 2005 relatif à la prise en charge des soins reçus hors de France, 19 May.

Code de la Santé Publique, Articles L.6211–2–1 and R.6211–46 to 56.

Code de la Sécurité Sociale, Articles L.332–3 and R.332–2.

Cour d'Appel de Colmar. 2002a. Chambre Sociale, No RG 00/04258, *Marianne Thébaud vs. CPAM Strasbourg*, 17 October.

Cour d'Appel de Colmar. 2002b. Chambre Sociale, No RG 00/04259, *Jean-Louis Vaquin vs. CPAM Strasbourg*, 17 October.

Cour d'Appel de Colmar. 2003. Chambre Sociale, No RG 00/04257, *Frieda Pfrimmer vs. CPAM Strasbourg*, 19 June.

Cour de Cassation. 2002a. Chambre Sociale, No de pourvoi 00–15.903, *Robert Magnan vs. CPAM des Hauts de Seine*, 28 March.

Cour de Cassation. 2002b. Chambre Sociale, No de pourvoi 01–20316, *Caisse Nationale Militaire de Sécurité Sociale vs. Jozan*, 26 September.

Cour de Cassation. 2004. Chambre Civile 2, No de pourvoi 02–30674, *CPAM de Montpellier-Lodève vs. Gérona*, 25 May.

Decree 2005–386 du 19 avril 2005 relatif à la prise en charge des soins reçus hors de France et modifiant le code de la sécurité sociale. Journal Officiel de la République Française, 27 April.

Decree 2006–306 du 16 mars 2006 relatif au régime d'autorisation des laboratoires établis hors de France dans un Etat membre de la Communauté européenne ou partie à l'accord sur l'Espace économique européen et modifiant le code de la santé publique (dispositions réglementaires). Journal Officiel de la République Française, 17 March.

Law 2003–591 habilitant le Gouvernement à simplifier le droit, 2 July.

Law 2004–806 relative à la politique de santé publique, 9 August.

Law 2004–810 relative à l'assurance maladie, 13 August.

Law 2006–1640 de financement de la sécurité sociale pour 2007, 21 December.

Ministère de l'Emploi et de la Solidarité. 1998. Ministerial letter, 29 June.

Ordonnance 2004-329 allégeant les formalités applicables à certaines prestations sociales, 15 April.

Tribunal des Affaires de Sécurité Sociale. 2000a. No du dossier G 166/99, *Frieda Pfrimmer vs. CPAM Strasbourg*, 14 June.

Tribunal des Affaires de Sécurité Sociale. 2000b. No du dossier G 229/99 et G 230/99, *Marianne Thébaud et Jean-Louis Vaquin vs. CPAM Strasbourg*, 14 June.

Union Régionale des Caisses d'Assurance Maladie. 2004. Guide Méthodologique: d'Aide à la Mise en Place de Coopérations Transfrontalières, January.

Germany

AOK Federal Association. 2003. Statement for the draft of the *Gesetz zur Modernisierung des Gesundheitssystems*, 20 June.

AOK Federal Association. 2005. Statement of the supervisory board for the proposal of the European Commission concerning the services directive, 9 February.

Association of the *Angestellten-Krankenkassen/Arbeiter-Ersatzkassen*. 2003. Statement. Formulierungshilfe für einen Gesetzentwurf der Fraktionen SPD und Bündnis 90/Die Grünen zur Modernisierung des Gesundheitssystems, 2 June.

Bundesgesetzblatt. 2003. *Gesetz zur Modernisierung der Gesetzlichen Krankenversicherung*. Part I, Number 55, 14 November.

Bundesgesetzblatt. 2006. *Gesetz zur Änderung des Vertragsarztrechts und anderer Gesetze (Vertragsarztrechtsänderungsgesetz)*. Part I, Number 66, 22 December.

Bundesgesetzblatt. 2007. *Gesetz zur Stärkung des Wettbewerbs in der gesetzlichen Krankenversicherung (GKV-Wettbewerbsstärkungsgesetz)*. Part I, Number 11, 26 March.

Bundessozialgericht. 2004. B 1 KR 11/04 R, 13 July.

Central Associations of Statutory Health Insurance Funds and *Deutsche Verbindungsstelle Krankenversicherung – Ausland*. 2003. Common recommendation. Leistungsrechtliche Umsetzungsfragen des GKV-Modernisierungsgesetzes, Kostenerstattung gemäß § 13 Abs. 4–6 SGB V und Kostenübernahme bei Behandlung außerhalb des Geltungsbereichs des Vertrags zur Gründung der Europäischen Gemeinschaft und des Abkommens über den Europäischen Wirtschaftsraum gemäß § 18 SGB V, 19 November.

Central Associations of Statutory Health Insurance Funds. 2001. Gemeinsames Rundschreiben vom 31. August 2001 zu den Auswirkungen der Rechtsprechung des Europäischen Gerichtshofs vom 12. Juli 2001 in den Rechtssachen "Smits/Peerbooms" (C-157/99) und "Vanbraekel" (C-368/98), 31 August.

Central Associations of Statutory Health Insurance Funds. 2005. Statement for the hearing of the Committee for Health and Social Security in the German *Bundestag* from 16 March 2005, 9 March.

Common Working Committee. 1999. The *Länder* Brandenburg, Baden-Württemberg, Bayern, Nordrhein-Westfalen and Saarland, the Central Associations of Statutory Health Insurance Funds, and the Federal Ministry of Health. Report. Auswirkungen der Rechtsprechung des EuGH zur Erstattung von Kosten für Medizinprodukte und Behandlungen im EU-Ausland durch nationale Krankenversicherungsträger, January.

Deutsche Sozialversicherung – Europavertretung. 1998. Europäische Fachinformation 9/98, Urteil des Europäischen Gerichtshofes vom 28. April 1998 in den Rechtssachen Decker und Kohll (Rs. C-120/95 und C-158/96), 5 May.

Deutscher Bundestag. 2003a. 15th legislative period, printed matter 15/1170, 16 June.

Deutscher Bundestag. 2003b. 15th legislative period, printed matter 15/1174, 17 June.

Deutscher Bundestag. 2003c. 15th legislative period, Ausschuss für Gesundheit und Soziale Sicherung, Wortprotokoll Nr. 15/29, 25 June.

Deutscher Bundestag. 2003d. 15th legislative period, printed matter 15/1525, 8 September.

Deutscher Bundestag. 2004a. 15th legislative period, printed matter 15/3511, 1 July.

Deutscher Bundestag. 2004b. 15th legislative period, printed matter 15/4135, 9 November.

Extended Committee of the Central Associations of Statutory Health Insurance Funds. 1999. Strategischer Umgang mit den EuGH-Urteilen *Kohll/Decker* vom 28. April 1998, 29 March.

Federal Association of Statutory Health Insurance Dentists. 2003. Summary of the statement for the draft of the *Gesetz zur Modernisierung des Gesundheitssystems*, 19 June.

Federal Ministry of Health. 1998a. Press release. Eine Auszehrung der deutschen Krankenversicherung muß verhindert werden, Issue 28, 28 April.

Federal Ministry of Health. 1998b. Press release. Zur Anwendung des Rechts der Europäischen Gemeinschaft im Hinblick auf die Urteile des Europäischen Gerichtshofes vom 28.04.1998, Issue 41, 5 June.

Frankfurter Allgemeine Zeitung. 1998. Seehofers Auslegung des Luxemburger Urteils wird in Frage gestellt, 3 June.

Gesundheitspolitischer Informationsdienst. 1998. Positionen zum Urteil des Europäischen Gerichtshofs. *Forum für Gesellschaftspolitik* (May), 105–124.

Second Statutory Health Insurance Restructuring Act. 1997. Neuordnung von Selbstverwaltung und Eigenverantwortung in der gesetzlichen Krankenversicherung, 23 June.

Siemens Betriebskrankenkasse. 2006. Probleme der Koordinierung der sozialen Sicherheit – VO (EWG) 1408/71 und Erwartungen an die neue VO (EG) 883/04 und die Umsetzungsverordnung: Die Verordnung aus der Sicht der gesetzlichen Krankenversicherung, Günther Lorff, 30 June.

Social Code, Book IV, Paragraph 3.

Social Code, Book V, Paragraphs 13, 16, 17, 18, and 140e.

Social Code, Book IX, Paragraph 18.

Techniker Krankenkasse. 2001. Medizinische Leistungen im EU-Ausland. Erfahrungen und Erwartungen der TK-Mitglieder, April.

Techniker Krankenkasse. 2003a. Press release. TK begrüßt das Urteil des Europäischen Gerichtshofes zur Behandlung im EU-Ausland, 13 May.

Techniker Krankenkasse. 2003b. Core statements for the draft of the *Gesetz zur Modernisierung des Gesundheitssystems* (GMG) as amended on 2 June.

Working Committee of the Central Associations of Statutory Health Insurance Funds. 2000. Position paper. Strategischer Umgang der GKV mit den aktuellen europarechtlichen Entwicklungen – Herausforderung Europa annehmen und gestalten, August.

Working Committee of the Central Associations of Statutory Health Insurance Funds. 2001. Press release, 19 July.

Working Committee of the Central Associations of Statutory Health Insurance Funds. 2002. Statement. Handlungsrahmen für die Weiterentwicklung der GKV in Europa, 2 May.

Working Committee of the Central Associations of Statutory Health Insurance Funds. 2004. Position paper. Europa für die Versicherten gestalten – aktuelle europäische Entwicklungen im Bereich der Gesundheitspolitik, October.

The United Kingdom

Administrative Court of the Queen's Bench Division of the High Court. 2003. The Honourable Mr. Justice Munby, *R (on the application of Yvonne Watts) and (1) Bedford Primary Care Trust (2) Secretary of State for Health*, Case No CO/5690/2002, 1 October.

British Medical Association. 2003. Press release. BMA response to ruling on Yvonne Watts case, 2 October.

British Medical Association. 2006. Press release. BMA responds to ruling on Yvonne Watts ruling, 16 May.

Court of Appeal. 2004. Civil Division. The Master of the Rolls Lord Justice May and Lord Justice Carnwath, *Secretary of State for Health and R on the application of Yvonne Watts*, Case No C1/2003/2399, 20 February.

Daily Mail. 2001. NHS goes into the export business, 27 August.

Department of Health. 1995. Health Service Guidelines (95)33. Patient referrals outside the UK and European Economic Area, 11 July.

Department of Health. 2000a. For the benefit of patients. A Concordat with the Private and Voluntary Health Care Provider Sector, 31 October.

Department of Health. 2000b. The NHS Plan. A plan for investment. A plan for reform, July.

Department of Health. 2001. Press release. New Scheme for sending groups of patients abroad – Milburn, 15 October.

Department of Health. 2002a. Evaluation of Treating Patients Overseas. Final Report, July.

Department of Health. 2002b. Growing Capacity. A new role for external healthcare providers in England, June.

Department of Health. 2002c. Guidance for Primary Care and Acute Trusts. Treating more Patients and Extending Choice: Overseas Treatment for NHS Patients, November.

Department of Health. 2003. Choice of hospital. Guidance for PCTs, NHS Trusts and SHAs on offering patients choice of where they are treated, July.

Department of Health. 2004a. Commissioning treatment in the EU, 1 March.

Department of Health. 2004b. Information for NHS trusts and PCTs, March.

Department of Health. 2004c. Patient information and FAQs, March.

Department of Health. 2005. Interim guidance on obtaining medical treatment outside the UK, 21 July.

Department of Health. 2006a. Going to an EEA country or Switzerland in order to get treatment, 4 October.

Department of Health. 2006b. Press release. Waiting lists fall to a record low, 29 September.

House of Commons. 2002a. Fourth Standing Committee on Delegated Legislation, 5 February.

House of Commons. 2002b. Parliamentary questions. John Hutton in answer to Andrew Murrison, Hansard Location 389 c871–2W, 22 July.

House of Commons. 2003. Parliamentary questions. John Hutton in answer to Tim Loughton, Hansard Location 400 c536W, 400 c528W, 25 February.

House of Commons Health Committee. 2001. The Role of the Private Sector in the NHS, session 24 October.

House of Commons Health Committee. 2002. The Role of the Private Sector in the NHS, session 9 January.

House of Lords. 2001. Parliamentary questions. Lord Hunt of Kings Heath in answer to Lord Clement-Jones, Hansard Location 627 c33WA, 14 September.

National Health Service Act 1977, Chapter 49, London: HMSO, reprinted 1995.

NHS Confederation. 2006. Press release. NHS Confederation comments on EC ruling on Yvonne Watts' case, 16 May.

The Daily Telegraph. 2001a. Thousand NHS patients treated abroad, 21 August.

The Daily Telegraph. 2001b. U-turn by Milburn on exporting NHS patients, 27 August.

The Express. 2001. Following the Health Secretary's decision to change the law to let patients facing a long wait seek hospital treatment elsewhere in Europe, we discover what they can expect; wish you were here?, 8 September.

The Guardian. 2001a. Health bosses propose sending patients to Germany, 30 July.

The Guardian. 2001b. We are the masters now, 10 August.

The Guardian. 2001c. NHS to fund operations in Europe, 27 August.

The Guardian. 2003. Judge opens floodgates on foreign surgery, 2 October.

The Independent. 2003. Thousand set for free surgery abroad after NHS ruling, 2 October.

The National Health Service Act 1977 and National Health Service and Community Care Act 1990 (Amendment) Regulations 2002. SI 2002/2759, London: HMSO.

The National Health Service (Travelling Expenses and Remission of Charges) Amendment (No. 3) Regulations 2001. SI 2001/4043, London: HMSO.

The Sunday Times. 2001a. A healthy decision, 26 August.

The Sunday Times. 2001b. A healthy opportunity, 15 July.

The Sunday Times. 2001c. EU hospitals give emergency surgery to Britons on NHS list, 19 August.

The Sunday Times. 2001d. GPs tell patients: Get treatment abroad, 22 July.

The Sunday Times. 2001e. NHS exports patients to Germany, 29 July.

The Sunday Times. 2001f. Patients will sue for surgery abroad, 5 August.

The Sunday Times. 2001g. Patients win fight for surgery abroad, 26 August.

The Sunday Times. 2001h. Ruling frees NHS patients to seek treatment abroad, 15 July.

The Sunday Times. 2001i. The hospital barrier, 22 July.

The Sunday Times. 2002. Patients to sue as NHS blocks surgery abroad, 29 December.

Miscellaneous

Administrative Commission on Social Security for Migrant Workers. 1996. Decision 161 of 15 February 1996 concerning the reimbursement by the competent institution of a Member State of the costs incurred during a stay in another Member State by means of the procedure referred to in Article 34(4) of Regulation (EEC) No 574/72. Official Journal of the European Communities, L 83, 2 April.

Administrative Commission on Social Security for Migrant Workers. 2000. Decision 176 of 24 June 1999 concerning the reimbursement by the competent institution in a Member State of the costs incurred during a stay in another Member State by means of the procedure referred to in Article 34(4) of Regulation (EEC) No 574/72. Official Journal of the European Communities, L 243/42, 28 September.

Council Conclusions. 2006. Common values and principles in European Union Health Systems, C 146/01, 22 June.

German EU Presidency. 2007a. Notes of the Trio Presidency. Health care across Europe: Striving for added value, 20 April.

German EU Presidency. 2007b. Press release, 27 March.

German EU Presidency. 2007c. Press release, 20 April.

Irish Department of Social and Family Affairs. 2005. Press release, 5 June.

MORI Social Research Institute. 2002. Many Patients "Willing to Travel Abroad for Treatment", 30 June.

Working Group of the *Euroforum soziale Krankenversicherung*. 1999. Auswirkungen des Wirtschafts- und Wettbewerbsrechts der EG auf die soziale Krankenversicherung, Report, Vienna, 3 August.

List of Interviews

Germany

G1: Bokeloh Arno, Bundesministerium für Gesundheit und Soziale Sicherung, Bonn, 19 September 2005.

G2: Reker Elisabeth, AOK Federal Association, Responsible for European law, Bonn, 19 September 2005.

G3: Burger Stephan, Bundesverband der Betriebskrankenkassen, Responsible for European law, Essen, 26 September 2005.

G4: Kücking Monika and Anouchka Jann, Verband der Angestellten-Krankenkassen/Arbeiter-Ersatzkassen-Verband, Responsible for European law, Siegburg, 10 November 2005.

G5: An official of the Siemens Betriebskrankenkasse, Telephone, 17 August 2006.

G6: A former high-ranking official of the German Federal Ministry of Health and Social Security, Telephone, 25 August 2006.

France

F1: Lhernould Jean-Philippe, Université d'Orléans, Professor of labor law, Orléans, 11 July 2005.

F2: Gouello Martine, Caisse Nationale d'Assurance Maladie, Mission des Relations Européennes et Internationales et de la Coopération, Responsible for European law, Paris, 13 July 2005.

F3: A high-ranking official of the Ministère de la Santé et des Solidarités, Direction de la Sécurité Sociale, Division des Affaires Communautaires et Internationales, Paris, 15 July 2005.

F4: Delétang Nicole, Centre des Liaisons Européennes et Internationales de Sécurité Sociale, Paris, 15 June 2006.

F5: Samantar Kulmie, Mutualité Française, Département International, Paris, 14 June 2006.

F6: Izard Jean-Luc and Séverine Métillon, Ministère de la Santé, Direction de la Sécurité Sociale, Division des Affaires Communautaires et Internationales, Paris, 16 June 2006.

F7: Bacq Gabriel, Caisse Nationale d'Assurance Maladie, Responsible for international relations, Paris, 16 June 2006.

The United Kingdom

UK1: Burke Simon, Department of Health, Responsible for European law, London, 12 October 2005.
UK2: A high-ranking official of the Department of Health, Loughborough, 13 October 2005.
UK3: Roberts Simon, Centre for Social Policy Research, Loughborough, 14 October 2005.

European Commission

EC1: Fages Géraldine, DG Internal Market, Brussels, 25 April 2006.
EC2: Fahy Nick, DG Health and Consumer Protection, Brussels, 27 April 2006.

European Court of Justice

ECJ1: Kühn Werner Miguel, Member of the cabinet of Advocate General Ruiz-Jarabo Colomer, Luxembourg, 4 May 2006.
ECJ2: Geelhoed Leendert A., Advocate General, and Watson Stewart, Member of the cabinet of Geelhoed, Luxembourg, 5 May 2006.

Miscellaneous

M1: Erbrich Malte, European Social Insurance Platform, Brussels, 26 April 2006.
M2: Palm Willy, Former director of AIM, since 2006 dissemination development officer in the European Observatory on health systems and health policies, Brussels, 28 April 2006.
M3: An official of the permanent representation of the Federal Republic of Germany in Brussels, Brussels, 28 April 2006.
M4: Lewalle Henri, Mutualité Chrétienne, Telephone, 29 May 2006.
M5: Spiegel Bernhard, Bundesministerium für soziale Sicherheit, Generationen und Konsumentenschutz, Vienna, 23 May 2006.

Index